BRAIN
HACKS

Keith Barry is the world's leading TV hypnotist, mentalist and brain hacker. His skills have been showcased in over forty international television shows, including his most recent series, *The Keith Barry Experience*. As a mind coach, Keith has also worked with many world-class athletes, businesspeople, influencers and actors to assist them in unleashing their subconscious potential.

BRAIN HACKS

EVERYDAY **MIND MAGIC** FOR CREATING **THE LIFE YOU WANT**

KEITH BARRY

with **GERARD CROMWELL**

GILL BOOKS

Gill Books
Hume Avenue
Park West
Dublin 12
www.gillbooks.ie

Gill Books is an imprint of M.H. Gill and Co.

9780 7171 9192 5

Designed by Bartek Janczak
Edited by Esther Ní Dhonnacha
Proofread by Jane Rogers
Printed by CPI Group (UK) Ltd, Croydon, CR0 4YY
This book is typeset in 12/18pt, Minion Pro

The content of this book is for information purposes only.
Readers should review the information carefully with their
professional healthcare provider. The information is not
intended to replace medical advice offered by doctors.

A CIP catalogue record for this book is available from the
British Library.

5 4 3

For Mairéad, Breanna and Braden,
the three most magical people I know.

CONTENTS

INTRODUCTION   ix

CONFIDENCE

1.   From the cradle to the stage   1
2.   From Jack the lad to king of clubs   19

RISK

3.   The girl in the red coat   41
4.   Bite the bullet   63

CREATIVITY

5.   The chaos of creativity   80
6.   Roll the creativity dice   97

SUCCESS

7.   Find your purpose   119
8.   The TARGETS formula   132

RESILIENCE

9.   Bob the Builder and the art of resilience   161
10. Everything comes in threes …   181

POSITIVITY

11. Happy headspace   199

12. What are you afraid of?   220

13. Disable the autopilot   236

INFLUENCE

14. Invisible influence   256

15. Influencing online   275

DECEPTION

16. The mind reader who can't read minds   287

17. It's all in the lies   306

A MAGICAL MIND

18. Don't forget to remember   321

19. Fun brain hacks   334

Acknowledgements   345

Endnotes   347

INTRODUCTION

THIS BOOK HAS THE POWER to transform your life. Within these pages are techniques and methods I have developed and refined over the past three decades that will help you transform the areas of your life that need to be transformed. It doesn't matter where you live, what age you are, whether you're in a relationship or not, whether you are currently employed or not, or whether you are rich or poor. I know these systems work and I know these techniques can transform your life forever.

I have used these techniques to inspire thousands of people all over the world to dig themselves out of whatever hole they were in, and kickstart a brand-new and totally improved life. I live by the philosophies and techniques in this book. Included are examples from my own life, some of them inspiring, some of them painful.

They are there so that you can understand how success can be achieved and problems can be overcome by anybody.

Although I am a magician, among other things, this book comes with a warning. If you are expecting a wave from a magic wand to make you healthy, wealthy and famous, then this book is not for you.

As well as being a magician, however, I am also a husband, a father, a scientist, a mentalist, a hypnotist, an escapologist, a businessman, a mind coach, and a brain hacker. I have written the book so that my hacks and visualisations are easy to understand and can be used by a reader of any age or background.

I've used these hacks and techniques on sportspeople from Olympians to international rugby players. I've used them on ordinary people in all walks of life and even Hollywood A-listers. I've helped well-known businesspeople and celebrities. While I don't pretend to have all the answers to all of the issues people face on a daily basis, I do believe I have a lot of tips and techniques that will help you in any walk of life.

If you've become one of those people who have an on-off relationship with the self-help section of your local bookstore, then you can finally stop spending your time standing with your head tilted at an angle, scanning the spines of books that may or may not help you achieve what you want to achieve in your life. You can stop picking them up, flicking through the pages for headlines or chapters that seem relevant to your life and your problems.

You can stop reading the backs of the books to see who the author is and what, if anything, anyone has to say about their methods. Finally, you can stop glancing at the price tag in the bottom corner of the book before deciding you can't really afford to buy it, only to go out and spend the same amount on something else you don't really need.

Ask yourself these questions.

> Why do you need to go to the self-help section of the store?
> Why did you pick up this book?
> Why are you reading this page?

The answer to all of these questions is simple, whether you know it consciously or not; you need, and want, to make changes in your life. These may be small changes, like getting over a fear of dogs, or bigger changes involving starting a totally new career or finding some way to pay your mortgage so that you don't end up in arrears.

The fact is that if you feel you are stuck in any sort of a rut or need help in life – whether that's in your home life, your career, your finances, your love life, your state of health, your social life or any-thing else – this book will help you move forward. I know because the hacks and visualisations contained in these pages are the very ones I continue to use daily in my own life.

You have the ability to attain the mindset you desire and change your life for the better, regardless of your circumstances. If you are ready to achieve a 'magical mindset' by not just reading this book, but by studying, applying, and repeating these hacks on a daily basis, then this book may just change your life forever. Read, study, learn, repeat, and live a magical life.

HOW TO USE THIS BOOK

As well as stories from my own life, in each section there are moments where you will be urged to put the book down for a while and focus your attention on what it is you are really trying to achieve and how best to move forward. To do this properly and help you keep you on top of your ideas, your targets and your progress, I suggest you

XII | BRAIN HACKS

keep a journal. This should be an expensive leather-bound journal or at the very least a good hardback copybook. Just keep it handy and use it regularly.

This book is divided into nine sections: Confidence, Risk, Creativity, Success, Resilience, Positivity, Influence, Deception and A Magical Mind. While it's probably best to read this book from beginning to end, it is written in such a way that you can skip to the relevant section that you need most. At the end of each section, there is a short list of everyday brain hacks, which can be used as reminders to help you get back on track quickly, and a tailored visualisation pertaining to the section topic. To complement these written visualisations, you can also hear an audio version of each one by visiting www.keithbarry.com/brainhacks and entering the password **BRAINHACKS21**. (There are also some pretty cool mentalism tricks in these pages that you can use to astound your friends and family. To complement these tricks, you can also watch a tutorial of each one on my website.)

Don't worry if you find it strange at first, or even feel a bit daft doing it. We all feel a little out of our depth the first time we try anything. But if you stick with it and keep practising for at least 21 days, these visualisations have the power to transform your life.

In one of the first experiments on visualisation, in 1967, Australian psychologist Alan Richardson visited a team of college basketball players and recorded each player's accuracy as they took free throw shots. He then split them into three groups for a month-long experiment. In the first group, students practised free throw shots for an hour every day. Instead of practising, though, the students in the second group were told to just visualise themselves making free throws instead. They were told to make the experience as realistic as possible. They were told to see the court and its surroundings, to feel the weight and texture of the ball in their hands, hear the sound of it bouncing off the floor, see the flight of the ball in the air and hear the swoosh of the net as it went in. Those in the third group were told not to play basketball for a month.

At the end of the month, all three groups were tested to check if they had improved. While the third group, who had done absolutely nothing, had shown no signs of improvement, the first group, who had physically practised, had improved their initial scores by 24 per cent. The biggest surprise, however, was the fact that the second group had improved by 23 per cent, even though all they had done was visualise themselves taking those shots.[1]

Since then, studies have shown that your brain doesn't know the difference between deep, clear, vivid visualisation of an action and actually undertaking the physical action itself.[2] If you visualise yourself achieving something you set out to achieve, then your brain thinks you have already done it and therefore believes that you can. Visualisation has become an important tool in achieving success for many people from all walks of life, including Michael Jordan, Tiger Woods, Michael Phelps, Oprah Winfrey, Will Smith and Arnold Schwarzenegger.

'I visualised myself being, and having, what it was I wanted,' said Schwarzenegger. 'Before I won my first Mr. Universe title, I walked around the tournament like I owned it. I had won it so many times in my mind that there was no doubt I would win it. Then when I moved on to the movies, the same thing. I visualised myself being a famous actor and earning big money. I just knew it would happen.' If you're a football fan, you may know that, as I write, Wayne Rooney is currently the record goal scorer for Manchester United, with 253 goals. What you may not know, however, is that Rooney visual-ised himself scoring those goals the night before every game. After finding out what colour jerseys, shorts and socks his team would be wearing the next day, so that his mental imagery would be more colourful and realistic, Rooney would lie on his bed and imagine the scene. He could hear the crowd, feel the grass under his feet, feel the touch of the ball on his boots and sense the atmosphere in the stadium before visualising himself scoring and playing well. 'I lie in bed the night before the game and visualise myself scoring goals or doing well,' he once explained of his visualisation technique. 'You're trying to put yourself in that moment and trying to prepare yourself, to have a "memory" before the game.'

But visualisation is not just for artists, sports stars or celebrities. I use it every single day of my life and you can use it too. Every single thing I have achieved in my life, from headlining in Las Vegas to writing this book right now, is a direct result of deep, repetitive visualisation.

CONFIDENCE

the ability to deceive yourself to believe in yourself

'I learned early on as an actor that confidence can be faked. If people feel you're confident, then they're confident.' – George Clooney

1.

FROM THE CRADLE
TO THE STAGE

THE ROCKY ROAD TO CONFIDENCE

Here's a little secret. Nobody is born with confidence. In the same way that you are not born with the ability to ride a bicycle, drive a golf ball onto a fairway or drive a car, you are not born with confidence.

Confidence is a trait or skill you pick up and learn as you go through life. The amount of confidence you have at this moment in time has been influenced by your experiences in life so far. People who lack confidence have, unfortunately for them, had their abilities, their looks, their thoughts and their ideas put down and knocked over time by teachers, coaches, schoolmates, peers, strangers or even friends and family. So those doubts you have in your mind that you 'can't do that', you're 'not good enough', 'not beautiful enough', 'not tall enough', 'not skinny enough', 'not intelligent enough' and everything in between have all been learned.

Confidence is like a brick wall. Every snide remark, every put-down and every bad online interaction can chip away at the mortar, dislodge the bricks, or even knock the whole wall down altogether.

Often unintentionally, some of this chipping and dislodging of bricks can come from our parents or siblings. Our brains are like sponges. Information from all kinds of sources drips onto that sponge daily and everything, both the good and the bad, gets soaked up. If you are constantly being drip-fed the idea that you can't do something, or that you are stupid or somehow less important than anybody else in the room, then you are eventually going to believe that. Consequently, you will have little or no confidence in yourself.

I was lucky enough to have very supportive parents and a pretty idyllic childhood, but I've also had my own confidence knocked on more than one occasion. My sister, Michele, and I had a great upbringing on the outskirts of Waterford City in the south of Ireland. We lived about six kilometres from the city centre, down a dark country road surrounded by fields in a then-rural area named Williamstown. Further out the road there were quite a few big houses built by doctors, lawyers and businessmen, earning the road the nickname Millionaire's Row – but we lived in a modest three-bed-room bungalow with a decent-sized garden situated next door to my mother's parents.

My grandfather, or 'Gaga', as we called him, grew his own vege-tables, and worked on the land for various neighbours. He was also the only person in my family who ever showed me a magic trick.

When I was very small, he used to do a trick with a piece of twine that involved putting it in his mouth, tying the middle of it to his finger, which touched his nose, and then pulling it through his finger with his other hand. I've only remembered him doing this recently but maybe subconsciously that little trick – which I still don't know how to do – sparked my initial interest in magic.

When I was old enough to begin my education, my primary school was just a short walk across the fields behind our back garden. My mother and I used to hop the ditch every morning to begin the journey. On the way, we would pass cattle and sheep, and in spring it wasn't uncommon to have witnessed a calf, foal or lamb being born before I sat down at my school desk.

Waterpark Junior School was an all-boys' school, and was quite strict. While corporal punishment was banned in 1982, it was 1996 before it was made a criminal offence, so sometimes crude ways of 'enhancing our knowledge' were used, like the 'splinter stick' and knuckle raps to your temple if you got something wrong or weren't paying attention. Having those things done to me in front of my friends didn't do much to instil confidence in my ability to learn.

The school was also quite posh, and we actually had elocution lessons most days. At the time, there didn't seem much point to me in standing up and rhyming off, 'How, now, brown cow,' and various other sentences, but in hindsight it probably helped me in the business I ended up going into. Apart from that, school in general was pretty enjoyable in those early years and I had a large group of school friends. We played outdoors together in all weathers after school.

As a child I had two main interests. I loved animals and I loved magic. One of the biggest TV shows of the time was *The Paul Daniels Magic Show* on BBC. With just three or four channels to choose from,

Paul Daniels' show was great family entertainment and was a staple of my Saturday evening routine for most of its fifteen-year duration.

At the age of five, I got a Paul Daniels Magic Set for Christmas. My first trick involved placing a ball under a cup, lifting the cup to reveal that the ball had disappeared and then, to the amazement of my audience – usually my parents and my sister – lifting it again to make the ball reappear. Once I had mastered this simple ready-made trick, I began to show it to various members of my extended family and delighted in the response that I got for my efforts.

My parents saw how much joy I got out of that little magic set, and Santa must have noticed too, because every year after that I would get a magic set for Christmas and my birthday. As I got older and the tricks became bigger and more elaborate, I revelled in the notion that I could completely fool and astound an ever-widening circle of family, friends, classmates, teachers and even complete strangers with a simple magic trick.

Although the world becomes a much more cynical place as we grow into adulthood, magic always brings me back to that childhood delight, that feeling I got and still get to this day, from seeing grown men and women stunned and amazed at little tricks like a handkerchief or a card vanishing in front of their eyes. I found that performing magic for friends and family was an amazing way to develop confidence at a young age. Magic gave me a belief in myself that I'm not sure I would have had if I hadn't discovered my passion so early in life.

A move to the Christian Brothers-run Mount Sion school in the city centre, however, jolted me out of my happy-go-lucky prepubescent existence. I immediately struggled to fit into Mount Sion, but the one good thing about it for me was that my dad's childhood home was five minutes away and I got to spend every lunchtime with my grandparents Paddy and Nancy. My grandfather worked in the local post office and my grandmother was a fantastic cook, baker and mentor. She was also decades ahead of her time, practising yoga and meditation before they were even on the radar in Ireland. If she were alive today, I'm sure the modern term for her would be 'thought leader'. My daily lunchtime visits saw me build a really great bond with both of them as I grew up.

Most of the kids who went to Mount Sion lived nearby, in the city centre, so I was seen as an outsider. Not only an outsider but a posh outsider. Unlike them, I called my mother 'mum' instead of 'mam' or 'ma', and as far as they were concerned, I was from Millionaire's Row and was a spoilt little rich kid and a target for their bullying – which often left me hobbling around school with dead legs, bruised arms or chewing gum in my hair.

In an effort to avoid the bullies, I tried changing my accent for a while, but my mother was having none of it at home, so I was a bit confused as to what to do. At the time, I was a pretty solid defender for football club Johnville FC, but after a year or so in secondary school, in an attempt to build up my confidence and face up to the bullies, I stopped playing football to take up Taekwondo with two of my few friends from Mount Sion, Cian Foley and David Burke.

I really got stuck into Taekwondo and, after a few years, had moved up to black tag, one grade away from black belt. But I never got my black belt. I stopped for two reasons: the fact that we trained outside and had been doing inclined press-ups on our knuckles on corrugated concrete (which wasn't great for my long-term hand dexterity if I was to continue doing magic); and the fact that we started learning full-contact street-fight-style Taekwondo.

I remember sparring one day and getting kicked in the groin. Now, I had a protective cup on, but it was still sore and there were tears. As I welled up, the adult I was sparring with punched me in the nose and kicked me in the groin again. I fell to the ground as he shouted repeatedly at me to 'Get UP!' and continued kicking me.

As I lay there, defenceless, one of the older guys in the class, a six-foot-six behemoth who has since sadly passed away, came over and tried to get my sparring partner off me. When he repeatedly told the man to stop kicking me, his response was to keep on kicking me as he told my saviour, 'If he's on the ground outside a nightclub, they're going to keep kicking him!'

When he eventually pulled the man off me, and I dragged myself to my feet, I began to have second thoughts about Taekwondo. I realised I was dealing with enough bullies in school without having to deal with a fully grown adult bully and I quit the club. Having begun to build my confidence through the sport, my last experience of Taekwondo left me feeling even more vulnerable than before I started.

STOP GIVING ENERGY TO PEOPLE WHO KNOCK YOUR CONFIDENCE

Even if you manage to get through school relatively unscathed, college or employment can bring a whole new set of people armed with chisels who add to that chipping and stripping away of your wall of confidence. After a while you begin to doubt yourself. You tell yourself, and even other people, that you are shy, an introvert. But shyness is just a word for not expressing yourself because you're unsure, you don't want to feel silly, stupid or inadequate. Thalia Eley, professor of developmental behavioural genetics at King's College

London, says shyness is only around 30 per cent genetic and that 70 per cent comes from your reaction to your environment. Being shy at a young age can come from domineering parents, coaches, teachers, bullies, or others who won't let you have an opinion.

If you are over eighteen and are reading this book, though, then you need to realise that you are no longer a child who can be told to stay quiet or persuaded that you will never amount to anything. You are an adult and now is the time to accept responsibility for how you react to your environment. You can't continue to spend your life trapped in a web of anxiety and shyness. You must take responsibility. It's time to be yourself and stop blaming others.

If people around you are constantly knocking your confidence, then the first thing you must do is use the word 'stop'. You need to actually tell whoever it is to stop doing or saying whatever it is that is making you feel uncomfortable or damaging your confidence. If they don't stop then you need to either phase their opinions out of your life or phase those people out of your life and stop giving them your energy. You need to show them and, more importantly, yourself that you have matured, moved on and taken charge of your own mind.

Now, you might say something like 'I don't like confrontation. I can't phase them out.' Well, nobody in their right mind likes confrontation. The only people who like confrontation are bullies – and very often those bullies don't realise they are bullies and don't realise the harm that they have done.

On rare occasions, I still bump into the bullies from my old school. Often, they'll come up to me and say how great it is to see me doing so well. As they speak to me, in my head I want to attack them, pay them back for their misdeeds, but, of course, that is not the correct response. I know the right thing to do is simply to continuously phase them out. As an adult you have to start to forget bullies. You have to get to a point where you no longer give those people energy. You need to stop their thought process interfering with yours.

As a thirteen-year-old, I still practised magic almost every day, but career-wise I wanted to be a vet and spent the summer of my first year in secondary school helping the local vet, Ken Kiersey. Ken was a farm vet, which often meant helping him inject cattle, and I even had to put my hand up the rear end of a cow once in a while. I'd come home covered in cow dung most days and my mother wouldn't let me into the house until I'd stripped off my work clothes, but I absolutely loved it and worked with Ken for a couple of summers in an effort to get some experience of what it would be like if and when I got my dream job in the future.

At 14, I got my first ever paid magic show, a kids' party for families of the employees of Kromberg & Schubert in the old Ard Rí Hotel up on the hill in Waterford City. My uncle Brendan had got the gig for me. I had taught myself a show and had rehearsed it over and over at home. Doing it at home, though, and doing it in front of a hundred crazy screaming kids was a completely different ball game.

The whole way through my act, my hands would not stop shaking. I could actually feel and see them shaking but I couldn't stop them. I could barely pick up my props and the kids basically tore me apart for an hour. Every trick I did they would scream, 'It's up your sleeve,' or 'It's in your pocket,' or whatever else they could throw at me. They even grabbed my props and pulled my pockets inside out.

Although I got paid a small fee for the experience, I was a bit the worse for wear afterwards and my confidence in my ability as a magician had taken a really good battering. My mother could see from my body language as I slumped into the car that the show hadn't gone well and by the time we reached my grandmother Nancy's house I hadn't spoken more than a couple of words.

Always a very positive woman, Nancy tried to boost my spirits by telling me that she knew a magician who could give me some advice. Full of enthusiasm, she picked up the phone and called him right there and then.

'My grandson is a magician and I'm just wondering if you could give him some advice?'

'Sure,' came the reply and she handed the phone to me.

Excitedly, I began with 'Hi, how are you? I'd just really like to learn some …'

He stopped me mid-sentence with just four words.

'It's a closed shop!'

'I'm sorry, what do you mean?' I asked innocently.

'Magic! It's a closed shop!' he repeated and hung up. That was it, the only advice I had ever had from a real magician. The combination of a very shaky first show and the lack of empathy from someone who had been there and bought the T-shirt, someone I aspired to be like, left me running really low on confidence for a long time after.

Slowly, over time, I realised the best reaction to people who knock you is no reaction at all. Give them and their thoughts no energy whatsoever. None. Zero. Zilch.

Constantly absorbing this negativity will become deeply ingrained within the neuro-circuitry of your brain and drag your confidence down. To eliminate this negativity you must immediately focus on your confidence wall. Instead of the negative comment chipping away at your wall, imagine yourself putting another brick into or on top of the wall. Add some mortar and smile internally because the person's negativity is actually helping you build even greater confidence.

Years later I became friendly with the magician who fobbed me off when he saw me in the newspapers and made contact, but I'll never forget that day and how I felt after it. It's something I've learned from, and I currently mentor a couple of young Irish magicians, Aidan McCann and Daniel Cremin.

When I told Nancy the details about my disastrous first show and that I thought maybe I wasn't good enough to be a magician, she gave me my first lesson in reality with the words 'Well, that's life, Keith. Sometimes things don't go as well as you'd planned. We all find ourselves in situations where we feel out of our depth or that we don't deserve to be there, but the thing you need to learn is that everybody feels like an impostor sometimes. The trick is to never give up and to keep doing the things you love until you realise you are as good as anybody else.'

WE ARE ALL IMPOSTORS

At the time, I had never heard of the term 'impostor syndrome', and I'm sure my grandmother never had either. In the decades that have passed since those words of advice from my grandmother, I have come to realise that absolutely everyone suffers from impostor syndrome at some point in their lives. Impostor syndrome is that feeling that you don't belong in a certain environment or situation, that you're not good enough to be there, don't deserve to be there. It's that feeling you get when you don't believe in your own abilities.

The term was first coined in 1978 by Dr Pauline Clance and Dr Suzanne Imes after a study into highly successful women who, despite earning degrees, passing tests, and being formally recognised by their colleagues as excellent professionals, believed they were inadequate or incompetent and attributed their successes to luck.[3]

In the 1980s further research suggested that seventy per cent of all people feel like fakes or frauds at some point.[4] In my experience, I've found the figure to be much higher.

Every single one of the athletes, businesspeople and entertainers I have worked with as a mind coach over the years has the same reaction when I reveal this simple fact to them. Invariably, they reply with a huge sigh of relief, 'Oh my God, so it's not just me!'

Society often dictates that we are all at different levels socially, which means people often feel they are less than the person they are dealing with, whether that's their boss or their colleagues, friends or neighbours. The reality is that many people inherit and gain positions, possessions and power based on bloodlines, favouritism, looks, education, religion or race.

The greatest illusion of modern society is the fact that the majority of people who are now known as online influencers don't show the reality of their lives off camera. Many of the world's top 'influencers' and reality 'stars' have massive confidence issues. The majority of these figures have more problems than followers and definitely more problems than the ordinary Joe Soap. The fact that they look confident and sound confident is the illusion. In reality, many of the online singers don't have the confidence to sing in real-life scenarios, lots of social media magicians don't have the confidence to pull off a basic trick unless it's pre-recorded in front of a camera and plenty of online comedians don't have the confidence to stand on a stage in front of real people.

I know CEOs of multinational corporations who act like 12-year-olds at the weekend and have a side to themselves that they would never reveal to their colleagues. Although they command huge salaries, have great pension funds, drive nice cars, live in big houses, they genuinely don't believe they should be in the position they are in. And they are not the only ones.

In my one-to-one coaching sessions over the years, lots of international athletes, celebrities, successful businesspeople and even global superstars have all confided the same thing to me. They don't really think they should be in the position they are in. They are almost always waiting for somebody to expose them as a fraud, an impostor.

If you've ever had that feeling, then I have some good news for you. Absolutely everyone on this planet has doubts about their looks, their ideas, their relationships, their capabilities, even their whole way of life, at some stage or other. So, if you feel like an impostor in situations from business meetings to job interviews, auditions, joining a new team or class, even just meeting other people, remember that the people opposite you are more than likely feeling exactly the same or at least have felt that way at some point in the past.

When I was 15, I was among a group of students who went to Edinburgh on a school trip. After visiting Edinburgh Castle and almost putting my front teeth through my lip when I smashed my face off a handrail on my first attempt at ice skating, a classmate, Fergus Power, and I stumbled upon a magic shop on a little hill in the middle of the city.

On my grandmother Nancy's advice, I had kept on doing magic, but I had never seen a magic shop before, didn't even know such things existed, so I was blown away when I walked through the door and saw the number of tricks, props, illusions, gadgets and books inside. The place was a kaleidoscope of magic paraphernalia and I spent most of my pocket money on a trick that produced 'smoke' from your fingertips when you rubbed them together and two books entitled *The Klutz Book of Magic* by John Cassidy and Michael Stroud and *Practical Hypnotism* by Ed Wolff.

When I read the hypnotism book I was immediately fascinated. On the front of the book was a hypnotic spiral which I cut out and put on a pin so that I could spin it in front of people's eyes as per the instructions inside. When I got back home and finished reading it, I couldn't wait to find out if this hypnosis thing was actually real. As usual, my parents and my sister were the first guinea pigs for my newly acquired hypnosis skills. Of course, when I tried it, it didn't work on them. So I was still unsure as to whether hypnosis was real or not.

The Klutz Book of Magic, however, had given me great new ideas and tricks and I wanted to try them out on the public. At the time there were a lot of talent shows being held in pubs in the Waterford area, but after my previous experience of performing in public, I was wary of following my grandmother's advice when she suggested overcoming my impostor syndrome by entering them all. I knew my dad had been an entertainer when he was younger and had starred in musicals and 'Tops of the Town' shows in the area for years, so I decided to ask him for advice. He said, 'Keith, if you practise, practise, practise, put the work in and know you have done the best you possibly can to be ready, then you can be confident of success.'

PRACTICE MAKES PERMANENT

When it comes to card tricks, there is an old magician's saying that you should 'practise until your fingers bleed, then put on plasters and practise until the plasters wear off. Then you know you're ready.'

While refining the tricks I'd learned from *The Klutz Book of Magic*, I spent weeks and months with a deck of cards in my hands for up to eight hours a day. I would spend that time practising shuffles, cuts, slices, lifts and tricks. I would hold the cards all day just to get a feel for them. I got into the habit of showing anyone who entered my vicinity a card trick, which is something I have carried over to the present day. I sometimes made mistakes, but by making those mistakes in front of my family and friends, I learned from them without fear – and each mistake I made at home helped me ensure it wouldn't happen in front of a crowd.

Even now, as a professional magician, I practise daily. I almost always have a deck of cards very near me. I practise showmanship. I practise sleight of hand in front of a mirror. I even practise speaking. In the middle of writing this section, I had a pitch meeting with an executive from a US TV channel. Every chance I got, in between working and spending time with my family, I practised for the pitch meeting. I practised so much that in the middle of the meeting I actually lost my voice for the first time in over five years. In the middle of the most important meeting of the year! Thankfully, it was at the end of my presentation, and I was able to hand over to my producer and chug a glass of water before signing off.

You, too, should practise whatever you need to practise, be that a presentation, a job interview or a wedding speech. Practise the way you hold yourself, the way you speak, the way you smile, everything. Practise on your family, on your friends and especially in front of the mirror. Record and review your practice sessions on your smartphone. Make your mistakes there and correct those mistakes as you go along.

By practising for weeks on end and forcing myself to do a lot of magic in front of a lot of people, my nerves eased slightly and my performance in the talent shows began to improve, although I never actually won any of them.

THE POWER OF SAYING HELLO

After entering almost every talent show in Waterford, at 15 years of age I borrowed one of my dad's suit jackets, even though it was too small for me, and made my way into the city with the plan of going into every local restaurant and asking if I could do some table-hopping close-up magic for their customers as they dined. By then I had become quite adept at close-up magic and the nervousness regarding tricks was all but gone. Meeting new people and putting a business proposal to them, however, was a different prospect.

If you want to be confident when attending a business or social event, or simply when meeting new people, I've found that having a couple of simple things prepared can make a huge difference. To get over the hump of meeting new people at social events, I found magic was a great way to introduce myself when I was younger. 'Hello, how are you? I'm Keith. I'm a magician. Do you wanna see something you will remember for the rest of your life?' was my regular opening line. I will even give you a few of my favourite tricks at the end of this book that you can also use to help break the ice in any environment.

But you don't need magic to have confidence walking into a room full of people. Preparing a couple of things, a couple of sentences or a couple of bits of information that you know are appropriate for the environment you are going into will go a very long way. If that environment is a blind date or a social gathering, then four or five questions about the other person's favourite movie, favourite band, favourite sports team can often get a conversation rolling. Five or ten simple lines or questions can get a conversation started. Once you have those lines out and you can get into the flow, you're off.

A simple hack to boost your confidence in talking to new people is to take every opportunity to do just that. When you go for a walk put your technology away. It blows my mind the number of people who have their heads down, hoodies up and earbuds in, retreating from the world during their walks. Instead of listening to headphones or scrolling through social media, simply say hello and smile at each person you meet. You may not get a reply from everyone, but you will get a reply from most. Sometimes you will even get a full-blown chat and when you do, you will be surprised at how easy it is. The weather, the traffic, the news are all common topics of conversation and there are no wrong ways to start a conversation.

Unless I am having a very odd off day (yes, it does happen, but not often) I am always ready to make eye contact and simply say hello to strangers. Even if you say, 'It's a cold day today,' and the other person thinks it's hot then you will get another couple of sentences out of that. You don't have to spend ages talking to somebody but the simple act of saying hello will expose you to meeting new people and starting conversations that will boost your confidence.

The first restaurant I went into as a 15-year-old was the Wine Vault, one of the best restaurants in Waterford at the time. I had already envisaged myself traipsing around the twenty or so restaurants in town in the slim hope of getting into any of them, so I was prepared to take no for an answer and move to the next restaurant. As it happened, the owner, David Dennison, had seen somebody do table magic while he was on holiday in France, and when I pitched him my idea of doing magic at the tables, he said yes straight away.

As I left the premises, delighted that I had landed myself a weekend job doing magic, I began to realise I had something else to worry about. I would have to introduce myself to complete strangers over and over again. For the next day or two I tried to come up with a way of breaking the ice between myself and the customers. I eventually ended up introducing myself to the Wine Vault's diners every Friday evening by saying, 'Hi, I'm the wandering magician and I was wandering if you'd like to see some magic?' While it may have been corny, the line almost always worked. I got paid the princely sum of £20 every Friday and sometimes got enough tips off the customers to double my pay.

While my magic skills had begun to earn me a few bob, the jury was still out on hypnosis – until one day in school, when I unexpectedly managed to hypnotise David Burke in the middle of double Irish!

As David began to strut around the classroom clucking like a chicken, I sat there as amazed as everyone else that my hypnotism had worked. Much to the amusement of my classmates, and the consternation of our Irish teacher, David strutted around the room clucking, squawking, and flapping his arms, totally unaware that everyone else was looking on astounded.

As we all laughed, David continued to cluck and peck until a shout from the teacher shocked him back to reality and he returned, bewildered, to his seat, where he promptly got detention for something he couldn't even remember doing. That was the first moment I realised hypnosis was real and I rejoiced in the fact that my practising had finally paid off.

Not only did that chicken incident change my life but it changed David's too. Afterwards, he asked me for a loan of the hypnosis book. Although we have remained friends ever since, I didn't get that book back until about twenty-five years later. He presented it to me live on the *Late Late Show* and revealed to the viewers that he had been a hypnotherapist in Waterford for over a decade. I now regularly call him for advice on hypnotic techniques, as I regard him as the best hypnotherapist in Ireland by a long mile.

At home, I was still learning new magic tricks and continued to try hypnotism on members of my family whenever we met up for parties or gatherings. My first realisation that hypnotism could be used not just for entertainment purposes but to actually help people was when I convinced my father's friend Michael to let me try and persuade him to give up smoking. Although I wasn't nearly as proficient at the technique as a teenager as I am now, I sat him down that evening in my house and when I was finished, he refused a cigarette for the first time in over thirty years. Michael never smoked a single cigarette ever again. After that, I knew I wanted to become a hypnotist as well as a magician, but there was something more important looming on the horizon: my Leaving Certificate.

Academically, my veterinary dreams went out the window when I scored a pretty average 365 points on my first attempt. Even after repeating my exams the following year and boosting my score by one hundred points or so, I was still nowhere near the level required for veterinary college. When I told my parents that I wanted to be a full-time magician and hypnotist instead, they weren't exactly overwhelmed by the idea. While they had watched me progress over the years, they saw magic and hypnotism as hobbies. Although they would continue to support my passions, they told me in no uncertain terms that I was going to college to further my education.

2.

FROM JACK THE LAD TO KING OF CLUBS

HOW TO OPEN DOORS WITH YOUR TOES

BEFORE LEAVING MOUNT SION, I did an aptitude test one day with one of the nicer teachers in the school, Mr Barry (no relation). At the end of the test, he said, 'Well, Keith, the results tell me you're not great at science, so whatever you do in college, don't do science.' I had applied to various courses and colleges but when my CAO offers came back and veterinary science was out the window, perhaps with my teacher's words of advice ringing in my ears, the rebel in me chose to study a four-year Bachelor of Science degree in University College Galway. Unlike secondary school, I loved college life. I made some great friends and made the most of Galway's vibrant nightlife, festivals and parties and, as it turned out, I excelled at science without having to study too much.

I went home every weekend and continued working my close-up magic in the Wine Vault. By then I had made a few contacts through my shows and got to know popular Waterford entertainer Conor Halpin, who generously gave me a lot of work as a kids' magician. When I was 18 and had completed my first year in college, Conor got me a summer job as a kids' magician on the ferry from Rosslare to Cherbourg.

While the trip took 18 hours, I only had an hour's work to do, had my own cabin and was getting paid £80 a day. The ferry was my first experience of mingling with other entertainers. On board there were Irish dancers, comedians and singers and for 18-year-old me it was all a big adventure. The ferry was my first introduction to the theatre of big stage shows, though, and with older, more experienced people involved, I suddenly found I was quite nervous in that environment.

While families in general were placid when it came to watching the singers, dancers and other artists, I found that as a magician I didn't get the same treatment. As the children's entertainer, I was seen by some families as the babysitter for the duration of my show. I would have kids from maybe fifty different families who always wanted to know how a magic trick was done. If they thought they knew, even if they were miles off, they weren't long in letting me and everybody else know their theories.

After a while, doing magic on the ship reminded me of being back at my very first kids' party in the Ard Rí and it began to knock my confidence again. At one point, my performance anxiety hit such a peak that I came up with a mid-show routine so that, under the pretence of looking for a prop, I could quickly duck behind my cloth-covered magic table and vomit into an empty bucket I had there. The trick was to get the kids to shout the magic words 'Wizzy wizzy woo' over and over so that they couldn't hear me puking.

At the end of one particularly nervous show I decided to throw in a gag. I told all the kids in the audience to go and get ten pence from their parents, who were sitting around the entertainment area looking on. When the kids returned, I told them to put their ten pence into their closed hands and shout the words 'MAGIC, MAGIC, MAGIC' out loud. When they did, I told them to shout even louder. Again, they all followed my instructions as the parents stuck their fingers in their ears to drown out the noise.

'Okay, kids,' I smiled, winking at the onlooking parents, 'you're now all holding a magic ten pence. Later on, tonight, when you go to bed, put that ten-pence piece under your pillow and when you wake up in the morning it will have turned into a twenty-pound note.'

As the adults laughed and groaned, I walked off stage happy to be finished for the night. I thought no more of it until I was awoken by a bang on the door of my cabin at seven o'clock the next morning. When I opened the cabin door, the chief purser, the ship's manager if you like, was standing there holding a piece of paper. It was a note that read, 'I owe you £20, the magician.' Beside the chief purser was a young kid whose parents obviously didn't think much of my gag and were pretty irate about having to fork out £20 to their child.

To save face, I gave the kid twenty quid out of my own pocket, but even then, the child's parents were quite snotty about it when I saw them afterwards. I got a slap on the wrist off the chief purser and spent most of the day replaying the scene in my mind and worrying about the coming night's performance. Were there going to be more kids demanding money? Were there going to be more angry adults waiting for me? What was I doing thinking I could be a magician in the first place?

That night I was more nervous than ever. I felt like everyone was out to get me: the parents, the kids, the chief purser. I was so nervous that my whole body had begun to tense up and for some reason I had curled my toes as tight as I could. Just before I went on stage, I found myself randomly mumbling the words 'It's going to be okay. They're my best friends, they're my best friends, they're my best friends…' over and over again to myself to calm myself down.

AFFIRMATIONS

I have since learned, of course, that affirmations like the one a panic-stricken teenage me had been blabbering to myself backstage that night have been around for donkey's years. The reason affirmations have been around so long is because they work. Most of the world's top performers, from sports stars to businesspeople, use affirmations. So, what are they and how do they work?

Many people have heard the phrase 'Every day, in every way, I'm getting better and better.' It's so old it's new again and a lot of people probably have heard it without realising it's an affirmation. Although that particular affirmation is a good starting point, I have discovered that the more detail you can add into your affirmations the more effective they will be. As with the basketball experiment in the introduction, affirmations work because our brains don't know the difference between reality and a good visualisation. When you regularly repeat affirming statements, your brain begins to take these statements as fact. I have since updated and added what began as a panic-stricken ramble into one of my regular pre-show affirmations and I use others every single day.

STOP NOW, grab your journal and take a moment to write down three short affirmations that really resonate with you at this moment in time.

For example, if you are nervous or scared of what other people think of you, then maybe you can use an affirmation like:

'Nobody but me decides how I feel. I am confident and capable at what I do. I own my mind; nothing and no one will enter it without my permission,' or 'I believe in my abilities. I trust each and every decision I will make today will be the right decision for me. I deserve good things and I am confident in my ability to achieve everything I want in life.'

Affirmations, when repeated regularly, can help trick your brain into believing you are brimming with confidence. Once your brain believes those affirmations, it's only a matter of time before you actually are brimming with confidence and belief in yourself.

Make affirmations a daily habit. From now on, every morning when you brush your teeth or wash your face, look in the mirror and repeat your affirmations to yourself. You can even set a reminder on your phone to do it again before an important event or meeting, before you go to bed or as often as you like during the day. You can even go old school, as I do, and have Post-it notes all over your office or bedroom with your affirmations written on them, so you see them on a daily basis. I also have them set as my home screen on my iPad, iPhone and laptop. Do not underestimate the power of affirmations.

CURL YOUR TOES TO CONFIDENCE

Back on the ferry that night, I was so nervous that I actually kept my toes curled tight as I walked on stage and was in a reasonable amount of discomfort as I began the show. While I might have updated my pre-stage affirmations since working on the ferry, I've kept curling my toes ever since.

Over the years, I have seen performers use various affirmations and other techniques to settle themselves down, from stretching to tapping themselves, to doing vocals or jumping up and down and shaking. I've even seen some experienced entertainers on the side of the stage vomiting, just like I did on the ferry. That's a place you don't want to be.

At 18 on the ferry, I was so nervous that my whole body was tensing up. At that point I knew I had to do something to get over it, and curling my toes when I go out on stage is just a thing that I accidentally discovered works for me. The toe-curling technique distracted my subconscious from being nervous on the ferry. My mind was too busy wondering what was going on with the discomfort in my toes to be nervous. Subsequently, I understood that curling my toes as I repeated my affirmation also served as a physical anchor to the affirmation and released feel-good hormones such as dopamine and serotonin into my body.

Thankfully, what I discovered that night worked and since then I have incorporated curling my toes into a creative visualisation that I use to gain instant confidence, which I will share with you at the end of this section. Although it started out of panic, now, whenever I curl my toes it settles my autonomic nervous system down and I feel calm and assured.

In second year in UCG, my girlfriend began studying psychology in Galway. While we lived miles apart, we got to see each other quite a bit some days and I'd often browse through some of her course books as she studied. Pretty soon I was engrossed in psychology as much as magic and hypnotism. It was through reading her psychology books that I began to develop my interest in the power of the mind, and when I combined my new knowledge with my earlier interests in magic and hypnotism it had a very big influence on where my career ended up going.

At 21, I graduated from Galway with a first-class honours degree in chemistry. I got an award for the highest marks ever achieved in a BSc in UCG up until then and had signed up to do a PhD, but I ended up taking a job as a cosmetic scientist in Dublin instead.

Although I spent my days inventing women's make-up and men's skincare products for Oriflame in Sandyford, I still wanted to do magic full-time at some stage in the future, and carried a pack of cards with me almost everywhere I went. On a specific night out with Damien, a friend from work, those cards came in handy.

I had never really gone out in Dublin before so after a few hours in the pubs around Temple Bar, when Damien suggested we try to get into the Kitchen nightclub I presumed it was just like every other nightclub – that you got in as long as you were dressed smartly enough and weren't absolutely stone drunk or causing trouble.

The Kitchen, though, was the most happening nightclub in Dublin, if not Ireland, at the time. When we arrived outside there was a queue to get in that stretched all the way around the block. When Damien saw the line of people outside, he turned to go somewhere else. I curled my toes, grabbed him by the arm, assured him we'd get in and remembered some words of advice my father had given me as a youngster.

CHANGE YOUR POSTURE

My father used to say, 'Pull your shoulders back when you enter the room,' or 'Stand tall and stick your chest out when you go on stage.' It was his way of saying, 'Look tall, be confident.' Your posture reveals a lot about how you are feeling inside. If you are standing slumped over or sitting curled forward with your legs crossed or your hands or elbows on your knees or across your body, you are taking up as little space as possible, which indicates a submissive or nervous position.

The good thing about posture is that by simply changing the way you stand or sit, you can completely change the way you feel. In 2012, social psychologist Amy Cuddy gave a TED talk explaining how just two minutes of posing in open body 'power poses' that take up space, such as standing with your legs apart and your hands on your hips like Superman or Superwoman, sends a signal to the brain that you're feeling confident. Your brain then lowers your levels of cortisol, the primary stress hormone, and it also produces more testosterone.

These poses can be done in a bathroom or a lift or even outside a building where you need to feel confident. They can even be done before you turn on your camera ahead of your next dreaded Zoom call. I find that combining the poses with positive self-affirmations immediately before an event always leads to an increase in my confidence levels. Try them before your next presentation, interview or public speech. The effects may surprise you.

To stand confidently while talking to somebody, keep your chin level with the ground instead of pointing down to it. Align your feet with your shoulders and keep your feet five to six inches apart and pointing in the direction of the person you are speaking to. To feel more confident in your next online meeting sit up tall in your chair, pull your shoulders back and stare directly into the camera when speaking.

That night outside the Kitchen, with a bemused Damien in tow, I pulled my shoulders back and lifted my chin as I breezed past the queue and confidently approached the burly bouncer on the door.

'Where do you think you're going?' asked the bouncer, stopping me with an outstretched arm.

MAKE EYE CONTACT

Numerous studies have shown that people are more likely to listen to you, and more likely to be impressed by you, when you look them in the eye. Avoiding eye contact can be seen as a sign of untrustworthiness and people are less likely to believe what you have to say. A lot of people are fearful of making eye contact. If you are one of those people, simply pick a point between the other person's eyebrows and speak to there. That way the person will think you are looking directly at them, but you won't feel as if you are.

As I answered the bouncer, I made sure to make eye contact.

'I'm the celebrity magician!' I replied confidently as Damien looked on, bewildered.

'Yeah, right!' said the bouncer. 'Do us a trick, then!'

I pulled out my pack of cards and did a close-up trick for him. The bouncer grabbed the microphone tucked into the lapel of his jacket and called the manager of the club at the time, Ricky Mooney.

'This fella at the door says he's the celebrity magician …'

When Ricky arrived at the door, he too asked me to do a trick for him. I did another card trick and straight after that, to Damien's disbelief, we were both ushered into the VIP section of the club.

After spending most of the night performing magic for the various guests, none of whom I recognised, I was asked to stay back for a lock-in, where I did a few more tricks and got Ricky's phone number. The next day I phoned him and told him I wanted to do magic in the Kitchen every Friday night, much like I had done in the Wine Vault as a kid. When he asked me how much I wanted, though, I had no idea and came up with the figure of £80. He agreed immediately, which made me think I should have asked for more, and I ended up performing in the Kitchen for about two and a half years.

The Kitchen was underneath the Clarence Hotel and was owned by members of the band U2. The VIP section had its own bar and was like a little cave where celebrities or other guests huddled in small groups around maybe a dozen tables. In total, the area held maybe sixty people, but mere mortals never got past the security who guarded a roped-off area in front of the velvet door that marked the VIP entrance.

For the first few weeks, I felt as if I shouldn't be there, didn't deserve to be there. I felt like an impostor. All around me were celebrities from all walks of life. Suddenly they had this unknown kid from Waterford in their faces asking them if they wanted to see a magic trick.

Although I was petrified of being rejected in the Kitchen at the start, I took confidence from other people's belief in me. Sometimes people were too drunk or simply didn't want to see a trick but, even then, I revelled in the fact that I was working in U2's nightclub and that Ricky and the rest of the staff who worked there believed in me.

Often there were big international stars in the VIP section, and I soon found myself doing magic for stars like Bono, Bryan Adams, Naomi Campbell, and most of the boy bands you can think of. The

Kitchen is where I made my name in Dublin, where I grew in confidence and began to realise that I wasn't really any different from anybody else. I began to realise that we are all the same, that we all have our own insecurities and that my grandmother was right when she told me I wasn't the only one who sometimes feels like an impostor.

Years later, in 2004, I had that very same feeling when I was asked to do a TED talk in Monterey, California. Back then I was (and to be fair, I probably still am) a cheeky Irishman who performed magic, but I had been asked to perform live on stage for some of the people behind the biggest tech companies in the world. For about a month beforehand I was petrified.

By then, though, thankfully, I had enough experience and know-how to overcome my nerves. I prepared for weeks for that talk. I used affirmations daily. I practised in front of the mirror. I practised in front of friends and family. I visualised myself being a huge success. On the day of the talk, I was extremely well prepared, but I was still scared and lacking in confidence.

As a mentalist, I need to psychologically connect with my audience but, at the side of the stage, I had a brief moment of impostor syndrome. What the hell was I doing there in front of those important people?

Just before I went on, I repeated my new and improved pre-show affirmation internally. 'I deserve to be right here, right now, at this exact moment in time. I have worked hard for this and earned the right to be here. I love each and every person in that audience like they are my family. Nothing will faze me tonight and I will put on the best performance I've ever done. I'm going to love every single second of being on that stage. The audience will leave here with a sense of wonder, knowing they have witnessed something unique, something they have never witnessed before. Tonight, I will get a standing ovation.'

I then curled up my toes for an instant boost of confidence, pulled back my shoulders and walked out to an audience that contained Larry Page, the co-founder of Google, and Microsoft guru Bill Gates, among others.

Thankfully, my TED talk went pretty well. I got a standing ovation afterwards and 'Keith Barry: Brain Magic' featured in the top 25 TED talks of all time for around fifteen years.

Like most people, I've had my wall of confidence knocked down quite a few times over the years, and it often took a long time to build it back up before I accidentally perfected my toe-curling technique which, combined with the creative visualisation that I will share with you at the end of this section, helps me gain instant confidence whenever I need it. To this day, I use it every single time I go on stage or make an appearance on TV or online.

ACT THE PART

One of my favourite quotes is from Jean-Eugène Robert-Houdin, a French watchmaker who went on to become one of the world's top magicians in the 1800s and whose name later inspired the great Houdini. Robert-Houdin said, 'A magician is an actor playing the part of a magician.'

When I did my first kids' party, at the age of 14, I was an actor. I'd learned a couple of magic tricks but that was it. I was only playing the part of a magician. Seeing myself as a magician allowed me to pull off all the things I pulled off as a teenager. Even now, I see myself as an actor playing the parts of a magician, a hypnotist, a mentalist, a business coach, a movie consultant and lots more.

As a hypnotist I learned very early on that the art of hypnotism is based on confidence. You have to convince people to do things they wouldn't ordinarily do, just by using words. Hypnotists are probably the most confident people in the world, yet years ago I used to imagine myself as Pierce Brosnan, the Irish actor who starred in four James Bond movies, whenever I walked into a crowded room.

Brosnan was the epitome of confidence every time I saw him. He was my role model for how to look confident. Whenever I walked into a room, in my head I was Pierce Brosnan. Instead of shying away, I wanted people to look at me. Combined with the other things I described earlier, acting the part was another tool in my confidence toolkit until I found I didn't have to act any more.

Perhaps a modern-day equivalent of Brosnan would be somebody like Will Smith or Robert Downey, Jr, Margot Robbie or Beyoncé. Pick a role model like these, or somebody else you admire who exudes confidence.

STOP NOW and imagine a life-size hologram of that supremely confident person standing in front of you.

> Notice the way they carry themselves, the way they walk, the way they talk and the way they act.
> Imagine yourself walking into that life-size hologram and morphing into that person. Notice how that makes you feel.
> Notice the confidence of that person being absorbed inside you.
> Allow it to flow through your body.
> Multiply that confidence by a thousand. Feel it grow.

> › Feel yourself permanently absorbing their confidence.
> › Do this as often as necessary to start adding mortar and blocks to your confidence wall to make it stronger. Emulate that confident person in your own way. Now, that doesn't mean you go around walking and talking like them, but if you can channel their confidence and go out there and meet new people, speak publicly and do new things, then you are well on the way to supreme confidence.

A while back, Bono asked me out to his house to do a little surprise gig one night. I got to know the U2 frontman a few years back and we have remained friendly ever since. My presence on the night, however, was supposed to be a secret, so I hid in another room and then stood behind a set of double doors for a few minutes until it was my time to perform.

As I stood there waiting, though, I could feel the nerves kicking in. From the other side of the doors came a clinking of glasses, as if a speech was coming, and then Bono's voice. My brain was flip-flopping, sending conflicting messages into my head every couple of seconds, and I was surprised just how easily I had reverted to being the nervous teenager again.

'Shit! This is for Bono!' I thought.

'Yeah, but he's just a normal guy,' the rational side of my brain answered.

'This is Bono's house, though. You better not mess anything up!'

'It's okay ... it's just Bono, I've known him for a long time.'

'You better not mess up in front of his friends!'

'But it's only twelve people. You do this stuff in front of twelve hundred people on stage!'

'Yeah, but this is Bono!'

By the time Ireland's most famous musician was ready to open the drawing room doors, his mystery entertainer had gone through every emotion under the sun. I'd been giddy, nervous, excited, panicked, I even roared with laughter internally at one point, before remembering my affirmations and curling my toes in time to pull myself together.

'Ladies and gentlemen, I'd like to draw your attention, please,' Bono announced to his guests, as he pulled the doors back to reveal yours truly standing there. 'We've got the Brain Hacker here … the one and only Mister Keith Barry.'

To make matters worse, when I stepped into the room, the dozen or so guests included The Edge and his wife Morleigh, Hollywood star Colin Farrell and his sister Claudine, and Guy Oseary, U2's and David Blaine's manager.

Suddenly, I was now not only performing for one international superstar, but for other people to whom I looked up as absolute stars of world entertainment – as well as the guy who managed the top magician in the world. Thankfully, everything went very well on the night and when I was finished, I got what remains to this day the most memorable standing ovation of my life.

Like almost everything else in life, confidence is an acquired attribute, a skill that can be attained by anyone. Sometimes in life you will have your confidence knocked, sometimes you will have it built up. Focus on the times you have it built up and forget about the times it's been chipped away or knocked.

The truth is that any moment can feel overwhelming and while there is no magic dust to overcome lack of confidence, if you regularly use the tips above you will soon build a solid wall of confidence.

Regular use of the brain hacks below will help you gain even more confidence and help you maintain that confidence for years to come.

EVERYDAY BRAIN HACKS FOR CONFIDENCE

> Tell whoever is knocking your confidence to stop. If they don't stop, then accept responsibility for how you react and how that reaction in turn affects your confidence. If you can't phase them out, then stop giving them your energy.

> Understand that you deserve every single success that comes your way. Whenever you feel like an impostor, just remember that the other people there are more than likely feeling exactly the same or have done in the past.

> Practise whatever you need to practise on your family, friends and in front of the mirror. Make your mistakes there and learn from them. Practise so much that whatever you are doing becomes ingrained at a subconscious level and you can be confident of doing it in public.

> Say hello to at least three strangers you meet every day until you are confident starting conversations with people you don't know.

> Write down three affirmations that suit three different circumstances in your life. Use these affirmations to programme your mind to be more confident.

> As you use the above affirmations and the following visualisation, curl your toes to act as an anchor and a trigger to give you a boost of instant confidence.

> Pull your shoulders back, stand straight and become a superhero for two minutes before important events.

> If you are fearful of making eye contact, pick a point between the other person's eyebrows and speak to there. The person will

think you are looking directly at them, but y
you are.

> Become an actor playing the part of a confident
  role model who you believe is super confident and
  until you gain your own confidence.

——— VISUALISATION FOR CONFIDENCE ———

An audio recording of me guiding you through this visualisation can be accessed on my website www.keithbarry.com/brainhacks. The code to access recordings for all visualisations and techniques in this book is **BRAINHACKS21**.

You will need one of your three affirmations for confidence for this visualisation, or you can use one from this chapter. I want you to read this visualisation three times. I then want you to close your eyes and try to follow the instructions to the best of your ability. Don't worry at first if you don't memorise it word for word. In fact, feel free to open your eyes and reread it. Don't worry either if it doesn't seem to work the first time you try it. I have found that visualisation takes consistent practice and the more you persist over the next few days, weeks and months, the better the results will be.

> Sit or lie down in a quiet spot where you can make yourself comfortable. With your eyes closed, visualise a purple light hovering over your body. This is your light of relaxation. Feel the light hovering over your feet and relaxing your feet as it slowly enters them. Focus on your feet and actively allow them to relax. As you do this, repeat silently to yourself over and over, 'My feet are relaxed, my feet are relaxed, my feet are relaxed.'

> Now allow that purple light to slowly spread up through your

legs into your torso, your arms and every other part of your body. As you feel the light entering each part of your body, tell that part to relax. Focus on relaxing each part of your body in sequence.

> Once your body is relaxed, shift your focus to your breathing. Inhale for 6 seconds and focus on inhaling pure relaxation. Hold for 3 seconds. Exhale for 6 seconds and focus on all the tension leaving your body as you exhale. Do this 20 times.

> Now I want you to imagine a gigantic cinema screen in front of you. Imagine you can see on that screen a vivid, clear picture of the most confident version of yourself possible. Notice what it is about this version of yourself that makes you confident. Add in as much detail as possible. As you visualise this most confident version of yourself, curl your toes and begin to repeat one of your three affirmations.

> Jump into the picture and feel the confidence spreading through your body. Notice the way you stand, the way you speak, the way you make eye contact, the way you own the space you're in. Magnify that vision of yourself and magnify your confidence times ten.

> When you feel that confidence boost, slowly reorientate yourself back to your room or wherever you are and allow your toes to relax. In any situation where you need a boost of confidence, simply repeat your affirmations internally and curl your toes, and your confidence will soar.

This process, it's very important to note, is like riding a bicycle. When you are learning to ride a bike, sometimes you fall off. But that's okay. As a child we commit to the process of cycling until we can ride a bike without stabilisers. The most important thing is to get back on that bike and try again until it becomes natural. If visualisation is new to you, it might feel strange or unusual and your mind might wander as you do it. That's okay. Always remember to come back to your breathing and your visualisation.

If you commit to doing this for the next 14 days, at the end of that 14 days every single time you curl your toes, no matter where you are in life, you'll find that confidence jumps back into your body. As if you are a magician, you can immediately gift yourself the wonder of confidence.

RISK

a decision that, when calculated correctly,
has a high probability of success

'He who is not courageous enough to take
risks will accomplish nothing in life.'
– Muhammad Ali

3.

THE GIRL IN THE RED COAT

HOW CALCULATED RISKS
MOVE YOU FORWARD

O N A COOL JANUARY day in 1966, a 17-year-old named Ken was hanging out with his friends after they had finished their day of schooling in Mount Sion, Waterford. As they walked home, their usual messing and playing was interrupted momentarily when an unknown girl with long blonde hair and wearing a bright red coat sailed past the group on a bicycle and stopped nearby. After the boys picked their jaws up off the floor, they turned to young Ken and bet him sixpence that he didn't have the guts to ask her out on a date.

Young Ken immediately weighed up his options. Option one was to do nothing, in which case he could simply ignore his friends, carry on walking and be no worse off than he was there and then.

Option two, though, involved having the confidence to ask the girl out and taking a risk on what her reply might be.

This second option brought consequences. Again, Ken did a quick calculation. If the girl said no to his request, well … he might get a slagging from his friends for a few minutes afterwards and feel embarrassed, but otherwise the result would be pretty much the same as if he hadn't asked her out in the first place. On the other hand, if the girl answered that she would like to go out on a date with him, then young Ken would not only be sixpence the richer, but he'd also have a date. He decided the possible benefits far outweighed the risk and he took option two.

Although nervous, Ken summoned up the confidence to approach the girl and invited her to his school dinner dance, where he was due to collect county championship winner's medals in both hurling and Gaelic football. Much to the amazement of his friends, the risk paid off, the girl accepted the date and Kenneth won his sixpence.

That first date went pretty well and on 23 July 1971, Kenneth Barry and Kitty Howlett were married in Ballygunner Church, Waterford. Three years later they were blessed with their firstborn child, a daughter named Michele, but it wasn't until 2 October 1976 that young Ken's bet truly paid dividends and he hit the jackpot in the form of yours truly. Of course, my parents probably didn't realise that at the time … and possibly still don't.

The small, calculated risk that young Ken took that day changed his life forever and, as I write this book today, my parents are both in their seventies, still happily married and full of adventure.

Risk is something we live with every day. When we get out of bed in the morning we risk falling over. When we have a shower, we risk slipping and falling. When we eat our breakfast, we risk choking. Every time we cross the street, drive a car, climb a ladder or take part in sport, we take a risk. If we didn't take any risks, we would never get out of bed, never be able to do anything at all, but I firmly believe we all have an obligation to live a fulfilled life, a life of freedom, a life of optimal potential. To live a fulfilled life, we must accept risk as an essential part of the process.

A life without risk means that you will never achieve your dreams. As Facebook CEO Mark Zuckerberg puts it, 'The biggest risk you can take is not taking a risk. In a world that is changing really quickly, the only strategy that is guaranteed to fail is not taking risks.' Now, that doesn't mean you go out and take massive risks every day, but regular well-calculated risk-taking is beneficial to all of us.

Taking well-calculated risks regularly will open you up to a life of adventure. It will allow you to live the life you want to live, as opposed to a life other people feel you should live. By taking calculated risks on a regular basis, you will open new possibilities, develop new skills, build your confidence, discover new opportunities and even begin to reduce the hold that fear may have over you. Even the ones that don't work out will have a positive effect by teaching you responsibility and enabling you to learn from mistakes.

The average person makes around thirty-five thousand decisions a day, a good portion of which contain an element of risk. A lot of these risks have become so familiar to us that we don't even notice taking them anymore.

When people are told they are at high risk of diabetes or heart disease they often continue to eat foods that are bad for them. This is because the instant emotional reward of a bar of chocolate or a bowl of ice cream seemingly far outweighs the risk of diabetes or a heart attack, because the danger seems much further away. It's the same reason that smokers can often be seen smoking at the funeral of somebody who just died of lung cancer. The perceived 'reward' of the cigarette is immediate, while their own prospective funeral seems far in the distance. The truth is that these people have not taken the time and effort to properly calculate the risk they are taking versus the perceived reward they are feeling in the moment. If they did, they would realise they are being reckless.

Research has shown that one of the biggest regrets people have in their lives is not taking action.[5] Even if people have gone through broken marriages, failed businesses or worse, the regret of not doing something is far more tangible than the regret of doing something. An Australian palliative care nurse, Bronnie Ware, wrote in her memoir that the number one regret people have on their deathbed is that they didn't have the courage to live a life true to themselves and not the life others expected of them. So how do you gain the courage to take regular calculated risks to do the things you might be afraid of doing in order to live a life true to yourself? To begin with, you first need to understand that there are two main parts of the brain responsible for assessing and reacting to risk.

The first one, the amygdala, is that flashing red light that goes off in your head when you sense danger. The amygdala operates at a subconscious level and often hijacks our brain so that the response to perceived threat or danger is so strong that we can't choose how we want to react. For example, if you have ever pulled a child out of the path of an oncoming car or made other instant decisions in the face of danger, that was your amygdala at work.

The amygdala is highly efficient at sensing danger, triggering a set of physiological responses designed to get us out of harm's way. If you've experienced physiological responses like a rapidly beating heart, sweating palms or stiffening muscles when faced with per-ceived immediate danger, like an angry, snarling dog about to attack you or a stranger following you home in the dark, that is the amyg-dala responding immediately. This causes a dump of adrenaline into your system, which in turn triggers your fight-or-flight mechanism. The amygdala is essential in life-or-death situations.

The second part of the brain involved with risk is known as the neocortex. The neocortex consciously assesses risk, gathers infor-mation and intellectually attempts to provide a solution to a risky situation. It tries to weigh up the pros and cons of a situation and then make the best decision based on the data available to it at any given time. The neocortex is why we have seatbelts in cars, why we brush our teeth daily and why we have doors, windows and roofs on our houses.

Since the amygdala is part of our reptilian or primal brain, and appeared earlier in our evolutionary development, it can sometimes override our neocortex, resulting in us feeling stressed and anxious in moments where stress is actually not required. To take calculated risks, you must first understand how your own amygdala is functioning. Assuming you are not in a position to get a brain scan to measure this, here is a simple exercise for you to do in order to understand better:

STOP NOW and think of a real-life situation where you regret not taking a calculated risk. Close your eyes and picture the moment again as clearly as you can.

> What was your response?
> Did you feel panic, anxiety, stress? What other emotions were you feeling?

> › Did you collect all the information necessary to help you make the decision?
> › Was your decision emotional, intellectual or a combination of both?
> › Did other people's opinions influence your decision?
> › Why do you regret not taking the risk?

What advice would you give your past self in order to take that calculated risk? In your journal, list five things you should have done differently.

Commit right now, in this very moment, to use that advice moving forward with every risk you need to calculate in life.

Do you believe your amygdala could be hijacking your neocortex in certain situations and preventing you from taking appropriate risks? If your amygdala is always on heightened alert, it is going to be more difficult to take necessary risk.

When I was 14, our house in Williamstown was hit by lightning. I remember it being so loud I thought a shotgun had been let off in the hallway. We all gathered in the hall afterwards to check on each other but our dog, a corgi named Champ, was nowhere to be seen. Eventually, we found him cowering and shaking uncontrollably behind the toilet. Everything that was plugged in that night – the television, the phone, the radio, and more – had broken but, other than that, no harm was done. Or so it seemed.

From that moment onwards, any time I heard a shotgun (which was quite often as I lived in the countryside, surrounded by fields and land that was often used by the local gun club to shoot pheasants), I would jump with fright and have a mild panic attack for about ten minutes afterwards.

My amygdala's prehistoric protection system had associated the sound of the gunshot with the house being hit by lightning and was warning me that the same thing was happening again, even though my neocortex later rationalised that it was just a gunshot from the fields nearby. I wasn't the only one it affected. At the sound of a gunshot, poor old Champ would go running for cover and often wouldn't be seen for hours afterwards.

The problem with this is that when you are assessing a moment of risk that could prove to be beneficial to your life, like changing jobs, starting a business, starting or ending a relationship, your amygdala will immediately hijack your neocortex, resulting in stress hormones such as cortisol and adrenaline being dumped into your system. As a result of this, you may feel too anxious or stressed to properly analyse all of the information at hand and may shy away from taking a risk when actually the best option may be to take that risk.

This is why taking smaller risks every day is key to taking control of your amygdala. When you get used to taking small, calculated risks, and are able to gather and process the information necessary to make an informed decision, you will find it easier to calculate bigger risks over time.

About eight years after the lightning incident, a mentor of mine, the renowned hypnotist Tony Sadar, explained what was happening and how to hack into my brain to take control of my amygdala. At the end of this section, I will share a visualisation designed to help you to do the same. It will help you take control of your amygdala in stressful situations so that you assess risk in a proportionate manner, and you will no longer worry about taking even the smallest risk.

TAKE SMALL, CALCULATED
RISKS REGULARLY

Taking small, well-calculated risks on a regular basis will have a profoundly positive effect on your life and will enable you to take bigger risks down the line. Very often in life, the smallest of risks can yield a huge, unexpected dividend. As my dad found out at a young age, something as simple as asking a question could change your life forever.

A small, calculated risk that yielded unexpectedly big results for me happened during my second year in college. After I visited a specialist in Dublin one day to have allergy testing done, my parents brought me out for lunch in Madigan's of Donnybrook on the way home. As the pub was situated close to the headquarters of national broadcaster RTÉ, I was hoping we might spot a few TV stars as we tucked into our carvery and, sure enough, after a few minutes I spotted Pat Kenny having lunch at one of the tables across the lounge. At the time, Pat was the host of the *Late Late Show*, the biggest chat show in Ireland, and I was excited to see him in real life.

As usual, I had a deck of cards in my pocket. I told my dad that I wanted to go over to Pat and show him a card trick. My dad replied, 'Okay, but just remember he's having his lunch and he might not want to see a magic trick right now.' While I was nervous that Pat might tell me that he didn't have time or didn't want to see my trick, I knew that if he turned me away, well then, like my dad when he asked my mum out on that first date all those years ago, I would be no worse off than I had been a few minutes before. I weighed up the possible outcomes and decided to take the small risk of approaching his table.

What actually happened was that Pat Kenny was very nice to me. He allowed me to interrupt his lunch and show him a trick where he signed a card and put it back in the deck only for it to appear folded over in my mouth seconds later. He even accepted one of the business cards that I had had made up to hand out at children's parties in Waterford. I went back to my parents beaming that I had met Pat Kenny and shown him a trick.

As it turned out, that little risk reaped a big reward as shortly afterwards the *Late Late Show* was having a newcomers' night for up-and-coming Irish people from the worlds of art, fashion, music and entertainment, and a researcher from the show called me and invited me along to audition.

Because the show featured solely newcomers, it was the only pre-recorded show of the year. My parents brought me to the RTÉ studios, where I did my magic piece in front of a live audience. Afterwards, I wasn't that happy about my performance as I felt that the people I had brought up on stage hadn't reacted as well as I had hoped. The next day my heart sank when I got a phone call to say that my act had been cut from the newcomers' show as the producers had the same impression. They didn't think the people reacted well enough either.

In the next breath, though, the researcher told me that they thought that my act was very good. In fact, they felt it was good enough to film live and that they wanted me to come back for the following week's live show. The live show went fantastically well. I got a dozen bookings the very next day and people immediately began to recognise me on the streets. (If you want to see that performance, you can check out my Facebook post on 13 May 2021.)

Like my dad's small, calculated risk of asking my mother on a date, my small, calculated risk of interrupting Pat Kenny during his lunch paid massive dividends for me. It became a turning point in my life, and you would not be reading this book now if I hadn't approached him. I realised that in order to strive to be the best version of myself, I needed to continue to take these calculated risks regularly. And I believe that you need to do the same. Here are some simple, small risk ideas for you to try.

Reach out to somebody you fell out with. The risk here really is minimal. If they don't want to talk to you, well, you won't be any worse off than you are now. But if they do talk to you then you might just rekindle a great friendship that will last for decades.

Put your technology down for a day. Turn off your phone, your computer, your iPad, whatever you use. What's the risk? You might miss a call. You might miss another social media post from your neighbour telling you how great their life is. So what? In this day and age, if somebody really wants to contact you in an emergency, they'll find a way. You're not going to lose out on much if you don't see a picture of what your online friend ate for dinner last night in that fancy restaurant. Again, the risk is minimal, and the potential rewards are huge if you spend this day wisely. You will, at the very least, gain some valuable time for yourself and allow your mind to unwind and calm down. You will have extra time to play with your kids, talk to your partner, tell people how you feel, go for a walk or try something new.

Have a yes day. After setting down a number of ground rules and perhaps a budget, declare to the people who matter to you that on a certain day next week you will say yes to whatever they ask of you. This idea was inspired by the movie *Yes Day* featuring Jennifer Garner. Since watching the movie, I have done it twice – once with my kids and once with my team. Are you willing to take the risk of a yes day?

STOP NOW and think of another three small risks that you will take this week. When you have come up with three, write them into your journal or notebook and act upon them. For all of these small risks, the possible downside is minimal. If it doesn't work, you are no worse off than you were previously. But often, you will find that taking a small, calculated risk could lead to something unexpected and fantastic, perhaps even a life-changing experience.

As we've learned, the human brain has a funny way of dealing with what it perceives as risk. While a computer or a robot might take a very calculated route to decide the possible outcome of certain events, we as humans often find our amygdala and our neocortex conflicting over other factors such as familiarity, emotion, memory, the effects of our decisions on others and whether the consequences or rewards for taking the risk are immediate or longer term.

Now that you know a little about how your brain works when faced with immediate danger, let's have a look at some of the different types of risk and some other tricks your brain can play on you when trying to calculate risk.

Our behaviours can be far riskier when we are doing something familiar to us, something that we do regularly, like riding a bicycle or driving. If driving is an everyday occurrence for you, but you only take one holiday abroad a year, then you may perceive driving to be safer than flying, whereas all of the statistics on the subject would say otherwise. If you ride a bicycle often, you are more likely not to wear a helmet, even though the mere fact that you are cycling more often means there is a greater chance that you will fall off.

Often, we use unconscious routines, known as heuristics, to cope with complex decisions. Have you ever noticed that when you are driving a new car, for example, you are more careful when parking or manoeuvring it into a tight space until you get used to the size of your new vehicle? After the feel and size of the car get banked in your subconscious mind, it remembers that information for you and you find you are free to talk, listen to the radio and not worry about the size of your new car anymore. This, of course, can be problematic if one day you have a trailer on the back, or a bike on the roof rack, so to make the best calculations we need to look at each risk from as many angles as possible – and we also need to know how to calculate and sidestep the potential pitfalls that our brain naturally leads us into.

TURN DOWN YOUR INNER KYLIE

In 1990, Aussie songstress Kylie Minogue had a hit single with a song called 'Better the Devil You Know'. The title comes from an old saying that goes 'Better the devil you know than the devil you don't,' implying that it is better to continue with something bad that you know rather than take a risk on something new that you don't know.

Often when we are trying to calculate a risk, our amygdala hijacks our brain and begins to sing in its best Kylie voice, telling us that maybe we are better off sticking with what we know. If you've ever bought the same type of car as your previous make, the same brand of clothes as ones you already own or even eaten in the same restaurant a few times in a row, then you have experienced the easiest option of all, sticking to the devil you know.

But doing the same thing as you've previously done, or deciding it's not worth the hassle to change things up, is a protective mechanism. Often, trying something new is admitting to ourselves that what we have been doing isn't working out. As humans, though, we don't like being wrong, so staying on the same path feels like a better option. If we are given more than one option, this makes calculating the risk even harder and our amygdala turns the volume up on Kylie again. In this situation, you need to remind yourself of what you need to change and why you need to change it. Changing things up requires action and this can make you uncomfortable, but you need to ask yourself this – if you don't do something different, how are things going to change?

Naturally, we all want an easy life, so we are often just too lazy to change. We look for any excuse not to rock the boat. While sometimes this can be a good option, it is not going to move you forward in life. As Einstein is rumoured to have said, 'Insanity is doing the same thing over and over and expecting different results.'

By the time I was twenty-three I had a pretty secure job with a steady income, but I was old enough and wise enough to know that being a cosmetic scientist was not my main passion in life. My weekends in the Kitchen had opened my eyes to an exciting new world and going back to the lab in Oriflame every Monday, while it was a very good job and a nice friendly environment to work in, just wasn't the same.

Pretty soon I was, like many people reading this book, bored and unhappy in my job. I knew that I wanted to get out of the cosmetics industry and get into magic full-time, but the problem was that full-time magicians were practically unheard of in Ireland at the time (and, for the most part, still are).

By that point I had taken hundreds of smaller risks in my life and had come up with my own way of calculating them each time. More often than not these risks had worked out for me, so I sat down in my apartment one evening and used the same strategy when calculating my potential career change.

MINE, EDIT, EVALUATE, DECIDE

The first thing you must do when calculating any risk is mine all the information necessary. Just as a diamond miner must dig for months or years to find the diamond in the rough, so too must you mine deep to gather all the necessary information that will help you decide whether to take the risk.

Once you have all the information necessary, you should edit it into two columns – gains and losses. What will you gain if the decision pays off and what will you lose if this turns out to be the wrong decision for you? Be sure to include the smaller losses and gains in addition to the obvious larger losses or gains.

When you have every scrap of information mined and edited, you must then take your time and evaluate whether the possible gains outweigh the possible losses and whether those gains are sufficient to take the risk. Even if the gains seem to far outweigh the losses, you must also look at things from a negative perspective and have a plan for what happens if things don't work out.

Then you need to make your decision and stick to it.

STOP NOW and think of a medium risk you need to decide on in the near future. Make this a situation slightly riskier than the three you listed previously.

> › **Mine** for all available information, making sure to dig deep beneath the surface. List all the information you find in complete detail in your journal.

> **Edit** and split the information into two columns labelled gains and losses. Summarise the information into concise and easy-to-assess bullet points.

> **Evaluate** the potential gains and losses and be confident you are listening to both your emotional response (amygdala) and your intellectual response (neocortex) in harmony.

> **Decide** based on the above and commit 100 per cent to your decision, whatever that may be.

Remember, not making a decision is actually making a decision to do nothing. If your decision is to not go ahead then that's fine. But whether you take the calculated risk or pass on it, make sure it is a deliberate, conscious decision and that you have calculated your reasons for that decision.

Although I didn't know it at the time, the strategy I used when contemplating my career change was one that I would use when faced with any risk ever since. I believe that if you follow this system of mining, editing and evaluating all information it will help you predict the outcome of any risky decision you are attempting to make.

When I began to mine information and investigate the risk of changing careers more seriously, I realised that while I had no doubt in my mind that I wanted to be a full-time magician, in order to pay my bills I would have to be guaranteed a regular wage as a magician before I could leave my secure full-time job in Oriflame.

Even then, I calculated that I would need to have some money put by in case things didn't work out. After performing magic for VIPs in the Kitchen at the weekends, I began to hand out business cards everywhere in an effort to get more work. One night at a corporate event, I took a small risk on a new trick that involved borrowing a valuable ring from a woman and making it disappear, only for it to end up on a key chain on my belt seconds later. The risk with that trick was that the ring could go flying off in the dark room and get broken or, worse, never be found again. I did the trick on businesswoman Jackie Lavin and remember being a bit nervous when she parted with what looked like an expensive diamond ring. Thankfully the trick went well, Jackie was astounded, and I handed her my card. That little risk ended up paying big dividends afterwards. From that single trick I ended up getting several bookings from Jackie and her partner, Bill Cullen, who owned the Renault Ireland franchise at the time.

From those and other gigs I began to save money every week with the idea of having enough reserves to give myself at least six months to try to build my name and make it as a professional magician. Soon I was getting so many gigs, from parties to weddings and other functions, that I decided it was now or never to jump full-time into magic. Even then, though, my amygdala was holding me back and I felt I needed something more to balance the risk of no longer having a steady income.

If I turned professional, I didn't want to be one of those people who just sat around waiting for the phone to ring for work. I didn't want to do kids' parties for the rest of my life either, so I began to think of other ways to make a living from magic. A marketing executive I met in the Kitchen one night introduced me to the owners of large Irish retail store Champion Sports. I suggested that magic would be a great marketing tool for their brand and after pitching the concept to them that I could attract more attention and publicity for Champion Sports, they offered me a contract to become their full-time in-house magician.

I went home and edited all of my information in my journal, calculated the money I had saved, and the contract offer from Champion Sports versus the steady wage I had in my job at the time. I calculated the number of hours I would need to work as a magician each week versus the hours I worked at the time, the possible travelling time and expenses involved versus my expenses at the time and other potential positives and pitfalls of leaving or staying in my job, including the worst-case scenario of having to give up and get another job. After some careful thought and evaluation, I concluded that the risk of leaving Oriflame to chase my dream of being a professional magician was worth it.

When I told my dad the news, though, he wasn't entirely convinced. He asked me to continue working and just practise magic part time. I reminded him that when he was younger he himself had left a secure job in Waterford Crystal to take up a new job in a completely different role in newly formed Tipperary Crystal. I told him I was taking a calculated risk, just the same as he did, and he was surprised when I showed him my journal and explained how I had gathered all the relevant information, factored in the pros and cons, and evaluated each one before making my decision.

I also explained that I'd prepared for what might happen if my risk didn't pay off. I had an education that would help me find another job if necessary, I had a supportive family to fall back on and I had been saving money from gigs while working in Oriflame, enough to keep me going for about six months. Upon seeing my calculations on paper, my dad admitted that he couldn't argue with me and gave me his full support.

Within a couple of weeks, I had signed the contract and handed in my notice in at the cosmetics company. I spent the next year or so travelling around Ireland to the various Champion Sports stores, where I performed magic to customers while they waited on store assistants to help find the correct size in whichever running shoes they wanted to try on. I also trained up other members of staff so that they could entertain customers with a few simple tricks.

Although my in-house magician idea seems bizarre even now, it became a huge success. After a publicity stunt where I made it snow outside the company's Grafton Street branch one winter's evening, passers-by began to phone in to radio shows wondering why it was only snowing on one street in the entire city that night. That generated huge publicity for the Champion Sports brand. In fact, it gained so much publicity that I got invited onto the *Late Late Show* a second time, where I made it snow in the studio, live on prime-time television.

BE POSITIVELY NEGATIVE

Another trick our brain can play on us when we are making a tough decision, like whether we should buy a new house, have children, start a new venture or even end an old one, is that we have already subconsciously made our decision before our conscious brain catches up with us.

When that happens, we then only look for information that supports our pre-existing view on the subject and we subconsciously filter out information that doesn't suit our purpose. In this case you need to perform reverse psychology on yourself and be what I call 'positively negative' about your situation. In other words, you need to use negative thinking for positive benefits.

Do not fall into the trap of asking the advice of people who you know are thinking the same way as you are, or people you know are likely to play it safe and give you the answers they think you want to hear rather than the truth.

When you mine the information on your prospective risk, you should look at it as you would when booking a holiday or buying a product online. As well as looking at the five-star ratings in the reviews you should go and look at the one-star reviews and see if there are any common themes or negative data that you need to take into account. For example, if you saw a cheap hotel with lots of great five-star reviews but the same hotel had a few one-star reviews from people who said they were robbed at gunpoint in the parking lot, it might make you reconsider your potential booking.

Whenever you find yourself edging towards taking the risk before you even mine, edit and evaluate all the data, this is where you need to negatively review the situation in order to find the true positives. Ask yourself several negative questions and think about the situation from a negative standpoint in order to gain a fuller picture and make a decision that is positive for you and your life.

Switching jobs or careers is one of the biggest changes most people will undertake in their lives. If you're not happy in your job, for example, and feel you can do better elsewhere, you have a limited number of options. You can always stay discontented in your job, but my advice is not to do that. Life is too short to spend most of your day in an environment you do not want to be in. But you must always be aware of the pitfalls you might encounter if you take the risk of leaving.

Most people can't simply walk out of one job and into another, so you need to prepare by researching potential positions. You may need to stay where you are and save some money for a while, like I did, in order to make the transition. In this situation you can either take the risk and leave or change your attitude to that environment and to those around you to enable you to be happier in your work. No matter what risk you take, however, you need to be aware of the pitfalls you might encounter if you accept the risk.

WHEN YOU'RE IN A HOLE, STOP DIGGING

The amount of time, money and physical or psychological effort you've already put into what you have been doing up until now, whether that is a career, a relationship or even a lifestyle, are all things that can stop you from taking a risk and changing your current situation.

Economists call this the *sunk cost* bias. It is much harder to let go of something you have worked hard on or put time or money into, even when letting go is the best option available. Sunk costs are something you did in the past that came with a price. They are almost always irrecoverable and although they happened in the past and therefore are irrelevant to your current situation, when it comes to making a decision, sunk costs can cloud your judgement. Letting go of something that you put time and effort into can feel like admitting to a mistake. But failure is only failure if you don't learn from it.

When I was around twenty-two, I decided I wanted to be an illusionist because I thought corporates in Ireland would pay more money for big illusions. When I weighed up the risk, I wasn't positively negative enough with myself to realise the downsides: illusions were really expensive, I didn't actually have anywhere to store them, and I had no clue how to market my new act. Still, with my subconscious mind already made up and my conscious mind blocking out negative information and only looking for information that suited my view that the risk was worth it, I took out a loan from the bank of £3,500, telling them I was buying a car.

I'd only been driving a couple of years and had never driven a high-top van before, but I risked hiring one and driving it onto the ferry and across to England to a company called Quality Props, where I purchased a number of illusions including the Table of Death, and a Mini-Zag.

Having arrived in the dark of night, I found that Quality Props was run by a guy with a workshop in his back garden. Still, I signed the waiver freeing him of any repercussions should I get crushed in one of his devices and he showed me how to operate the props.

The Table of Death illusion was basically a large wooden table with around forty menacing 12-inch stainless steel spikes standing upright on a hinge at one end. The trick involved being handcuffed to the table and trying to escape before the steel spikes came crashing down and gave you a whole lot of body piercings that would never heal. Besides the spikes slamming down prematurely and killing you, the biggest danger with the Table of Death was the fact that your foot was positioned very, very close to a huge metal spike.

On my first attempt at the trick, in the dark, in this guy's back garden, I miscalculated where my foot was and the spike came down swiftly between my big toe and my second toe, pinning my shoe to the table. I couldn't do a whole lot apart from ponder how close it had been as the guy said, 'I told you to mind your feet!'

I packed my new illusions away and drove home, where I stored them in my partner's and my tiny apartment in Dublin. After practising the tricks over and over in our cramped living area, I only ever performed the illusions once on stage – in a hotel in Kilkenny.

After the Table of Death had almost lived up to its name again, the second illusion, the Mini-Zag, involved my beautiful assistant of the time (and future wife) crawling into a box, from which I made her disappear and reappear.

As part of the live act, I lit a torch soaked in lighter fluid and waved its three-foot flame in through the box to show the audience that the box was now 'empty'. Because of the lack of space in our tiny apartment, however, I had never actually lit the torch when we practised and didn't realise the flame would be so big. This little miscalculation saw me almost cook my assistant live on stage! Needless to say, I had to go solo after that show. Although I had sunk a lot of time and money into my new props, I dumped the illusions soon afterwards. I reckoned they were too dangerous to sell to anybody else.

STOP NOW and think about something you persist with in your life that is not giving you the results you want. Decide if you have fallen victim to the sunk cost bias by calculating how much time, effort and resources you have sunk into the project. Be realistic about your projected outcome. Rather than continue to dig a hole that will only get bigger and bigger, sometimes the best thing to do is throw away your shovel and stop digging.

4.

BITE THE BULLET

HOW SMALL MISCALCULATIONS CAN TEACH YOU BIG LESSONS

A FUN RISK I SOMETIMES take is observing complete strangers and predicting what they will do in a certain situation. The risk in me getting that wrong is minimal, but the reward live in front of an audience is very big. Back in 2009, I was on the Dermot and Dave radio show on 98FM, when I was asked for a different type of prediction. They wanted to know what I thought the outcome would be for the upcoming Heineken Cup final, where Leinster were due to play Leicester. I told the lads that I believed Leinster would win by three points.

At the outset, making a prediction like that seems like a massively risky thing to do. However, what most people hadn't realised was that I had known for a long time that I was going to make a prediction on that final at some point. As a mentalist, I had studied Leinster, Leicester and all of the other teams for weeks and weeks as the competition evolved. In the run-up to the final, I wasn't just studying the way they played on the pitch; I also studied the body language of every individual involved in both teams. I examined everything, from the weather and the condition of the pitch to the referee and the attitudes of the individual players, to come up with a prediction that Leinster would win the game by three points.

Of course, the risk for me in making such a bold claim at the time was purely reputational. The odds of Leinster winning by three points were 19/1, but I felt I had calculated the risk properly and thought it was worth it to predict that margin. When I make these types of prediction, however, they are always purely for fun and entertainment, so I was surprised to see both Dermot and Dave immediately bet €50 each on that exact result.

What I hadn't factored in when making this prediction was the idea of people actually gambling on the prediction. I don't ever encourage people to gamble on my estimations because of course they can be wrong. As a result of Dermot and Dave gambling on the result live on air, however, thousands of people at home did the same. Although my calculations were still valid, I hadn't mined all of the information necessary and now the risk of people losing real money far outweighed the potential reward of me being right.

A few days later I was sitting in Dundrum House with one of my best friends, Bart, watching the last moments of the final. In what had been a tight affair, the teams were level when Johnny Sexton stepped up to take a kick for Leinster with ten minutes to go. Sexton's shot sneaked inside the right-hand post to give Leinster a three-point lead and despite a nail-biting finale, they hung in to win by that margin.

While I was delighted that Leinster had won and that my prediction had come true, it was only the next day when I saw the papers that I realised that bookmaker Paddy Power had lost half a million euro on the match, €225,000 of which had been won by those betting on a three-point win for Leinster at odds of 19/1. The reward for me afterwards was massive – I was headline news for weeks and sold out my next tour – but I learned a lesson that no matter how detailed you are with your own calculations, sometimes unexpected circumstances, like thousands of people betting on a prediction, can swing the pendulum more towards the downside of the risk than the upside. What started out as a small risk for me ended up being a bigger risk involving more people.

TAKING BIG RISKS

If you want to take big risks, like changing jobs, starting a new business, or ending a relationship, you must make sure the rewards are big enough, maybe even life-changing. The reward must always be greater than the risk taken. If the gain is too small, then a big risk is never going to be worth it.

Sometimes I take really big risks that most people would deem unnecessary. I have survived driving blindfold, dangling in a straitjacket suspended upside down 150 feet in the air from a crane, being locked in a shed rigged with explosives and even having a bullet shot at my face. Some of these I look back on now and wonder if I was mad at the time. Some of them, I realise now, I hadn't calculated properly and while they worked out at the time, they could have gone horribly wrong.

Known as the black trick of magic, the bullet catch is the most dangerous illusion in the world of magic. The trick usually involves a gun being loaded with a bullet (signed by a member of the audience) which is then fired at the magician in question. The gun is handled and fired by a firearms expert to demonstrate that the person firing the gun does not come into contact with the person catching the bullet.

The bullet is often fired through a pane of glass, which shatters to demonstrate that the gun has actually fired the bullet and that it is en route to being caught by the magician in question. Bullet catches have previously involved the magician catching the bullet in a bottle, on a plate or even on the tip of a sword, but lately the trend has been to catch it in the mouth, sometimes in a specially made metal box held between the teeth.

At the time of writing, at least fifteen people have died as a result of trying to pull off this trick. Some of these deaths have been what may loosely be termed 'accidental', like Adam Epstein, who died in 1869 when shards of the wand used to stuff balls into his rifle broke off inside the barrel and killed him when it was fired. Chung Ling Soo performed the catch regularly in the UK using a trick pistol with secret compartments. Overuse of the pistol, however, wore the parts down and in 1918 the bullet hit him in a lung; he died on stage.

Other bullet catch deaths, however, were not so accidental, such as the death of Arnold Buck in 1840, when the volunteer who loaded his gun secretly stuffed nails into the barrel as well. In 1890 deLine Jr was shot and killed on stage by his father, who was later jailed, while in 1922, H.T. Sartell, known as the Black Wizard of the West, died on stage when his wife purposely fired live bullets at him.

Some of the latest people to do it have had very narrow escapes. Steve Cohen did the bullet catch in New York in 2012. He stood 20 feet from the shooter in an underground firing range with a sheet of tempered glass hung halfway between them. Tempered glass was used because, instead of cracking into larger shards, the glass would form beads, which were supposed to fall straight down. When the bullet hit one bead of glass, however, the bead travelled onward and hit him in the chest, and he was rushed to hospital suffering from a huge haematoma all along his right side.

Still, despite the obvious risks, the trick has been attempted by professionals and even amateurs since then. On 26 June 2017, Monalisa Perez fatally shot her 22-year-old boyfriend, Pedro Ruiz III, in Minnesota. As the duo filmed a video they hoped would go viral on YouTube, Ruiz was shot in the chest with a semi-automatic pistol from about a foot away after he persuaded his girlfriend that a hardcover encyclopaedia would stop the bullet. Perez was seven months pregnant with the couple's second child at the time.

Even the great Harry Houdini was famously persuaded by his magician friend Harry Kellar that to attempt the trick was a step too far. 'We can't afford to lose Houdini' was one of the lines used to dissuade the legendary escape artist from a planned attempt.

Even with the knowledge of all these accidents and deaths, I decided to take the major risk of performing the bullet catch myself in Collins Barracks in 2004.

When researching the trick, I contacted the author of a 1986 book named *Twelve Have Died*, the title referring to the number of lives the bullet catch had claimed up to that point. When I asked him for advice, Ben Robinson – who lost four front teeth in his own attempt at the trick – was so scared of inadvertently encouraging me and perhaps adding another name to the list that he didn't even want to talk to me. 'The only advice I will give you', he said, 'is don't do it!'

The risk of serious injury, or even death, meant that safety was my biggest concern for the duration of the event. For me to go ahead with the trick, I needed to have just one bullet signed by a random audience member and then placed in the gun.

All eyeballs were to be on that bullet from then until the end of the trick. As I would have to lose sight of the bullet to do the trick, I also had two 'hidden ninjas' behind the scenes whose only job was to stare at the bullet and never let it out of their sight. It was the only way I could be confident that it was the only bullet that could be placed in the chamber of that gun.

Despite having done everything I could to ensure the integrity and safety of the catch, I was extremely nervous as I walked, with my hands handcuffed behind my back, down to the far end of the enclosed courtyard in Collins Barracks and the spot where I was due to stand. At the other end of the yard, an Irish Olympic marksman had previously shown the audience his skills with a handgun by hitting three or four targets from the same distance with the same pistol.

As I hit my marker and turned around to face the shooter, my amygdala's red light for danger was still flashing incessantly. *What the hell am I doing here? Am I insane? How did I ever think this was a good idea?* I was extremely nervous – but in situations like that it's important to be nervous. Your amygdala's function is to keep you safe, so nerves are a good thing. If you're not concerned about the outcome, you will be reckless with your risk-taking. In the few seconds it took the marksman to aim at my head, I was praying that I wouldn't be one of the unfortunate ones who died while doing this trick. What happened next, though, another miscalculation on my part, almost ruined the whole spectacle.

While I had told almost all the people involved in the bullet catch how the trick worked, I had forgotten to tell the paramedic who was on standby just out of shot at my end of the courtyard. When the bullet smashed through the glass, I jolted backwards and a tiny drop of blood trickled out of my mouth. The paramedic instinctively ran out to help me.

While he was concerned that I might be injured, I wanted to make sure that the audience could see the signed bullet between my teeth. As the armourer walked up with a tray for me to spit the bullet onto, I had to tell the confused paramedic to quickly get out of the shot or else the camera wouldn't be able to see me. If you look at my bullet catch on YouTube, you will see him run out and then look back to see where the camera is.

A lot of people later thought he was part of the trick, when in fact he was just trying to do his job and save me. I should have told him beforehand not to come running unless he saw lots of blood pouring from my face or chest. That little miscalculation could have seen him block the camera's view so my bullet catch couldn't be aired on television – and, as it was such a risky stunt, there was no way I was going to do it again.

THE BULLET STOPS WITH YOU

While the bullet catch was one of the most nerve-racking things I have ever done, it was a fantastic learning curve for me when it comes to taking risks. I realised that when other people are involved you must build them into the equation. This is probably one of the hardest things to do when calculating risk. You can never really legislate for what somebody else is going to do, so, where possible, try not to involve other people in the process of analysing risk. I've had other reminders of that on occasion since then.

Every night for my final act in my 'Eight Deadly Sins' tour around Ireland I would sit in a chair and be wrapped in a hundred foot of rope by two random audience members. The volunteers were each incentivised to tie me up tightly by a €500 bet that I could escape from the rope in less time than it took them to tie me to the chair. After tying me up, the duo would then wrap my head in clingfilm and leave me to escape as a countdown clock ran in the background.

One night, during my Waterford show, two guys came up on stage and had tied me quite loosely. I immediately thought it was going to be easy to escape. Just as that thought entered my head, however, one of the guys, a big burly lad, took one end of the rope and suddenly yanked it hard. He pulled it so tight that my whole body crunched over in the chair, to the extent that I thought he had broken my ribs.

When I asked him what he did for a living, he answered that he tied down big loads on trucks every day. While I escaped that night, I was left with huge rope burns all over my arms and torso for about two weeks afterwards.

During the same escape in the Olympia one night, one of the guys who came up on stage began to tie the rope in all sorts of different knots. These were big intricate knots that I had never seen before. When I asked him what he did for a living, he replied that he was a sailor.

When the sailor and the other audience member left me to try and make my escape that night, the rope was so tight that I couldn't get my hands out. I kicked back in the chair, fell over on my side and winded myself. My instant reaction to inhale, though, was thwarted by the clingfilm wrapped around my head and I passed out, tied to the chair on stage in front of a live audience.

At the time, one of my assistants was sitting in the balcony doing the countdown. On seeing me lie motionless on the stage, he actually jumped out of the balcony and dropped down onto the stage to come to my aid. As the curtains came down, he popped a hole in the clingfilm, and I was able to breathe and I came round.

Having somebody who was a professional at tying a rope come up on stage never entered my mind when I was calculating the risk involved in this stunt. By not taking into account what the other people involved might do, I was injured in Waterford and almost died in the Olympia during what had become a pretty routine trick for me at the time. To rub salt into my wounds, the two guys who had tied me up came around to the side door of the Olympia after the show with their hands out to receive their €500 winnings! My miscalculation had not only almost killed me that night, but it hurt my pride and cost me a thousand euro as well.

When trying to factor in other people's involvement in your risk, there are a few things you need to ask yourself. Are these people you know and trust or are they strangers? Are they experts in the decision you are about to make? Do they have a record of helping you or others? Will their advice assist you in calculating the risk or hinder you? Could they have ulterior motives or, like the sailor who tied me up, could they be incentivised in any way to lead you towards a certain result? An everyday example of this is a mortgage or insurance broker who receives a commission from a certain bank or company for your business. They are more likely to lead you towards their commission than the best deal on the market.

For me, while they seem very dangerous at the time, those bigger, crazier risks are almost always worth it. In those instances, my amygdala, my nerves, are keeping me alive. Although nervous, I'm calm and paying attention to everything. I'm paying attention to the armourer, the bullets, the marksman, or the straitjacket, the locks, the crane, depending on the stunt I'm doing.

These bigger risks have a huge reward for me: being able to fill theatres and travel the world doing something I love. If I played it safe and just did card tricks all the time, then nobody would come to my shows, my career would have stalled long ago, and I might have had to get a 'proper' job. When I hung upside down from a crane with my head wrapped in clingfilm and my body tied into a straitjacket in Waterford in front of ten thousand people, I made an indelible impression on my kids, who were in that crowd. The adventure makes it worth it.

DON'T BE RECKLESS

You must understand there is a major difference between gambling and calculated risk-taking. Although, as a professional, I regularly perform seemingly crazy stunts, I would never advise someone to do anything life-threatening or take risks that are detrimental to their health. There are many times in life when we have to decide if we need to take major risks. If you simply want to take a risk without actually needing to do so, my advice would be not to. Be mindful of the traps that our brains can lead us into when making risky decisions. Don't make a big decision when you are emotionally vulnerable. Make sure everything else in your life is stable before taking bigger risks. You need to ensure that if the risk doesn't pay off you are in a headspace that can handle that. Don't make risky decisions on the spur of the moment.

Everyone still has something they want to do, some risk they haven't taken – whether that's writing a book, starting a business, moving to a new house or telling somebody how they feel. Of course, not every decision you make will work out, that's why it's called a risk, but life would be very dull if we all did the same thing and nobody took any calculated risks.

I have learned that taking regular smaller risks promotes confidence, adds excitement to life and often throws up unexpected opportunities. I've also learned that regular risk-taking brings regular failings. But regular failings bring regular learning, which in turn brings self-improvement, something we should all be constantly striving for. Very often our fears keep us from achieving our dreams, but you'll never achieve your dreams without taking calculated risks. A lot of the time the reward for risk-takers can be far greater than the sum of those fears.

STOP NOW, grab your journal and write down the one big risk you need to consider taking this year, the one with the potential to be life-changing, and use the tactics I've outlined in this section to help you decide whether or not to take that risk.

As Jim Rohn, a pioneer of self-development, once said, 'I'll tell you what changed my whole life. I finally discovered that it's all risky. The minute you got born it got risky. If you think trying is risky, wait until they hand you the bill for not trying! Better to live thirty years full of adventure, than a hundred years safe in the corner.'

EVERYDAY BRAIN HACKS FOR TAKING CALCULATED RISKS

> Very often in life, the smallest of risks can yield a huge, most unexpected, dividend. Simply asking a question could change your life forever. Calculate three small risks every week. Write them into your journal or notebook and act upon them.

> Whenever your brain hears Kylie singing 'Better the Devil You Know', remember it's your amygdala trying to protect you by playing it safe. Turn the volume down and analyse the risk properly.

> You need to mine as much information as possible from every source possible about the risk you are going to take. Then you need to edit that information down into two tables, the gains on one side and the losses on the other. You must evaluate the situation using the information to hand and when you have done that decide whether or not the risk is worth it. Don't hesitate with your decision. Make it immediately.

> Whenever you find your brain edging you towards taking a risk before you fully mine, edit and evaluate all of the data, be positively negative and look for the one-star reviews in addition to the five-star reviews.

> When you invest a lot of time, money or effort into something it's often difficult to let those sunk costs go and change what you need to change. But often when you find yourself in a deep hole the best thing to do is throw away your shovel and stop digging.

> When trying to factor in other people's involvement in your risk, you must ask yourself if you can trust them, if they are experts, or if they could be incentivised to have ulterior motives. Remember that when you take that risk, the bullet stops with you.

> Don't take risks that are life-threatening or potentially detrimental to your health. Don't make a decision when you are emotionally vulnerable. Understand whether you are reacting to other people's opinions or to your own true emotion and belief.

VISUALISATION FOR CALCULATED RISK-TAKING

An audio recording of me guiding you through this visualisation can be accessed on my website www.keithbarry.com/brainhacks.

Read through the following several times before beginning the visualisation:

> Sit or lie down in a quiet spot where you can make yourself comfortable. With your eyes closed, visualise a purple light hovering over your body. This is your light of relaxation. Feel the light hovering over your feet and relaxing your feet as it slowly enters them. Focus on your feet and actively allow them to relax. As you do this, repeat silently to yourself over and over, 'My feet are relaxed, my feet are relaxed, my feet are relaxed.'

> Now allow that purple light to slowly spread up through your legs into your torso, your arms, and every other part of your body. As you feel the light entering each part of your body, tell that part to relax. Focus on relaxing each part of your body in sequence.

> Once your body is relaxed, shift your focus to your breathing. Inhale for 6 seconds and focus on inhaling pure relaxation. Hold your breath for 3 seconds. Breathe out for 6 seconds and focus on all the tension leaving your body as you exhale. Do this breathing 20 times.

> Now I want you to imagine a gigantic cinema screen in front of you. Imagine you can see in bright, vivid detail a moment in time when you know you should have taken a calculated risk but didn't. A moment when your emotions hijacked your system, preventing you from taking the necessary risk.

> Notice yourself on the screen back in that moment, losing control of your decision-making ability and allowing negative emotions to override your intellect.

> As you watch this movie of your past, pause the picture in your mind and make a commitment right now that you will stay calm when making any decisions involving risk from this moment onwards.

> Switch the paused picture of this out-of-control past version of you to black and white and see it pixelating and dissolving away into the distance.

> Replace that out-of-control, emotional version of you with a calm, collected vision of yourself.

> See yourself in that moment breathing in for 6 seconds, holding your breath for 3 seconds, and then exhaling for 6 seconds. As you see this, actually breathe with this technique right here, right now.

> Feel your mind and body relaxing the moment you begin this breath work. See yourself calm, collected and tapping into the inner strength and resources necessary to take this decision. As you visualise this, push your tongue gently to the roof of your mouth to anchor the feeling of controlled relaxation.

> Now visualise a future risky decision where you feel you need to be in full control of your emotions. Visualise this moment

clearly on the screen. See yourself calm and collected and relaxing your mind using your breathing. See yourself triggering that relaxation by touching your tongue to the roof of your mouth.

> Notice, as you are assessing the decision, how calm and self-assured you are. Make a commitment that from this moment onwards you will tap into this calmness, stay in command of your emotions and ultimately be firm in making your final decision, whatever that decision may be.

> Repeat these steps as necessary, visualising different risky scenarios as you do so.

> Slowly open your eyes and reorientate yourself back to your surroundings.

If you commit to doing this for the next 14 days, every single time you practise your 6.3.6 breathing, no matter where you are in life, you'll find that you can take control of your emotions in order to calculate accurately the risk involved and make the decision best for you. Any time you need to control your emotions and release calmness in any risky situation simply press your tongue to the roof of your mouth and calmness will flood into your body.

CREATIVITY

the ability to create unique ideas using magical thinking

'Every child is born blessed with a vivid imagination. But just as a muscle grows flabby with disuse, so the bright imagination of a child pales in later years if he ceases to exercise it.' – Walt Disney

5.

THE CHAOS OF CREATIVITY

HOW TO THINK LIKE A MAGICIAN

BEFORE YOU BEGIN this chapter, I want you to try to connect the nine dots below with no more than four straight lines and without lifting your pen or finger from the paper or going over the same line twice. When you have either found a solution or given up, read on.

Creativity is a trait regarded with envy by many. It is assumed that if somebody is creative and has a vivid imagination then they must have had this mysterious way of solving problems and coming up with ideas gifted to them at birth.

The truth is that we are all capable of creativity. Like confidence, resilience, influence or any other skill, creativity must be practised and honed regularly, which is why children are far more creative than adults.

How many times have you witnessed children get lots of presents for Christmas only to spend longer playing with the large cardboard box that the toys came in? My own children spent half of one Christmas holidays using a large cardboard box as a house, then a car and then an indoor slide on the stairs.

What adult goes into a toy shop, sees a big cardboard box and buys it thinking, 'That'll make a great indoor slide'?

Researchers in Berkeley, California, recently found that four- and five-year-olds are smarter than college students when it comes to figuring out how toys and gadgets work.[6] This is because young children spend much of their day, in school and at home, practising being creative. They play, they draw, they make jigsaws, they build things, they colour pictures, they paint with their fingers, and they use their imagination for a very large portion of every single day.

Children also have very few boundaries in their minds, which is why their creativity is amazing. But as we get older, school teaches us to focus on facts, logic and reality. Grown-up stuff gets in the way of playing pretend and we often go very long periods of time – weeks and even months – without giving any time at all to being creative and our imagination dwindles down to nothing.

We all have the ability to generate new ideas, problem-solve and be creative, some of us more than others, depending on our life experiences, our education, desire or confidence, but often as adults our own self-imposed rules get in the way.

THROW AWAY THE RULEBOOK AND THINK LIKE A MAGICIAN

When I made up my mind that I wanted to be a professional magician, everyone who I talked to about my plans, outside my close family and friends, laughed at me. Every single one of them. When I handed in my resignation at Oriflame, my boss was taken aback. I had a good job and had even been given my own line of men's cosmetics to produce. She couldn't understand me wanting to leave.

'What do you mean you're quitting? What are you going to do?' she asked.

When I answered with 'I'm going to be a magician,' she thought I was joking and laughed.

'No, seriously,' she said with a smile. 'What are you going to do?'

Back in University College Galway, after completing my degree, I had signed up for a PhD. When I went to tell Professor Spillane that I had changed my mind and was going to try to become a full-time magician, he couldn't understand it. He too started laughing. 'What do you mean you're going to be a magician? A magician? Like … magic? Seriously?'

The reason everyone laughed is because they all had rules in their heads that couldn't be broken. There is no exam in magic in the Leaving Certificate, no degree in magic in any college in the country, so therefore, in their heads, there couldn't possibly be a career in magic.

While my parents were and still are a constant source of support, when it came to magic, their advice was always 'Magic is great … as a hobby.' They were concerned parents and weren't sure magic was a viable option as a job, because they had never heard of anybody being a full-time magician, so therefore there were no rules for that.

Society lays down rules for us all of the time. 'You can't do that.' 'You're no good at this.' 'You're too old for that.' 'You have no degree for this.' 'You can't make a living doing that.' We get used to following orders, following rules, but one thing I have learned as a magician is that rules kill creativity.

Now, you do need certain rules in order to live a safe and happy life, but when it comes to being creative, the first thing you must do is throw away the rulebook. Like children, most magicians simply don't allow themselves to follow any rules in order to be truly creative when coming up with tricks and illusions.

As the magic and mentalism consultant on the movie *Now You See Me 2*, I was asked if I could do a giant version of three-card monte that could be filmed in one take. Whenever I get asked questions like this the answer is always yes. I may have no clue at the time how I'm going to do it, but I will always say yes and, invariably, by the time it comes around to doing it I will have it worked out. Three-card monte is a street trick in America and can sometimes be seen at race meetings, festivals or carnivals in Ireland. The trick involves a hustler laying down three cards, usually two black kings and a red queen. The hustler turns the cards face down and moves them around their table while a spectator bets on where they think the queen is.

Often there is a secret accomplice, acting the part of a spectator, who is sometimes seen winning money to encourage passers-by to bet on the game. Through sleight of hand, though, the innocent bystanders will never win. Even if they pick the correct card, the hustler will use a sleight of hand move known as the Mexican turnover, resulting in the cards being switched without anybody noticing.

When I sat down to try to figure out how to do a giant three-card monte trick for the movie, the first thing I thought of was the other name for the trick. In Ireland, because you are looking for a queen among two kings, it's called 'find the lady'. I thought, 'Well, if I don't limit myself to the usual rules of only using cards, then why not make things more exciting for the movie? Wouldn't it be cool if we used a real woman and two men in "find the lady"?' I immediately wrote my idea on a Post-it note.

Next, I had to come up with a way the trick might be done. As the trick would actually be revealed in the movie, I had to come up with a method that was easy to reveal. When I started brainstorming my ideas with other people on my creativity team, I came up with the idea of using either identical triplets or quadruplets, or three sets of identical twins. I brought all these ideas together and then began to wonder how the trick could work.

Normally at this stage of the process I would be at home making a model of my trick from something like cardboard, Play-Doh or Lego. All of these are great for working out problems or building models of something you want to make in real life. In fact, there is a whole new creative industry based on playing with Lego; multinational corporations are now paying a lot of money to bring Lego creatives into their offices to teach people how to be more creative.

On the set of *Now You See Me 2* I happened to have an actual modelling department to work with, which was great. First, I asked them to make huge playing cards that a person could stand behind without being seen. I told them not to limit themselves in any way, to come up with a variety of cards in different shapes, sizes and colours.

The next thing I had to do was think of a method of combining the giant playing cards with the people that would actually work. After hours of doodling and messing about with bits of cardboard, I went back to the modelling department and told them that I wanted them to build the outdoor set with a trap door in the wall behind and a trap door in the street that looked like a manhole.

With the casting team, we then found three sets of identical twins and, once the set I had created with the set designers was built, I had the twins practise and practise the trick over and over again. Jon Chu, the director, wanted the scene to be shot in one take and in the end, that's exactly what happened. The three sets of twins moved seamlessly in a choreographed sequence, flawlessly dropping in and out of trapdoors to magically move the lady behind these giant cards in sequence. What began as a random idea ended as a beautiful piece that was later revealed in the movie.

If you are still struggling with the nine-dot puzzle from earlier, here is one solution that can be done in four lines or less without going over the same line twice.

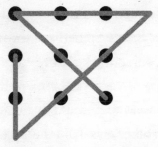

Now, you may notice that this solution involves going outside the nine-dot square to make the four lines connect with all nine dots, and you may think this is unfair, against the rules. But nobody said you couldn't go outside the square. If you thought you weren't allowed do this, that is a rule you imposed on yourself and is an example of how, when we try to be creative, we can impose our own rules on problems that have no rules.

Still, I bet you'd be surprised if I told you that when children were faced with the nine-dot problem above they confounded even the researchers when they came up with a solution containing just three straight lines. Give it a go and when you've reached a solution or given up, read on.

CREATE A CREATIVE ENVIRONMENT

Okay, so not everybody will have a props department on hand when they are trying to be creative, but if you are surrounded by kids running around yelling, dogs barking or other distractions then you are not doing yourself justice.

If you are trying to be creative, a good idea is to have either a whiteboard or Post-it notes to structure your ideas. You should also use your journal or hardback copy to splat down every idea that comes to mind inside or outside your creative space.

When I started out in magic, I used to stick Post-it notes all over my wall at home. In fact, my office wall is still covered in Post-it notes from previous shows. Sometimes those notes could just have a doodle on them, sometimes a word, or even a thought. While filming *Now You See Me 2*, I was based in the Landmark Hotel in London during the week and would fly home to my family at weekends. I had my own office on set, but I didn't know if my ideas were safe in that office as there was no lock on the door, so in order to protect them I did most of my planning in my hotel room. I had all my different colour pens with me and had Post-its stuck up all over the room. When I went home for the weekend, I took them down and put them into a scrapbook so that I could work on them at home.

When I first walked into *Now You See Me* scriptwriter Ed Solomon's office in Los Angeles, I was blown away by the order and organisation of his thoughts. Ed is probably best known for writing the *Bill and Ted* movie series, but he also wrote *Men in Black* and *Charlie's Angels* among lots of others.

In his office overlooking Main Street, Santa Monica, Ed had all four walls completely covered in giant whiteboards. On those whiteboards he had notes in every colour under the sun to compartmentalise his thoughts and ideas. He had a system for every colour. Ed knew that if something was written in blue it belonged to one part of his script-writing process, yellow to another, green to another.

I took inspiration from Ed Solomon's office that day and have used whiteboards in my own creative process every day since. Blue is the colour I use for the boring part of a magic trick, so I use blue marker to write down my methods. Blue for you could be the process of getting from A to B in whatever you need to do. I use green as my starting point and red as my end point and I also use other colours to match things in between.

Now, when I walk into my office or wherever I am being creative, this colour coding allows me to instantly find the method, the outcome and the ideas for the trick I'm working on, in the middle of lots of other notes and random ideas.

In London, my hotel room was a bit stuffy, so I bought a humidifier for £40 and it's something I now use wherever I am trying to be creative. You can also use various scents to improve the atmosphere in your creative space and boost your mood. My two scents of choice are frankincense and neroli, which comes from the blossom of bitter orange trees. Strangely, I have found that these two scents help relax my brain and help the process of creativity. I say 'strangely' because I have had no sense of smell since birth.

At home, I also surround myself with books. I use old and new books on all kinds of subjects to inspire me and help conjure up new ideas. I also use Lego, cardboard and Play-Doh to build models of my ideas. Play-Doh is a great tactile experience. You can build anything, from a character or an object in a book to a house you are thinking of designing. You can also get some great ideas from watching fantasy movies or even by watching somebody else be creative.

Buy a piece of art, or posters with quotes or words that inspire you, words that mean something to you. If you can't afford one, be creative and make one. Hang them up in your creative space and let those positive messages sink into your subconscious. Purchase a mini indoor fountain or other water feature; water features have a calming effect and can increase positive mood.[7] Running water also improves air quality by creating a flow of negative ions, which improve oxygen levels and mental alertness.

My current office has a couple of lamps with vintage Edison bulbs in them that emit an orange hue. Orange light has been proven to promote creativity, attention and focus. A study at the University of Liège in Belgium in 2014 showed that subjects exposed to orange light showed 'greater brain activity in several regions of the frontal lobes related to alertness and cognition',[8] which is probably why creative companies such as Rothco and Accenture use orange lighting and orange paint in many of their offices.

STOP NOW and take a good long look at your creative space. How can you improve it?

> What inspirational quotes can you put on the walls that will inspire you?
> What is your lighting like?
> What can you see from the window?
> What colours are the walls?
> What do your surroundings smell like?

Decide on three things right now that you can change in your environment to help get your creative juices flowing.

KEEP IT CLEAN WITH A CHAOS BOX

A tidy workspace is also a necessity. Okay, everyone can have a bad day or two where they don't get time to tidy things up, but the rule should be that wherever you are trying to be creative should be tidy. Numerous studies have found that working in a cluttered environment means that subconsciously some of our focus is drawn to the clutter, whatever is lying around on our desks or in our field of vision.[9]

This clutter competes for space in our brain with the task that we are trying to achieve and can even make us procrastinate more or put us in a stressed mood. So, if you are studying for an exam or trying to come up with a plot or storyline for that book, declutter your desk and the area in which you are trying to be creative.

If your creative space is cluttered, it can take time to find what you are looking for. Every minute you spend looking for a pen, a

Post-it note, a file on your computer or that scrap of paper you wrote your idea on the day before is time wasted.

The first thing to do if your desk is cluttered is simply take everything off it until it's bare. After a quick wipe down and polish, you can then begin to put things back in order of how often you use them. A computer or laptop might be the obvious first thing back on your desk, but do you really need that half roll of Sellotape, that empty ink cartridge or those cables that are attached to nothing? Put your bin right beside your desk, not in the far corner of the room. That way it will be easier to instantly throw away anything you don't need. Now throw away anything that is not essential.

Get yourself a small desk organiser, or at least a plastic cup or box to put your coloured markers and other useful items in. If you need to keep files, use coloured tabs or coloured folders to easily distinguish their importance and, if possible, keep them in a drawer or cabinet and off your desk. Use a smaller whiteboard or a daily diary for to-do lists and tick items off when you've done them. This will remind you what you have to do and will also give you a sense of achievement with each task you tick off.

Purchase an interesting-looking box and label this your 'chaos box'. Put anything you feel will add to your creativity, or perhaps inspire you down the line, into your chaos box. This box can contain literally anything; scraps of paper, puzzles, medals, business cards, magazines, comic books – anything that could potentially promote creativity.

Occasionally, turn your chaos box upside down onto the floor and sift through it with an open mind and creatively play with whatever is inside. You never know what ideas your chaos box might inspire. I had an idea one time for an effect where I would throw an imaginary ball to a blindfolded spectator onstage and they would catch the imaginary ball seconds after I threw it. I couldn't find a way to achieve the effect. I went to my chaos box and emptied it out. After a few seconds I noticed an elastic band around a deck of cards, and I knew I had found the solution. How did I use an elastic band to solve the problem? That part will remain a mystery! Constantly refresh the box with new items. This way chaos and tidiness can exist together to help promote creativity.

STOP NOW and create your chaos box. Put in an item that has real historical meaning to you; some interesting newspaper or magazine articles; some Play-Doh, modelling clay or Lego; and three other things which you think could promote your creativity.

The easiest way to ensure your desk is always clutter free is to tidy it up at the end of each day; that way you will be starting with a clean slate and a focused mind tomorrow.

Now, back to the problem of joining the nine dots with just three lines. How about this for a solution?

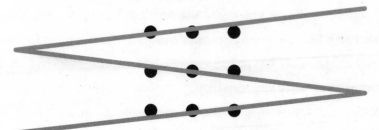

Okay, so this time the lines are not going through the centres of the dots. But again, there was no rule saying the lines had to go through the centre of the dots. If you thought there was, then you just made that rule up as well. Kids, though, came up with even better solutions and lots of them. What if I told you all nine dots could be joined by just one straight line? Have a go and then read on.

START WITH 'WHAT IF?'

We can all write books and paint pictures. We may not become famous or make money from it, but we can all create to please ourselves or others. Sometimes, when we are faced with a task or problem, we think we know the answer before we try to solve it and are defeated when it doesn't work out the way we expected.

To be truly creative you must look beyond the obvious 'solutions' and have an open mind. You must have a childlike curiosity and approach. If you are trying to resolve a problem, often the best option is something you may not have considered. You need to forget about the age-old concept of thinking outside the box and, like a magician, remember there is no box to begin with.

You must start with the end result clearly defined in your mind but park the obvious answers and start the creative process by asking imaginative questions of yourself: magical questions, if you will. The words 'what if?' are a great starting point. When I came up with my stage show 'Brain Hacker', I wanted it to be a fun, mind-blowing show and used my imagination in fun, childlike ways in order to write it. The creative process for that found me thinking about potential mind tricks everywhere.

When I was walking around, I'd spot somebody across the road and ask myself, 'What if I could walk up to him and tell him what he did for a living or tell him the PIN for his bank card?' When I thought about that question in depth and how I might use that in my live show, I began to ask myself more 'what if' questions. 'What if my chest was an imaginary bank machine and a member of the audience stood in front of me on stage and imagined punching their PIN in? What if I could do it blindfold?' I then imagined how it would work, the method to the trick. The method took a long time to perfect but by the time 'Brain Hacker' went live, I performed it on stage every night, revealing hundreds of PINs during the tour. While watching a talent show on TV, I saw a ventriloquist and wondered, 'What if I could take a random audience member and turn them into a human puppet? Say they're sitting on one chair, and I've got a large mannequin dummy on another chair. Then, while in a trance, with their eyes closed and earplugs in their ears so they can't see or can't hear anything, what if I could control their mind, body and soul so that whatever happens to the giant puppet happens to them?' These are pretty imaginative questions, but both of those tricks came from random ideas and show that if you spend enough time and come up with enough different solutions to the problem you will eventually find one that works.

STOP NOW and grab your journal. Answer the following 'what if' questions as a creativity exercise.

> What if you wanted to make a coin disappear out of your hand in order to astound your friends and family?
> What if you could use other props to achieve this?
> What if you could use misdirection?
> What if you could use an accomplice?

Start to think about three simple methods you could use to achieve this trick. To help you start the process I'll give you an idea for the disappearing coin trick. As I write this, I'm wearing a hoodie with a zip down the front. Under misdirection, I could move one hand up over the other quickly, and while doing that I could flick the coin into my open hoodie, creating the illusion it has vanished. While it's not the most deceptive way of doing it, it's still a method.

Perhaps you could take a cloth or piece of paper as cover for a split second. The more you think about it, the more options you will have. Come up with at least three solutions for the disappearing coin trick and see what works best. When you decide on the most deceptive method, I want you to come up with a presentation for that trick, a story if you like. Come up with a viable story about how you can make a coin 'invisible' and amaze your friends and family with your new trick.

Now write down three 'what if?' questions relevant to something you currently want to create or a problem you are trying to solve.

For example, if you own a bar that has social distancing in place due to a pandemic you might ask yourself:

> What if I hosted fitness classes in the car park and served non-alcoholic drinks and healthy food afterwards?
> What if I held cocktail-making classes on a Monday night?
> What if I delivered drinks to customers on a Friday evening and put on a virtual comedy show for free for those customers?

METAMORPHICAL THINKING

An exercise I use all the time to promote creativity is something I call metamorphical thinking. In magic, a trick known as a metamorphosis usually involves changing something or somebody into something or somebody else. With metamorphical thinking I continuously imagine random objects magically morphing or changing into completely different objects.

An example of this wacky kind of thinking is when I was trying to come up with the finale for my show 'Insanity'. I was travelling on the Tube in London when I decided to use metamorphical thinking to imagine the train I was on changing into an airplane. I then used the same thinking to imagine all the passengers on the train morphing into bright yellow bananas. The plane then morphed into a church, and I could see the time on the clock in the church. I then imagined the bananas standing up and raving like lunatics inside the church, which then turned into the Olympia Theatre. Finally, I imagined all the raving bananas morphing into the actress Meg Ryan.

Now, this might seem like a crazy way to be thinking while sitting on a train, but it is often this wacky thinking that produces great ideas. The end of the 'Insanity' show was one of the most memorable finales I've ever done. There was music blaring and, like the bananas on the train, the whole audience were up out of their seats and raving like lunatics. Meg Ryan, too, was an important part of the magical reveal!

STOP NOW and think about something you want to create. Start by morphing an object in front of you into another object in your mind. Then morph that object into something else. Do this repeatedly until a solution, even a part solution to move you towards your creation, comes to mind. Once it does, be sure to immediately write it down in your journal.

For example, if you wanted an idea to write a kids' book, you might:

> Morph your iPhone into a talking salmon.
> The salmon morphs into an alien with fish scales.
> The alien in turn morphs into a Rubik's cube.

You now have the beginning of a book with an underwater alien who loves using technology to solve all kinds of problems and their ambition is to become the world's fastest Rubik's-cube-solver.

If you have come up with your coin trick and tried it on your kids or your family, by now you will have begun to open your mind to the creative process and you might even have solved the nine-dot puzzle in just one line, like the kids did. If not, then here is the solution.

Who said the lines had to be the width of a pen or marker and couldn't be the width of a large paintbrush? It must have been you!

6.

ROLL THE CREATIVITY DICE

HOW EDISON'S BALLS CAN
SOLVE YOUR PROBLEMS

ONE OF THE THINGS I constantly say to my kids is 'never give up'. I say it so regularly to them that I have even begun saying it to their friends when they call over to play with them. My kids have got used to me dancing at the front door in a super positive mood, telling their friends to never give up. More often than not, they roll their eyes and tell me I'm a weirdo, which only enhances my super positivity and dancing, and I usually answer loudly, 'Yeah, I'm a weirdo! I don't care!' before making a rock fingers symbol and saying, 'Remember, guys … NGU!' to their laughing friends.

Now, while this might embarrass my own kids, I know the other kids' parents are not going to give out to me for telling them to never give up. Maybe somewhere down the line those three words will come back to them when they are stuck on a problem or trying to figure out how to do something new.

PREPARE TO FAIL

When being creative, you must reduce your sensitivity to failure and keep going. If you don't, you will get frustrated and decrease your productivity, possibly give up altogether.

It took Thomas Edison a thousand failed attempts before he invented the lightbulb. When he was asked why he made so many mistakes, he told the journalist in question that he didn't make a thousand mistakes, that the lightbulb was in fact an invention with a thousand steps.

In the previous chapter I mentioned that during my 'Brain Hacker' show I would hack into someone's mind on stage to reveal their PIN in front of a packed theatre. What I didn't mention was that I failed close to a thousand times before I got the trick to work.

The method for figuring out someone's PIN is based on what is known as 'psychophysiological thought reading' or, in simpler terms, muscle reading. Every single thought we have results in tiny subconscious physiological changes in our muscles. After a lot of practice, I developed the ability to read those tiny changes in physiology and make it look like I am inside someone's mind extracting information, whereas, unbeknownst to the person, I am feeling for the changes in their physiology.

With the PIN trick, I would have the person focus on the number and extend their first finger as if they were about to enter it into the bank machine. I would then have them imagine the keyboard of the bank machine on my chest as I gently held their wrist. As I moved their wrist around my chest area, I attempted to detect any tension while the person focused on the first digit of their PIN. When I felt the tension, I would reveal the number and would then repeat this for the next three digits to reveal their full PIN.

As you can imagine, perfecting this trick required me to get it wrong thousands of times in order to learn from my mistakes, but as the late creativity expert Ken Robinson once said, 'If you're not prepared to be wrong, you'll never come up with anything original.'

Of course, I couldn't fail every night during my paid live shows so my family, friends, and a number of control groups went through the arduous process of assisting me in perfecting the method over a long period. (A control group is simply a diverse group of people I've never met before who are paid for their opinion on what I am presenting to them. It's an effective way of getting honest feedback and helps accelerate my learning process.) That way, by the time I did the trick on stage, I was able to nail it almost every night.

You can try this trick yourself for fun. Like I said, it takes a lot of practice, but if you do manage to extract someone's PIN please send the relevant name, address and PIN to me!

PIGGYBACK

The vast majority of major inventions are not created by one person, but rather a number of people improving on existing concepts.

Abbas ibn Firnas was almost seventy years old when he jumped off a cliff in Yemen during the ninth century wearing self-made wings combining wood, silk and feathers. Having studied the flight of birds for over twenty years, ibn Firnas, a polymath and engineer, glided in the air for around ten minutes before an abrupt landing left him with an injured back and pondering the means of a more comfortable touchdown.

Although he is not widely recognised for it in the West, Firnas' flying machine diagrams went on to become the basis for future aviation. When the Wright brothers became the first people to fly, they had considered all the previous attempts at flying and simply modified and advanced those techniques and had more success.

While Thomas Edison and Nikola Tesla, the inventor of the alternating electrical current, got the credit for bringing electricity to the masses, other inventors had already started to develop methods to produce electricity. Both Edison and Tesla adopted a 'what if' attitude and ended up getting the credit for improving what were essentially other people's methods.

Albert Einstein worked in the patent office in Bern for seven years, exposing himself to other people's inventions and innovative ideas on a daily basis and opening his mind to the large scope of creativity to be found in different areas.

When I am writing my shows, I make sure that I research people who have done something similar in the past in order to learn from their experience. For my live show 'The Dark Side' I wanted to perform a comedy piece based around psychics. My research took me to some very strange places, and I ended up studying the historical records of Hitler's and Stalin's psychic advisors. I developed a brand-new routine, which turned out to be the hit of the show, directly from that research and by piggybacking on their so-called psychic abilities.

Often there are historical accounts of somebody trying to do what you are trying to do. Maybe you can tweak and enhance their ideas, maybe there is more technology around now to help you. All problems are opportunities for creative solutions and if you dig deep enough you are sure to find that somebody else has probably solved a similar problem already.

FIND A MENTOR

Rarely will you see a professional athlete train with somebody who is not as good at their chosen sport as them. Instead, they seek out better, wiser, more experienced mentors and try to improve by learning from them and training with them. When you are trying to achieve something or learn something, try to find people who are better than you at your chosen subject. Brainstorming with and listening to advice from these people is absolutely key to the creative process.

I have dozens of people whom I go to regularly to brainstorm with, depending on what I need, but Tony Sadar, Doc Shiels, the late Paul Goldin, the late Billy McComb and my dad have been my main creativity mentors.

My dad was a successful businessman and is a good husband and a good parent. He has a wealth of knowledge on various subjects, so I often go to him for advice. He was a popular singer in his day and starred in Tops of the Town shows and other big stage productions around Waterford when he was younger, so he has also taught me a lot about the business side of show business. Once, when I was a teenager, a local businessman decided that he wouldn't pay me for a number of shows I had performed. When I asked him about it, he'd say that he was a bit tight that week and he'd pay me my £30 the next week.

When this went on for a month, however, my father gave me another lesson in life. He decided to pay me what I was owed out of his own money. My dad then visited this man at his house and told him that as he had paid me, the man now owed him £120 and that he wanted it there and then. Faced with an adult instead of a kid, he paid up and my dad came home with advice that I have never forgotten. 'Keith,' he said, 'it's called *show business* for a reason. If you want to make a living out of magic, then you need to look after the business side of things as well as the show side.'

When I first moved to Dublin, I joined the Society of Irish Magicians, where I met Tony Sadar. Tony had been a top stage hypnotist in Ireland and ran a clinic where he helped people give up smoking, lose weight and lose their phobias. It wasn't until a couple of years later, though, that I asked him if he would help me with hypnotism. Over the next year or so I trained under him before passing an exam for the National Guild of Hypnotists in America to become qualified. Tony has always been around to bounce ideas off or pass on his knowledge. In the course of my career I got to know the late Paul Goldin and he too became a mentor. Paul had a master's in behavioural psychology and logistics and had previously worked for the US government helping survivors of the Jonestown massacre, in which 918 people died in 1978. Paul taught me how to do advanced instant induction hypnosis, which enabled me to hypnotise people within seconds of meeting them, and other tips and tricks that nobody had ever shared with me before.

Tony 'Doc' Shiels is one of the most creative people I know. Doc is a highly regarded surrealist artist, writer and entertainer, and he is also known as a magician, a trickster and a hoaxer. A book written on a creature in Cornwall known as 'the owlman' acknowledges that Doc Shiels is single-handedly responsible for that myth. Although he has never admitted it to me, it is probably no coincidence that crop circles were very prominent in Cornwall, where he lived for many years. Doc was also involved in monster-hunting expeditions and indeed took one of the most famous photographs ever taken of the Loch Ness monster. He is a fount of knowledge and a prolific creator and the person I most often turn to if I'm in a creative rut.

While most people are very protective of their ideas, even worried about them being stolen, I'm very willing to discuss my ideas with people. An idea will always remain just an idea unless you share it with somebody. Stop holding on to your ideas because you are nervous someone might steal them.

When I was working on my theatre show 'The Dark Side', I wanted to perform a piece of magic that would happen inside the mind of the person on stage, while the rest of the audience would understand how it worked. My aim was for it to be a surreal experience for the person on stage, but a peek behind the curtain for the rest of the audience.

When trying to figure out this mental illusion, I called Doc and explained my very rough idea. We sat in Reidy's bar in Killarney over a pint (or two) of Guinness and began to flesh things out. He reminded me of his 'psychic touch' effect from his book *The Cantrip Codex*, where the onstage volunteer could feel the performer's bio-electrical energy tingling on the back of their head. We used that as the basis for the trick.

Imagine you have your eyes closed and the index fingers of my hands rest gently on your eyelids. You know my hands cannot move from your eyelids without you knowing. You know we are alone on stage and no one else is nearby. Now, I use hypnotic language to put you into an altered state of mind as I begin to tell you a story about ghosts. If you suddenly felt an icy tingling sensation on the back of your head at this point, you would probably lose your mind. That's exactly the reaction I received every night on stage!

Regardless of what I am creating, I nearly always use another creative person as a sounding board or a brainstorming partner. I have a hugely diverse group of people I can reach out to and brainstorm with, spanning across all age groups and ethnic backgrounds. Make it a habit to surround yourself with strange and delightful people and be sure to continuously expand this group. Be sure to practise the law of reciprocation: if they are willing to help you, please make time to help them when they need you!

Spend the next week researching coaches and mentors in your field of interests. Find three who you think could help with your creativity. Reach out to all three expressing your interest in them mentoring you. Ensure you have always at least one mentor.

SET DEADLINES

One of the things that I find spurs my creativity is setting deadlines. The outcome, however, of hitting that deadline must be enough to excite your brain so that you'll push on through problems and obstacles. Otherwise you're not going to put in the hours needed. The concept of 'waiting for inspiration' is an excuse for a lazy mindset. Creative thinking requires discipline and scheduling!

Whenever I want to do a new show, I always book a theatre, name my show, and put it on sale before I even have one idea for what's going to be in it. I'm always careful on the name choice because that will give me inspiration as to what's going to be in the show but, apart from the name, at that stage there is no show. Once I have my show named, I get the artwork done up and I put the show on sale.

For me, having thirty dates booked, knowing that I have to write a show for them is a real way to concentrate my attention on one project. I don't have a choice then. I've got to get creative. In this instance the exciting outcome is being on stage in front of a packed audience and having a sold-out tour. To get there, I need to think of themes that are provocative for the audience.

Once the date for my 'Dark Side' show was locked in, I researched the dark, bizarre side of magic and based a lot of my show around Aleister Crowley, one of the strangest men who ever lived. During one of my creative walks in nature, I saw a pigeon flying overhead one day and wondered how I could rip a pigeon's head off live on stage to mess with people's heads. No pigeons were harmed in the show, but the audience didn't know that, and the trick had the desired effect.

Sometimes deadlines can hit you when you least expect them. On the opening night of 'Eight Deadly Sins', the plan was to reveal the eighth deadly sin in ultraviolet light on the walls of the Olympia at the end of the show.

But on the night in question, as we were setting up, we were told that we weren't allowed write on the walls because the Olympia is a listed building. After consulting with the manager, we were told that we were allowed write in UV ink on the floor of the stage, so we did that instead. When we turned off all the lights, however, nothing showed up. We couldn't understand it. We were about an hour away from opening and had suddenly lost our big reveal ending.

We tried brainstorming everything under the sun to solve the problem and eventually came up with the thought that perhaps the stage was too clean, and the light was bouncing off it. With no other viable option, as the guys got the stage ready, I ran outside and down the street to a building site, where I asked a couple of surprised labourers for a bag of dirt. When I got back, the technical director of the show, Joe Cleere, and I got a brush each and swept the dirt into the floor. We switched on the UV lights and just minutes before I walked on stage it worked. We were off the hook.

STOP NOW and decide on a creative task you want to accomplish. Set a realistic date for when you want to accomplish it and lock the date into your diary. Schedule creative sessions daily to focus your mind on metamorphical thinking.

DO SOMETHING DIFFERENT

If you are stuck in a rut or find that what you are doing is not working, then a simple tip is to change your position, change your environment or just change what you are doing altogether.

Einstein often interrupted his brainstorming sessions to play the violin.

Listening to music, reading a book, watching a movie, going for a walk or doing some other form of exercise can all change your physiology and give you a fresh perspective on your problem. Exercise is known to boost endorphins and release stress, leading to an increase in creative thinking and problem-solving skills.

Often, I'll change chairs after an hour. I'll go for a walk in nature, do some breath work or do some exercise, and come back and sit in a different space. Walking on your own in nature can sometimes give you enough headroom to come back with an idea. The trick is to look for inspiration everywhere and not to wait for it.

Yesterday, for example, I was in a bit of a creative rut. I got up and had a coffee, did a bit of exercise, and came back to work, but instead of going into my office I lay on the grass outside. As I lay there, a rose petal flew across in front of me and I came up with a whole new trick involving a levitating rose for my next show.

In a 2012 study called 'Fluid movement and creativity', published by the American Psychological Association, scientists from Tufts and Stanford Universities concluded that creativity can be enhanced by certain types of physical movement.[10] When I am in a creative session, either alone or with someone, I will often pace around the room and swing my arms wildly to change my emotional state and promote fluid thinking. Next time you are in a creative rut, jump up and do ten jumping jacks to change your emotions.

Another thing I find helpful when stuck in a rut is listening to binaural beats. Binaural beats are two sounds under 1500 Hz played at slightly different frequencies (less than 30Hz difference) in each ear. They work best when listening through headphones and are a type of auditory illusion. When our brain hears these two sounds in different ears it gradually creates a third frequency, and this helps induce a mental state akin to meditation.

You can find binaural beats online and the use of different frequency ranges has been linked to better sleep, reduced anxiety, increased concentration levels, better creativity – one study even noticed a reduction in tinnitus after a three-month period of use.[11]

One of the most important exercises I regularly practise is to sit alone in my office with a blindfold on, listening to binaural beats through noise-cancelling headphones while focusing on a creative project. Now, my wife has assured me that I look absolutely crazy while doing this, but I find it helps me to come up with loads of fresh ideas.

DOODLE

Remember when you were in school, and the teacher told you to stop doodling on your copy or schoolbook and pay attention? Well, you're not in school anymore and, in my opinion, doodling can lead to great creativity.

When in an altered state of mind while creatively visualising, I sometimes do a form of writing called automatic writing. I simply place an A4 piece of card on my lap and place a pen onto the centre of the paper. After using the relaxation process I have shared with you to induce relaxation and to increase creativity, I allow my hand to move while focusing on whatever it is I'm trying to create. I generally draw twenty or so doodles in a sitting and afterwards focus on them to try and make some sense of them.

When I was working on *The Keith Barry Experience* for RTÉ, I wanted to come up with a big new trick for the show. I knew I was limited to an indoor studio with low ceilings so I couldn't do an escape that involved heights. I also knew the audience would be sitting all around at different angles, so I sat down and started doodling this space. Out of nowhere I drew four boxes. Then I drew a stick man in front of one of the boxes and thought, 'What if these boxes were actually doors?' Then I thought, 'What if I hung a hammer over one door?' and then 'What if I hung a giant hammer over every door?' From that doodle I ended up doing a giant Russian roulette trick which involved me avoiding giant sledgehammers smashing through three of the four doors, with *Dancing With the Stars* judge Julian Benson being in full control of the outcome!

I doodle every day, whether it is to decide where I'm going to plant things in the garden, how I'm going to lay out a stage show, or how to come up with a trick. Sometimes I come up with a drawing that I don't even know what to make of, but when I look at it for a while, I find something useful – and occasionally I draw something that turns out to be a nugget of gold.

STOP NOW and grab your journal.

> Use the purple light of relaxation to relax deeply for 10 minutes and think about the solution or idea you are trying to come up with.
> Doodle for the next five minutes with your eyes closed and simply allow your hand to move wherever it wants to move.
> Fill at least ten pages during this process.

Open your eyes and analyse your doodles. If you don't discover anything useful then put the results in your chaos box for inspiration in the future.

SLEEP ON IT AND INDUCE CREATIVE DREAMS

Did you know that the idea for Google came to Larry Page in a dream? The *Terminator* movie came to director James Cameron in a fever-induced dream, while the *Twilight* series of books also came to author Stephenie Meyer in a dream. There are many stories of books, movies, songs and even business ventures coming to people in dreams.

If you've ever had to learn the periodic table in school, then perhaps you have heard of the man who invented it. Dmitri Mendeleev had recognised a pattern in the elements, but it was only when he fell asleep that he saw the table of elements in his dream. When he woke up, he wrote down what he had dreamt and, although some minor changes were made after that, the periodic table you learned in school is still pretty much the same as the one that came to him in a dream.

Salvador Dalí and Thomas Edison realised the power of dreams early on and both came up with interesting ways to harness that power. Whenever Dalí came across a problem, he would take a nap in an armchair with some spoons in his hand and a plate placed carefully on the ground underneath. He'd think about the problem while drifting off, but as soon as he fell asleep the spoons would drop and clang off the plate, waking him up in time to be inspired by what he was dreaming about. Instead of spoons and a plate, Edison held metal balls in his hand for the same effect.

In 1993 psychologist Dr Deidre Barrett asked her Harvard Medical School students to imagine a problem they were trying to solve as they lay in bed before going to sleep. The study found that half of the participants had dreams that addressed their chosen problems.[12] 'We're in a different biochemical state when we're dreaming,' Barrett says, 'and that's why I think dreams can be so helpful anytime we're stuck in our usual mode of thinking.'

In 2004, researchers at the University of Lübeck in Germany trained participants to solve a long, tedious maths problem before giving them an eight-hour break. When the participants returned for retesting, researchers found that those who had slept during the break were more than twice as likely to figure out a simpler way to solve the problem than those who had not slept.[13]

Before you go to bed tonight, take a Post-it note or a piece of paper and write down a sentence or paragraph about the problem you want to solve, or the project you are trying to create, that you want to dream about. Read it five times before closing your eyes and commit to that one thought every night until you have that dream.

If you want to try *advanced* creative dreaming, then set your alarm clock at two-hour intervals during the night so you wake in the middle of your dream. Be sure to immediately write down all the details you can remember when you wake up. Of course, unless you are a vampire, you cannot do this on an ongoing basis, but if you do it sporadically you will extract some amazing information from your dreams.

If you are feeling tired when trying to figure something out during the day, try the same thing as Dalí or Edison. However, instead of spoons or metal balls, hold a deck of cards loosely in your hand as you settle down for a nap with the problem on your mind. There's nothing like a game of fifty-two pick-up to inspire creativity.

I meet people all the time who say that they wish they were creative. Often when people say they are not creative they really mean they are not good at the arts; they can't paint, draw, sing, dance, write songs, act. But you don't have to be artsy to be creative.

Have you ever measured something without using a measuring tape, hammered a nail in without using a hammer, made a play tent or made up a game for your kids? If the answer is yes, then you are creative. In fact, we are all capable of being creative in some way, we just need to recognise and acknowledge this.

If you are struggling with creativity, then somewhere along the line it has been suppressed. Your mind is like a muscle: it needs exercise on a regular basis. You can start by doing crosswords or puzzles, even jigsaws or adult colouring books. A Rubik's cube is also a great tool to promote problem-solving and creativity.

ROLL THE CREATIVITY DICE

Here is a great way to help get creative juices flowing. Write these six sentences into your journal or into your smartphone notes and every workday for a week roll a die to select one of the six options below to make a random creative decision.

1. Pick up a random book, go to a random page, read that page, and use that new information to spur an idea or concept.

2. Call a creative friend and ask them a question based on a problem you are trying to solve.

3. Watch a random TED talk to inspire you.

4. Empty your chaos box and play with the contents.

5. Watch a comedian on YouTube. Stress is the enemy of creativity. Laughing will release feel-good chemicals into your system to boost creativity.

6. Listen to classical music. This genre has a calming, relaxing and stress-reducing effect on the brain and has been found in studies to help students perform better in exams.[14]

When you have these written down, simply roll the die and allow it to decide what you do for the next 15 or 30 minutes of your day. These six tasks are all designed to promote creativity – and of course you can use your imagination to design brand-new lists every week!

Always keep your journal or notebook close to hand. How many times have you had a great idea while driving, shopping or doing something else unrelated to what you were thinking about? At least if you write everything down, and I mean everything because there are no bad ideas, then it will still be there minutes, hours, and days after you thought about it.

Soon you will realise that you have more ideas than you think, but the fact that you haven't been writing them down until this point means most of them never got any further. Maybe an idea won't get any further than a line or two in your notebook or journal, but at least it's in there, and you never know when you might come across a problem that can be solved by that note.

Anyone can be creative, but you must believe you have the ability to improve on existing solutions or see how to do things differently. You must allow your imagination to take centre stage, let it fly and take you beyond your expectations. Explore all options, ask yourself magical questions. Think like a magician. Creative thinking starts with the determination to succeed.

EVERYDAY BRAIN HACKS FOR CREATIVITY

> Try to come to your solutions like a magician. Don't impose rules on yourself that aren't there. Think outside the dots.

> Get yourself a whiteboard and some coloured markers. Use them for different stages of your problem or project.

> Change three things about your environment today to help promote creative thinking.

> Keep your clutter out of your peripheral vision and out of your mind, leaving you free to focus on your creativity. Use a chaos box to store items and search through it occasionally for inspiration.

> Ask yourself 'What if?' magical questions. Begin at the outcome and explore every avenue on the way there.

> If you're not prepared to be wrong, you'll never come up with anything original. Mistakes are there to be learned from.

> Work with others who have experience in the topic at hand. Share ideas and try to improve on the historical solutions to your problem.

> Give yourself a timeframe to achieve the results you are looking for. That way you are more likely to focus your attention on the problem at hand.

> Change your position, your environment or what you are doing to refresh your mind and gain a new perspective.

> Start with a doodle and see what you come up with. Analyse it again later and see if your outlook has changed.

> Induce problem-solving dreams by writing down your ideas before you go to bed.

> Pick six different things to inspire creativity and roll a die every day to see which one you will use.

———— VISUALISATION FOR CREATIVITY ————

An audio recording of me guiding you through this visualisation can be accessed on my website www.keithbarry.com/brainhacks.

Read through the following several times before beginning the visualisation:

> Sit or lie down in a quiet spot where you can make yourself comfortable. With your eyes closed, visualise a purple light hovering over your body. This is your light of relaxation. Feel the light hovering over your feet and relaxing your feet as it slowly enters them. Focus on your feet and actively allow them to relax. As you do this, repeat silently to yourself over and over, 'My feet are relaxed, my feet are relaxed, my feet are relaxed.'

> Now allow that purple light to slowly spread up through your legs into your torso, your arms and every other part of your body. As you feel the light entering each part of your body, tell that part to relax. Focus on relaxing each part of your body in sequence.

> Once your body is relaxed, shift your focus to your breathing. Inhale for 6 seconds and focus on inhaling pure relaxation. Hold for 3 seconds. Exhale for 6 seconds and focus on all the tension leaving your body as you exhale. Repeat this breathing pattern 20 times.

> Imagine you are in an empty room. The room is painted light orange on all six sides with no windows or doors. This is your room of creativity. The only object in the room is a clear glass full of coloured markers.

> Focus on a creative issue where you need to gain some insights or a problem you need to solve. Think of this thought like a seed being planted in your mind. Your subconscious will immediately begin to nurture that seed and look for possibilities, solutions and inspiration to encourage that seed to grow.

> Now imagine you are using the markers to write down any images, doodles, thoughts or ideas that come to you on the orange walls in your room of creativity. Do it with no judgement or hesitancy. Follow the ideas and see where the journey takes you.

> When the ideas begin to dry up, wipe the walls clear in your mind and start with blank walls once again.

> Now spell out your objective by writing it clearly and concisely on the walls of your imaginary room.

> Repeat the above process and once again write down any images, thoughts or ideas that come to you on the orange walls in your room of creativity.

> Don't be impatient. Sometimes answers will come super-fast, other times slowly. The more you practise this, the more you'll tune into your inner stream of consciousness and the faster the answers will come.

Slowly open your eyes and return to your waking state. Grab your creative journal and write down as many ideas as you can remember. Follow those ideas and allow them to open a path of creativity, consciously and subconsciously.

SUCCESS

achieving something you want to accomplish with
absolute precision

'You can have anything you want if you want it
badly enough. You can be anything you want to be,
do anything you set out to accomplish, if you hold
to that desire with singleness of purpose.'
– Abraham Lincoln

7.

FIND YOUR PURPOSE

WHY SHOULD YOU BEGIN WITH WHY?

ENGLAND INTERNATIONAL footballer Marcus Rashford grew up on the Wythenshawe estate in Manchester. A sprawling concrete jungle, some twenty-eight square kilometres in area, Wythenshawe was once the largest housing estate in Europe. Here, in an area recently described by the *New York Times* as an 'extreme pocket of social deprivation and alienation', young Marcus lived in a small terraced house with his four siblings and his single mother, Melanie.

In a constant struggle to pay her bills and feed her five kids, Melanie had three jobs. After her shift as a clerk at the local book-makers' she would spend her evenings cleaning for two different companies. Often things were so tight that she went without meals herself to ensure that her children had something to eat.

'As a family, we relied on breakfast clubs, free school meals, and the kind actions of neighbours and coaches,' Rashford wrote in an open letter to the UK government in 2020. 'Food banks and soup kitchens were not alien to us; I recall very clearly our visits to Northern Moor to collect our Christmas dinners every year. It's only now that I really understand the enormous sacrifice my mum made in sending me away to live in digs aged 11, a decision no mother would ever make lightly.'

Although Marcus Rashford grew up wanting to be a professional footballer, his main purpose for doing that was to make enough money to dig his family out of poverty and change their lives for the better. By the time he was 18 and made his debut for Manchester United's first team, he had hit that target.

Still, Rashford knew there were other families who struggled as much as his had, so when he began to light up the Premier League and gained international selection for England, he set his sights higher and tried to help as many of them as possible.

When the Covid pandemic closed schools across the UK in March 2020, the then 23-year-old Rashford wondered where the children who were no longer getting free school meals would be fed. He knew that for a lot of them, those free meals were their only meals, and he contacted a local charity to make a substantial donation.

After discussion with the charity's CEO, however, he decided to offer his full support to a campaign he hoped would raise £400,000 for local children. It raised over £20 million and reached four million kids across the UK within a month. His open letter in June 2020 saw an outpouring of support so substantial that the government made a U-turn and extended the school meals programme to feed children during lockdown. Since then, Rashford has campaigned for an end to child poverty in the UK and has also spearheaded campaigns to increase social welfare payments, increase literacy among young people and help parents to cook cheap meals for their kids.

'There were times when there wasn't any food there and you would just go to sleep,' Rashford said of his upbringing. 'It should never be normal to feel how I felt. When you get to the position that I'm in now, I feel like, if they are in need and they don't have anyone fighting for them, I should be the one that does it really. I think in life you have to have something behind you that is pushing you. When you come from a place of struggle and pain, a lot of the time it switches, and it becomes your drive and motivation.'

While working on the *Now You See Me* movies, I became friendly with actors Woody Harrelson and Mark Ruffalo. As well as being a bona fide Hollywood star and a family man, Woody is an environmentalist at his core. He has risked his freedom campaigning for environmental causes, including one protest where he scaled the Golden Gate Bridge with an activist group to raise awareness of the plight of America's ancient redwood trees. Two decades ago he formed a company that makes paper from wheat stalks and other agricultural waste instead of trees in an effort to save the forests.

He is a committed vegan and has lived off the grid for years. He even has a 1970s environmentally friendly tour bus which runs on vegetable oil. Recently, Woody narrated a Netflix documentary called *Kiss the Ground* to teach people how regenerative agriculture and planting can help reverse the effects of pesticides and even global warming to revitalise the planet.

Woody's purpose is to educate people on how we can be friendlier to the environment, and he lives his life true to that purpose every day. He talks the talk, walks the walk, and lives a life of environmental education, sustainability and activism – all to help people undertake a healthier, more sustainable way of living and help save the earth.

Mark Ruffalo is probably best known for playing the angry green giant the Hulk in the *Avengers* movies, but he also has a green heart and is a huge environmentalist. When energy companies threatened to frack for natural gas near his farm in New York State, Mark researched the process and became aware of the high environmental cost of fracking.

To release gas trapped inside rock beneath the earth's surface, fracking uses huge amounts of water and has been shown to release potentially carcinogenic chemicals. Mark now travels America denouncing oil pipelines and hydraulic fracking for natural gas. He has testified in Congress on the need for regulation of substances known as PFAS, long-lasting toxic chemicals used in packaging, household cleaning products and fire-fighting foams among other things, and he has also campaigned for clean water.

When Mark contacted me a while back and asked if I would assist in preventing fracking in Ireland, I did my own scientific research on the process and came to the same conclusion that it's not good for the earth and it's not good for us, so I added my name to the cause. After strenuous efforts to stop it, thanks to the input of Mark and others, fracking has since been banned in Ireland.

Like Woody, Mark is known as an actor, but he is also a family man, a philanthropist and an environmentalist. 'I have been gifted with this outsize media coverage, celebrity,' he said recently. 'I could decide, well, I can use that to do car commercials and make a lot more money … I could use that for any number of things to ingratiate and enrich myself. I feel like, from this blessing that

I've been given, that I want to give people the voice that don't have a voice.'

Both Woody and Mark still love acting, have other hobbies and interests, but, like Marcus Rashford, have very definite greater purposes. All three have used their voices as celebrities and committed themselves to the greater purpose of helping people and saving the planet.

I learned a long time ago that to be happy and successful, everybody needs a sense of purpose in life. For me, purpose is a pursuit or activity which adds value and meaning to your life. Without purpose, I don't believe you'll jump out of bed and tackle every day with the discipline necessary to hit your targets. Without a sense of purpose, there's not much to get up for in the morning and it's very easy to inadvertently sink into despair and depression.

Purpose is the number one thing that separates peak performance individuals from average people. A lot of people just plod along in their lives with no real sense of direction. Peak performers, on the other hand, from top athletes to businesspeople, absolutely know their purpose. They know why they are doing what they're doing. To define your own purpose or multiple purposes you need to ask yourself, 'Why?'

ASK YOURSELF WHY

Most people don't put enough deep, meaningful thought into their whys. Why they're in the job they're in, why they're with the partner they're with, why they are where they are in life, why they're doing things that are actually detrimental to them. If you don't know your whys, you end up going through life lost. And there are a lot of people lost right now. If you haven't already done so, you owe it to yourself to figure out where you are in life at the moment, how you got here and what your purpose in life actually is.

When asked why they do the things they do, or work in the job they work in, most people will answer, 'I'm doing it for my family' – which is the most obvious but laziest answer. While Marcus Rashford's first thoughts were for his own family, he didn't stop there. He saw the bigger picture and tried to ensure that no other child had to endure what he, his siblings, his classmates, his friends, and most of the families in his area had to endure.

When probed about why they are doing what they do, some of the busiest businesspeople in the world will give the same answer: that they are doing it for their family. Yet those same business-people will barely see their families, because they're so busy with their work, and spend a lot of their time wondering why they are so unhappy.

I have actually had some clients tell me that their sole purpose in life is to make money. Now, these people are already very rich financially, but they tell me they want to be the richest person in the world. If you want to do something purely for money, I'm not going to judge you for that, but what I will judge you on is not having a purpose or, indeed, multiple purposes.

All over the world, people volunteer and give up their time to teach, coach, or care for others. People help out at sports clubs, on Tidy Towns committees, Meals on Wheels groups and other com-munity services. We are all psychologically hardwired to help other people. Inherently, we all want to serve and help others and a lot of us are already doing just that without realising it.

The only way to figure out your purposes is to write down the word 'why?' and ask yourself questions like:

> › Why don't I ...?
> › Why do I ...?
> › Why am I unhappy in ...?
> › Why am I happy in ...?
> › Why am I successful in ...?
> › Why am I unsuccessful in ...?
> › Why do I spend so much time ...?
> › Why am I worried about ...?
> › Why do I put up with ...?

STOP NOW, grab your journal and write ten questions about yourself beginning with 'why'. Take time to look at those questions and figure out what you are doing right now. Are you are aligning yourself to your purpose? If you're not, then ask yourself, 'Why not?'

While I also do what I do for my family, to inspire my children and to help them fulfil their potential in life, another major purpose of mine is to serve other people, either by entertaining them and bringing them some escapism from their everyday lives, or by helping them better themselves through my executive coaching or mind coaching. Sometimes that purpose has included literally saving people's lives over the years and I'm very grateful to be able to do that.

Adventure and being more environmentally friendly are other purposes of mine. I love travelling to new places, doing new things, meeting new people and helping them. I'm learning more about the impact I have on the environment and am trying to do my bit to help. Having recently decided to only cut my grass once a month, I now leave a strip of dandelions for the bees after finding out that one-third of our bees here in Ireland are threatened with extinction. Maybe you could do the same.

I also want to leave a legacy of some kind. My purpose in writing this book is to share my knowledge in the hope that I can help at least one other person change their life for the better. I hope it will positively affect hundreds, perhaps thousands of people. But if it profoundly affects just one person, I will be very happy. That would mean I left some kind of legacy on this planet.

Everything I do in life, from where I live, to where and how I work, to how I spend my time, revolves around my purposes. They are the reason I jump out of bed every morning with a smile on my face, ready to attack every single day as if it is my last. My purposes excite me.

When you're examining your purposes, your whys, you need to put deep, meaningful thought into them. You can't just sit down for five minutes and think about them. You need to invest a lot of time to figure it all out.

TAKE A REORIENTATION DAY

One of the things I insist on with all the clients I work with is that they take a 'reorientation day' every month. A reorientation day is a half-day or, ideally, a full day of between six and eight hours, where you take a journal to a really quiet place and work on yourself, your purposes, your whys and your targets.

In order to keep each purpose in mind at all times you must first write them down. I recommend buying yourself an expensive journal in which to write your whys, your minor and major purposes, and your targets, and to record your progress. The reason for this is simple. If these records are going to be important to you, then they need to be kept in an important place. If you purchase an expensive leather-bound journal, you will value it more and you will want to know where it is at all times. You should use this journal at least once a week and preferably every day to record your progress.

Your reorientation day can be a trip to a quiet spa or retreat, an empty beach or into the wilderness, but wherever you go there must be no distractions: no phone calls, no emails, nothing but you and your journal. It's time to just sit and reorientate your conscious and subconscious mind to optimise your focus on your whys and your targets in life.

On this day, every month, take time to focus on your different purposes in life and make sure that the actions and behaviours you have taken in the previous month align with those purposes. If they didn't, then you must figure out why not. Over the years I've found that while highly successful people will always take the time to have a reorientation day, a lot of other people won't. The ones who won't, however, are invariably stuck in the same place a year later. People say they don't have time to take half a day out of their lives. They can't leave their families. They can't take a half-day from work. They're too busy.

But the average worker spends twelve and a half hours a week digitally distracted during business hours.[15] That's over a half a day a week on Facebook, Twitter, Candy Crush or other apps while you are supposed to be working. Then there's all the time you are digitally distracted in work or at home, like when you're sitting on the couch half-watching TV, sitting at the table half-eating your dinner, or sitting on the loo half … well, you get the idea. If you can spend that much time on your phone or computer, how can you tell me that you don't have time to enhance your life?

People will easily spend a couple of hours, for two or three days a week, in the gym but won't put any effort into improving their mindset. That, to me, is like having a car that you wash and valet and polish but never have serviced. Well, if you never service the engine, no matter how shiny and sparkly it looks on the outside, sooner or later that car is going to break down. I see it all the time. With experience, I've learned that if a coaching client says they don't have the time for a reorientation day, or even that they just won't do it, then it's not going to work. I'll give them their money back there and then, saving both of us wasting our time.

I recently interviewed Suzanne Jackson of SoSueMe for my YouTube channel. Suzanne at the time of writing has 297,000 followers on Instagram and a team of fifteen people working for her. She is listed as the number one Irish influencer in the world, but she didn't get there by magic. During our chat, Suzanne told me that she creatively visualises regularly, she self-hypnotises, she even visualised the house that she now lives in. She has taken reorientation days without realising that was what she was doing. When my clients get into the habit of doing this, they are astounded at what comes out. I've had clients come to me with businesses worth €5 million that are now worth sixty times that.

Everyone can spare four to eight hours in a month to improve their mindset. For example, schedule a recurring half-day on the last Thursday of every month. Don't have a glass of wine on a Friday evening, so you can get up early on the first Saturday of the month. You can always find the time. You need at least four hours to sit or lie in a quiet place and do the work. You can't put yourself in an altered state of mind, think about your targets and purpose deeply and write down your thoughts and progressions in half an hour or even two hours. It's just four to eight hours out of 730 hours in an average month to productively change your life forever.

The successful people I coach use these techniques but, because it's not easy to sit down with a journal and get inside your own head, most ordinary people simply won't do it. Everyone is looking for an instant fix. Often, people who go to a hypnotist or psychologist are looking for a quick fix. A lot of people reading this book are probably looking for a quick fix, an instant cure. People want a snap of the fingers that tells them, 'Life is rosy, I'm going to be rich, I'm going to be famous, I'm going to have health, wealth, love and money.' But that's not how it works. I can help you. I can give you tools and techniques. But the real magic must come from inside you. You have to find your purposes and find your passions to find that magic. If you just put half an hour a month into yourself, into your mind, then you're not going to hit your targets. That's why a reorientation day is so important.

STOP NOW and put a reorientation day in your diary. Inform anyone who needs to know that you will be completely off the grid that day. Decide where you are going to go for your reorientation day. If it is somewhere that requires booking, such as a hotel or spa, book it right now!

When I was about 15, I was in a cabaret act that included an Elvis impersonator, a comedian and a singer. Every Saturday night we would be driven from the town centre in a clapped-out old minibus to the Grand Hotel in Tramore, where we would entertain holidaymakers from the hotel and the caravan park across the road.

Our 'promoter' (and bus driver) thought that Keith Barry wasn't a great stage name, however, so he decided to give me a new one instead. Every Saturday evening, when it was my turn to take to the stage, he would announce, 'Ladies and gentlemen … boys and girls … all the way from Las Vegas, Nevada … please welcome the Great Maldini!'

As the hotel function room went wild with expectation, 15-year-old me would bumble out from behind the curtains and hack my way through my routine, which involved taking eight tennis balls out of a crystal glass box, making them disappear in a bag and spinning the box to reveal the eight balls back inside it again.

While the Grand Hotel in Tramore was a far cry from the glitz and glamour of Las Vegas, the promoter's tongue-in-cheek introduction every Saturday night lit a fire in me to find out more about this mysterious showbusiness place. If I wanted to entertain as many people as possible, maybe Las Vegas was the place to be.

When I naively asked my dad if he'd heard of Las Vegas, he regaled me with stories of Frank Sinatra, Dean Martin and even the real Elvis Presley headlining shows on the famous Vegas strip.

I was impressed by these stories and eventually saw clips of some of them on TV, but these were all huge stars. I was a 15-year-old kid from Waterford and thought there was no way that someone like me could headline in Las Vegas. That was until I discovered that another kid from Waterford had already proved my theory wrong decades earlier.

Brendan Bowyer began his career with Waterford band The Royal Showband in 1957. While I had heard songs like 'The Hucklebuck' on the radio and on my mother's record player, I had no idea of the successful career Brendan Bowyer had enjoyed. I couldn't believe that the Beatles actually opened for his Waterford band in the Empire Theatre in Liverpool or that, from 1975, Brendan and his band spent half of the year headlining their own show on the strip in Las Vegas, with the real Elvis Presley actually coming to watch him!

In total, the late great Brendan Bowyer played residencies on the Las Vegas strip for twenty-five years. He proved me wrong. I realised that a kid from Waterford could headline on the strip in Las Vegas and from the time I found that out, I resolved that I would do just that.

8.

THE TARGETS FORMULA

HOW TO CONSISTENTLY HIT
YOUR TARGETS IN LIFE

WHEN I WAS a child in Waterford, we lived down a quiet country road with no streetlights, which meant that in the cold, dark evenings of winter, my sister and I would rush through our homework so that we could go next door and play indoor games with our grandparents. The most popular games in the house at the time were cards and darts. Years of playing darts with her parents from a young age ensured my mother was so good at it that she represented County Waterford and the province of Munster in competition.

On those dark winter evenings, the whole family would spend hours on end throwing darts through plumes of my grandparents' cigarette smoke at an old dartboard hung on the kitchen door. At first, my sister and I were allowed stand a bit closer than you would in competition, and our sole objective was to merely hit the dartboard and save the back of my grandparents' kitchen door.

As we got better, we learned the rules of the game and how, beginning with a score of 501, every dart thrown reduced our total until the first player to get down to zero was hailed the winner. We learned that hitting triple twenty with all three darts ensured you got the highest score possible in each round but, as the final game-winning dart had to hit a double, we also learned about the value of practising aiming for smaller numbers.

It was only when I got older that I realised how much those games had taught me about hitting targets – not only on a dartboard, but in life. As a child my mother used to tell me, 'You're not going to get what you want if you don't aim at it,' meaning there was no point in aimlessly throwing darts at the board. If I needed to hit a specific number to win the game, then I had to focus intently on that target and aim for it. When I got older, I came to the conclusion that the same could be said for anything you want to achieve in life.

At first, when things worked out more for me in life than they did for some of my friends or colleagues I thought it was coincidence, but after a while I realised there were simply too many coincidences for that to be true. I sat down one day and thought about how I had hit most of the targets I had aimed for in life and noticed that I had been using the same approach most of the time. The ones that I missed were invariably times when I had veered off track, got distracted, lost my focus or given up too soon. Over the next few weeks, I spent a lot of time thinking about targets and the scientist in me came up with a formula, which I will explain later in this chapter, to help me stay on track and hit those targets again and again.

So what is a target? A target is a clearly defined objective that you want to accomplish within a set period of time. Some people prefer the term 'goal' or 'dream', but for me, a goal is just an aspiration that may or may not be attained, while dreams are figments of our imagination. Without clear targets to aim at, goals may remain goals and dreams may remain just dreams. While a goal can be vague and you may fail to reach it because you are distracted, a clearly defined target is something your subconscious mind can lock onto like a heat-seeking missile. Once that target is clearly seen in your mind, then, just like a missile, you will find your way over, under, around and through anything that gets in your way.

In its simplest form, a target is something to aim at. While in darts that target could be the triple twenty or any smaller number, in life that target could be anything from getting a promotion in your job to buying a bigger house, going on holiday or cutting something out of your lifestyle.

I have used my TARGETS formula, brain hacks and visualisations to turn my passion into my career, to get my own TV shows in Ireland and America, to headline on the strip in Las Vegas and gain success in my life over and over again. The reason acronyms like TARGETS are used so much in schools, businesses and other walks of life is that they help us remember. TARGETS stands for:

> Take aim
> Act
> Record your progress
> Gamify
> Expect obstacles
> Team up
> Success

TAKE AIM

As my mother said, 'You're not going to get what you want if you don't aim at it.' In life, if you simply keep firing darts aimlessly, you will miss your targets and possibly even lose your darts. You'll get fed up playing the game and will settle for something less exciting instead.

When I took up darts, my first target was simply to hit the board. When I was able to do that, I moved back further and tried to focus on getting higher scores, hitting the triple twenty as often as I could. After a lot of time and focused practice, I was finally able to hit any number I wanted the majority of the time. If you want to hit your targets in life, the process is exactly the same.

In order to take aim, you must first have something to aim at. Do you want to drop a size in time for that upcoming wedding or party? Do you want to move house? Do you want to go on a date? Do you want to stop smoking? Do you want to travel the world? Do you want to ace your exams?

I recommend you have four different types of target in life to aim for at any given time. The first type would be your easier short-range targets. The second type would be medium-range targets which would take a longer time to hit. The third type would be long-range targets that could take a few months or even a few years to hit.

Finally, my fourth suggestion would be a target so crazy, so out-landish, that ordinarily it wouldn't even be in your sights. This is your magical target. Most people miss out on having these nutty, crazy, magical targets in life. These targets may be far-fetched and therefore not seem as important as the other ones but, in my opinion, they are just as important as your other targets, and they can be so rewarding when you hit them.

As I sit here writing this book, I have a large whiteboard in front of me where I have drawn a target with my short-, medium-, long-range and magical targets in marker. The whiteboard is in a prominent place in my workspace so that I see it every day. That way I will be reminded continuously, if only subconsciously, of what I'm aiming at. I can use that whiteboard to record my progress, tick off my successful hits and set new targets on a daily basis.

Right now, one of my short-range targets is to grow a YouTube series. I have already completed four or five interviews for the series, and it will probably begin to air in the next couple of weeks. When it does, I can wipe that target off the board. Another short-term target was to connect with a UK TV producer. I did that today and I have a meeting with another UK producer next week, so I can now wipe that off the board.

As I glance up now at the whiteboard from my desk, I've reminded myself of a short-term target to create content for my social media channels before the weekend. I have a medium-range target of having 30,000 followers on YouTube and 100,000 followers on TikTok by the end of 2021 and I am already working on how best to achieve those targets. Two long-range targets of mine are to land a new TV show when the pandemic is over and expand my business internationally.

You will notice that several of my short-range targets lead into my medium-range ones and they, in turn, lead me on to the long-range targets. For example, the short-range target of meeting with a TV producer leads into the medium-range target of pitching to TV networks, which in turn leads into my long-range targets of landing a new TV show and expanding my business internationally.

One of my crazier, more outlandish magical targets is to climb Kilimanjaro in my underpants with the Ice Man, Wim Hof. Now,

period. Now, reduced sleep has its drawbacks, but if you are serious about hitting your big targets you need to take massive action.

We all sometimes plod along, get busy being busy. In the past couple of years, though, we've all had to stop and pivot, change our lifestyles and adapt how we work, how we meet, how we shop. Even then, we soon get busy at these new things.

At some stage, however, you have to stop and put time into yourself. A lot of people I coach are so busy that they don't stop to think about themselves. It's not that they're doing stuff wrong. It's that they're not doing this stuff at all. They're simply not activating their subconscious minds, finding their purpose for doing things or setting their sights on their targets with precision.

When the pandemic hit in early 2020, live shows were put on hold indefinitely and I went from selling out theatres across Ireland to having literally nothing to do. For a while I had no sense of purpose. I felt irritated, angry and anxious. With no way of entertaining people, or even helping people on a one-to-one basis, I felt like I didn't belong, had nothing to offer anymore, and I got really down for a few weeks.

But then I took a reorientation day. I spent eight hours alone with my thoughts and my journal and I realised that with hard graft and dedication I could pivot with the pandemic. I took massive action and went into super-activation mode. I learned as much as possible about hosting online meetings and began to work 14–16 hours a day until I figured it all out. I bought the necessary equipment and educated myself enough that I could move all of my shows, webinars and coaching online. Now I can reach more people than ever before, from all over the world, all from the comfort of my own home.

With my new studio set up, I decided a short-range target that I would aim at was to get back on Ellen DeGeneres' highly popular US daytime show. I knew the show had an average viewership of 4.1 million people per episode and that it was a great shop window for me in America. As I had been on it before as a young magician, I contacted my agent to see what he thought.

'Well, you're not going to get back on Ellen, Keith,' he said bluntly. 'There's thousands of people trying to get on that show every day.'

By then, I hadn't been on Ellen's show for about thirteen years, so I expected more obstacles this time around, but I didn't expect my agent to be so pessimistic about my chances. I didn't know any directors, producers or anybody else associated with the programme, but I was determined to get back on it and decided to take massive action.

Starting from zero, I googled researchers and producers of the show and sent out thirty emails. When I got no response, I looked up phone numbers for the show and began calling them. Again, I got no response. I waited a week and then sent out another thirty emails and made another twenty phone calls, with the same result.

Still, I gamified the experience by telling anyone who would listen to me that I was going to be on the *Ellen DeGeneres Show* before the end of the year. I even told my audiences in my online shows and corporate gigs and promised myself a reward if I did get on. I was all-in dedicated to hitting my target of getting on *Ellen*. I do that with every aspect of my life. If I decide I'm going to do something, I go all in, whether that's family, fitness, work or whatever it is I want to do.

In the end, it took me ninety-two emails and forty-six phone calls, but I got on the *Ellen DeGeneres Show* in October 2020 and it went really well. As a direct result of being on that show I began to get more corporate gigs online from America, which helped me hit my medium-range target of pitching my TV show ideas to some of the big US channels.

Because of the way I structure my life and the work I put in, I firmly believe I will have landed a TV show shortly after this book is published. The true aim of all of this, however, is to allow me to get back on stage to fulfil my purpose of entertaining people and allowing them to escape reality for a while.

Some people take baby steps to get where they want to go, and that's definitely necessary at times, but you have to realise that the smaller the steps you take the longer the journey is going to be. You must also start that action immediately. How many times have you heard somebody trying to lose weight or somebody trying to give something up say, 'I'll start Monday.' Why Monday? What's wrong with today? Right now? Do it now! My success is nothing to do with intellect. I don't believe I am any more intelligent than you. I don't believe I was 'born' to do my job. I don't believe I have a gift. I do believe that I achieve the things I achieve because I regularly take massive action towards them. Always keep your targets in sight and don't limit your actions to hit them. If you've got a target in your mind, always take massive action.

STOP NOW and decide what massive action looks like for you. Are you willing to put in the effort and dedication for three months of super-activation mode? Ask yourself:

> How much energy are you willing to put in to hit your target? What resources are you going to put in?

> > How much money and time are you going to put in?
> > How many extra phone calls, emails and dreaded video meetings are you willing to make?

All of these things need to be considered thoroughly. Decide what are you willing to sacrifice to hit your targets and then prepare your diary to allow time to act on that. Then you need to magnify that action times three or four. Take massive action. Don't just do enough. By just doing enough you'll never hit the kind of long-range targets that you want to achieve. Now throw your first dart. Put this book down. Go! Take action! Throw away your sweet stuff, crush your cigarettes, hire a trainer, book a flight, work out a business plan, whatever it is you need to do. Start immediately.

RECORD YOUR PROGRESS

The modern game of darts involves an electronic scoreboard that records each player's progress. With every dart they throw, they check the number on the scoreboard and analyse and adjust their aim so that they hit the required targets to win the game. You too should record your progress towards your own targets.

You must have metrics to know whether you are moving in the right direction, or even moving at all. If you find your aim is off, then you can recalibrate your actions. If you find that your timeframe for hitting your target is not long enough, then you may have to move the target a little further away. If you find that you are hitting your short-range targets sooner than expected, you might be able to move your medium-range targets closer.

Define a realistic timeline for each target and then analyse and monitor your progress daily. Record that progress or lack of progress in your journal or on your whiteboard and re-evaluate things as necessary. If you are off track, redirect your focus, change direction if needed and get yourself back on track.

The physical act of recording your progress creates a link between the spatial part of your brain and the verbal part which ultimately helps people remember things better. But don't just record your progress. Discuss your progress with a trusted confidant, advisor or coach. That way you will have constant reminders of what you are aiming at and how near you are to your intended target.

Recording your progress has other benefits. Ticking something off your list, wiping it off your whiteboard, or telling your friend you hit your target is an added bonus that will give you a sense of satisfaction and achievement and remind you that you are on track.

GAMIFY THE EXPERIENCE

Set yourself a little competition every week. When you hit your short-, medium-, or long-range targets give yourself a little reward. This reward, however, should never take away from achieving your targets. What I mean is if you are aiming to lose weight, the reward should not be food-related. If you are aiming to curb your addiction to technology, the reward should never be a video game, a new phone or anything technology-related.

Some targets require hard, difficult graft to hit them, so gamifying your progress will keep you focused and excited about the next reward. For example, if you have a long-range target of losing three stone, you should have a reward for every time you hit a short-term target of half a stone and a bigger reward when eventually you hit that long-range target. That reward could be a new pair of runners, a new book, a massage, time off work, a fishing trip with your friends – anything that isn't food-related. My passion is magic, so I will often reward myself with a new trick or illusion whenever I hit my targets. It's a great fun way to keep your interest and you will soon find that the process of ticking off old targets and setting new ones is very satisfying.

Gamification is fuelled by dopamine, the chemical your body releases when you experience something pleasurable or satisfying. One of the biggest dopamine providers in life is receiving a reward for doing something, which is why parents all over the world use rewards to incentivise their kids to do chores, go to bed early or study harder.

Dopamine neurons can learn to predict when something satisfying is on its way and will release good vibes beforehand. By recording your progress, you will often get a little chemical hit of dopamine in the build-up to actually hitting your target. This is why fitness apps have activity rings that need to be closed or steps that need to be taken before you can get your next reward or progress to the next level. Gamification helps keep you motivated and on track for the next part of the challenge.

Decide now on some rewards you are willing to give yourself should you reach certain milestones along your journey towards a certain target. Write these rewards into your journal so they are at the front of your mind at all times.

EXPECT OBSTACLES

The number one mistake people make when setting targets is a failure to expect obstacles. Now, you may think that expecting obstacles is negative thinking, but it's not. It's being prepared. If you expect obstacles and pre-emptively prepare for them, they will be so much easier to overcome.

As I write this, I am in the middle of one of the busiest periods of my life. Everything I do now is online, which means I could have a gig in Ireland in the morning, one in the UK in the afternoon, one in America that evening and another one in Australia at 2 a.m. the next morning.

When preparing for the shift to online gigging, I sat down and wrote out my short-, medium-, and long-range business targets. I also sat down and went through every obstacle to hitting my targets that I could possibly imagine. What if my Wi-Fi dropped in the middle of a corporate gig? What if my internet access went down in the middle of a live virtual TV appearance in the US?

To help prevent this, I contacted my internet provider and explained my situation. Between us, we tried to figure out the best, most stable system to use, resulting in me now having two different internet systems hardwired through my devices. If one drops off, the other one immediately kicks in.

Even with that problem solved, I tried to come up with other obstacles. What if a storm came and I was left without electricity for a couple of days? Usually once a year or so, there is enough wind to knock out the electricity in my house, so I pre-empted that by buying a generator that will now kick in if that does happen. You need to expect problems. Sometimes no matter how hard we try we cannot imagine the obstacles that will land in front of us out of the blue, but if you can pre-empt at least the ones you can envision, then you will be well equipped to deal with the ones you can't.

By the time I perform an escape while chained and padlocked in a container full of water, I will have already spent time anticipating all of the obstacles I can think of that might prevent me from escaping that container uninjured. Everything from the locks not working to the chains rusting to the water being too cold and causing me to go into shock has all been anticipated and pre-empted.

Good darts players expect noise from the crowd, they expect bad lighting, they expect their darts to break, they might even expect the board to fall off the wall and have to be replaced mid-game. Expecting obstacles is so important. In fact, it's one of the most important things to do when you aim for a target. If you expect these things, they won't faze you when they do happen. You don't have to be worried about obstacles. Most of them will never happen but if they do, and you are ready for them, then your aim will stay true, and you will still be on your way towards hitting your targets.

STOP NOW, grab your journal, and think about your current targets. Try to pre-empt as many obstacles as you can for each one. What could go wrong? What might prevent you from hitting those targets? Write down three possible solutions for every obstacle you can think of.

TEAM UP

Most people will struggle to meet their targets on their own. I know I certainly can't hit mine without some help from my team. They help me with my website, to take bookings, to edit videos, to inspire me, to teach me; and you should get help from others too.

Teamwork can come in many forms. If you are trying to meet new people and you ask a friend or neighbour to come along for support, that's teamwork. If you are trying to lose weight and you join a slimming club, that's teamwork, taking the advice and help of others. If you are trying to get fit and you join a gym or sports club, that's teamwork. If the gym is closed and you are using a workout app on your phone, you are involved in teamwork.

It's okay to ask for help. Technology nowadays allows us to create target teams all over the world at the press of a button. If you are brave enough, put your targets on your social media or join a like-minded online group for support. The more people you trust who know about your targets, the more support you are likely to have, and you will also feel more accountable for your actions. Surround yourself with a target team that can help you reach your targets and vice versa. Always be willing to give back in equal measure to the people on your team. One of the most fulfilling things we can do as human beings is help each other.

SUCCESS

As one of my main purposes in life is to entertain people, my first really long-range target was to become well-known enough in Ireland to be able to sell out my own stage shows.

As well as following the other steps in my TARGETS formula, every day I visualised myself standing on a stage in front of hundreds of people. I could see myself doing it. I could hear the laughter and applause. I could feel the endorphins pumping through my body. If I hit my target, I knew that was what success would look and feel like.

You too need to be able to define and visualise what success looks like to you. You need to know what it will look like, what it will feel like, what it will sound, smell, and possibly even taste like. If you haven't clearly defined success in your mind, how will you know you have succeeded?

STOP NOW and spend time thinking about your targets.

> **Take aim** and plan the necessary steps to hit your short-range, medium-range, long-range and even magical targets.
> What **Actions** do you need to take to get there?
> How can you **Record** your progress?
> How can you **Gamify** your progress?
> Have you allowed yourself to **Expect obstacles**?
> Who can you **Team up** with?
> What will **Success** look like?

When you have figured this out, grab your journal, write everything down and start throwing your darts.

After hitting the short-range target of getting well-known in Dublin by blagging my way into the Kitchen, doing various private parties and gigs for local celebrities, and making my first appearance on the *Late Late Show*, my first medium-range target was to get my own TV show on RTÉ.

I wrote that first medium-range target down in black permanent marker on one of the walls in my bedroom at the time. That way it was the first thing I saw when I got up each morning and the last thing I saw before I went to bed. It was always right in front of me and therefore was always in my mind. I also wrote it into my journal. Once I had **Taken aim** at my target and written it down, I immediately began to take **Action** towards that target.

Part of that action was to come up with ideas and write a pitch that I could present to a TV studio. I wrote a pitch and then searched for a list of production companies that could help me pitch my ideas to the national broadcaster. I **Recorded** my progress by ticking off the ones I had contacted, and I also wrote new ideas for my pitch into my journal.

While I was firmly established in the Kitchen at the time, another magician was also very well established in a different nightclub across town. In my head, I **Gamified** the whole experience by telling myself that it was a race between the two of us to get a TV show. Although the other magician had no idea about our imaginary race, the thought of him beating me to a TV show really spurred me on.

While I had **Expected obstacles**, one that I didn't expect was almost all of the production companies telling me it couldn't be done. Door after door was closed in my face until I finally **Teamed up** with Midas Productions.

I got a meeting with some executives from RTÉ at their headquarters in Donnybrook. At that meeting, I read their minds and performed a trick where a card signed by one of the executives ended up stuck on the outer glass of the window of the building we were sitting in. The meeting was a **Success**, and I landed my first ever TV show, *Close Encounters with Keith Barry*.

A short time after landing the deal I went to the Blackpool Magic Convention, the biggest convention in the world for magicians, and rewarded myself by purchasing a trick called Smash and Stab, which I then redeveloped into the Spike Trick and which went on to become one of my trademark tricks.

Hitting that first medium-range target and getting my own TV show enabled me to hit my first long-range target and become well-known enough in Ireland to be able to sell out my own stage shows and follow my purpose of entertaining as many people as possible.

START AT THE END AND WORK BACKWARDS

Most of the time it's important to work your way back from your long-range or biggest target in order to work out what steps you need to take to stay on track and hit that target. If you begin at the biggest target and work your way backwards to where you are now, you can then add in smaller targets and timelines that will act as stepping-stones on the way to your main objective.

If, for example, you want to complete the Dublin City Marathon, you know that to do that you need to be able to run 26.2 miles on the last Sunday in October. That's your long-range target. In that instance, a short-range target could be running a 10km race by August and a medium-range target could be completing a half marathon by September.

These targets and timelines, however, can be broken up further, depending on your current fitness level and the time you have available to hit your target. For a newcomer or a non-runner, your first short-term target could be to complete a 5km race, a 1km run, or simply to buy a decent pair of running shoes and begin running in the first place.

By using my TARGETS formula and **Taking aim**, **Acting** on each of these targets, **Recording** your progress, **Gamifying** the experience by collecting medals from each race or rewarding yourself with something else, **Expecting obstacles** like bad weather, illness or injury, and **Teaming up** with others from a local running club or people who have the same objectives, you will give yourself a great chance of **Success** and completing that marathon.

Even though I hit my first long-range target of selling out my live shows in Ireland, I knew that sustaining a full-time career in magic was going to be hard in such a small country and I figured that the best chance of doing that was in America. I remembered my boyhood dream of headlining in Las Vegas and began to focus on that as another long-range target. I knew if this was to happen at all it would take years of hard work, so I filled the timeline to that target with lots of other short-range, medium-range and magical targets.

With my Las Vegas target up on the whiteboard and written into my journal, I then had to figure out the small and medium targets that I would need to hit along the way in order to help me hit the big one that I was really aiming for.

The first time I flew stateside with the idea of 'breaking' America was shortly after *Close Encounters with Keith Barry* had aired in Ireland. Over the next five or six years, I would fly via Newark to LA and would spend anything from a couple of weeks to a couple of months there in an effort to hit the big time.

While I had meetings with agents, promoters and other enter-tainment people some days, there were often long periods when I hit obstacles and didn't have much to do except hang around. I tried to use these periods to practise and think of ways to get noticed. To get any attention from the movers and shakers in LA, I knew I had to infiltrate the Hollywood scene in much the same way as I had done in Dublin a few years earlier, so I spent most nights trying to blag my way into every big nightclub I could find.

When I did get into the clubs, I then blagged my way behind the red ropes and into the VIP sections. I got friendly with the nightclub bouncers and got to know the three biggest promoters in town – the Alliance, Brent Bolthouse and Sarah Pantera – and pretty soon I was able to get in everywhere. Known for running some of the best nights in town, these promoters had a list of celebrity friends as long as your arm and soon I was spending my nights doing tricks for Justin Timberlake, Kelly Osbourne, Paris Hilton, Harrison Ford, the *Jackass* guys and others.

In the days before camera phones and social media, Hollywood celebrities could let their hair down on big nights out without fear of ending up in the papers the next day. One night, Sarah asked me to arrive early to the opening of a new nightclub as she wanted me to entertain a friend of hers before the club opened. As hundreds of people queued up outside, I was ushered straight in to find Sarah and her friend were the only ones inside. Sarah introduced me to her friend, a striking blonde girl.

'Keith, meet Scarlett … Scarlett, meet Keith.'

Before I even had a chance to do a trick for her, future Black Widow Scarlett Johansson asked whether I drank and promptly ordered a bottle of Jack Daniels. Scarlett was lovely and after some small talk I did a trick for her where she signed a card and put it back in the deck, only to look up and see her signed card stuck to the ceiling over her head. She screamed the place down in disbelief. It was one of the most surreal moments of my life.

In that five-year period of travelling to LA, I began to get a name as 'that crazy Irish magician'.

I was sitting in a restaurant in LA around lunchtime one day when Josh from the Alliance came over to me and asked, 'Keith, I'm here with a friend. Any chance you'd do a trick for him?'

I said 'Sure, no problem,' and followed Josh over to his table. What Josh hadn't told me, however, was that his friend was Keanu Reeves. Now, I was a bit nervous, but I curled my toes and somehow remembered the spoon bend that happened in *The Matrix*. I picked a spoon off the table and went to melt it, Uri Geller style, in front of his eyes when Keanu suddenly jumped up out of his seat.

'What are you about to do?' he asked.

'I'm just going to show you a trick ...'

'No, no, no ... I can't see this,' he answered. 'I'm scared of magic! I can't see magic!'

With that, he turned on his heels and ran out of the restaurant. Josh threw a hundred-dollar bill on the table for their food and ran out after him, leaving me wondering what the hell had just happened and with a great story to tell my future wife, who was flying over the next day.

By the time she landed, though, I had a better story for her. We were both invited to a party that night in Keanu Reeves' house in the Hollywood Hills, where I continued my hustle and did magic for everybody ... except him.

I appeared multiple times on the Jimmy Kimmel and Ellen DeGeneres shows but it would still be a couple of years before I got my first big break in the US.

At one point I asked the three biggest nightclub promoters in LA to bring the celebrities down to see my show at the Henry Fonda Theatre on Hollywood Boulevard. Justin Timberlake, Elisha Cuthbert and lots more were in the audience that night, but the real purpose of the performance was to show the invited TV network executives and live entertainment executives what I could do.

Although CBS hadn't televised a magic show in over fifteen years, a pitch meeting with an executive from the network after that performance prompted them to offer me a huge four-show TV deal in 2006. The first one, *Keith Barry – Extraordinary*, aired to huge acclaim.

There were plenty more reorientation days after that, and lots more targets to hit, but by using my TARGETS system and continually focusing on what I wanted to achieve, I always got there in the end.

In 2009, a full 18 years after performing in the Grand Hotel in Tramore, I walked onto the stage at the Planet Hollywood resort and casino on the Las Vegas strip as the headline act. This time, though, I wasn't the Great Maldini. This time, the whole hotel and casino were branded with Keith Barry logos. My name was in lights on the front of the building and the two giant pillars at the hotel entrance were each plastered with a huge poster of my face. Everything inside the hotel, from the walls to the reception desk, staff badges, and even the bedroom key cards, bore the Keith Barry logo. It had taken a while to hit that target, but it was an amazing experience.

I went on to win Best Magician in Las Vegas that year and was also awarded the prestigious Merlin Award for Mentalist of the Year – the equivalent of the Oscars for magicians – by the International Magicians' Society.

As well as the visualisation that follows at the end of this section, I have used my TARGETS system to hit short-, medium-, and long-range targets for the last twenty years or more. I truly believe if you do the same then you can hit the bullseye on every single target you set for yourself.

EVERYDAY BRAIN HACKS FOR SUCCESS

> Ask yourself why do I …? Why don't I …? Why am I …? The only way to figure out your purposes is to ask yourself 'why' questions.

> Take at least four hours every month, preferably eight hours, to sit quietly with your journal and figure out if you are still aligned to your whys and still on track to hit your targets.

> As my mother told me when I was a child, 'You won't hit the target if you don't aim at it.' Clearly define your short-, medium-, long-range and magical targets.

> When you have taken aim at a target, act on it. Don't wait for the lost Italian tourist to turn up in his Ferrari.

> Write your targets on a whiteboard or in a journal. Tick them off as you hit them or adjust your progress after setbacks.

> Set yourself a competition and reward yourself when you hit your targets. Make sure that reward doesn't hinder your progress.

> Write down things that might prevent you from hitting your targets. Try to pre-empt them and prepare for them like a heat-seeking missile in order to go under, over, around or through them.

> Teamwork comes in many forms. Don't struggle to meet targets on your own. Create a 'target team' or join an online group of like-minded people.

> Visualise success. Know what it will look like, feel like, smell like and even taste like. That way, you will know when you've hit your target.

> Begin at the biggest target and work your way backwards to where you are now. Add in smaller targets and timelines that will act as stepping-stones on the way to your main objective.

———— VISUALISATION FOR SUCCESS ————

An audio recording of me guiding you through this visualisation can be accessed on my website www.keithbarry.com/brainhacks.

For this visualisation you will need your target drawing as mentioned in the TARGETS formula chapter, with your current targets defined clearly inside. Take a mental snapshot of that sketch so you have those targets fresh in your mind.

Read through the following several times before beginning the visualisation:

> Sit or lie down in a quiet spot where you can make yourself comfortable. With your eyes closed, visualise a purple light hovering over your body. This is your light of relaxation. Feel the light hovering over your feet and relaxing your feet as it slowly enters them. Focus on your feet and actively allow them to relax. As you do this, repeat silently to yourself over and over, 'My feet are relaxed, my feet are relaxed, my feet are relaxed.'

> Now allow that purple light to slowly spread up through your legs into your torso, your arms and every other part of your body. As you feel the light entering each part of your body, tell that part to relax. Focus on relaxing each part of your body in sequence.

> Once your body is relaxed, shift your focus to your breathing. Inhale for 6 seconds and focus on inhaling pure relaxation. Hold for 3 seconds. Exhale for 6 seconds and focus on all the tension leaving your body as you exhale. Do this 20 times.

> Now I want you to imagine you are outside in the woods, breathing in clean air and pure relaxation. Visualise your target sheet with your targets defined clearly in your mind's eye. Now see yourself as a Zen archer of days gone by, smoothly and calmly loading arrows into the bow one at a time and shooting them at all of your targets. See the arrows flying through the air with precision, hitting your targets each and every time.

> Fire as many arrows as necessary to hit each and every short-, medium-, long-range and zany target on the sheet.

> Decide what actions you can take today to progress towards those same targets.

> Now switch the picture in your mind to what success looks like to you, having hit all those targets. Allow the feeling of success to spread through your body. Excitement. Joy. Satisfaction. Feel that deep sense of purpose within you resonate deeply in every muscle, nerve and fibre in your body.

> Allow your subconscious mind to accept this future as your new reality. See yourself succeeding and understand that you have the precision, just like the Zen archers of the past, to hit every target every time.

> From this moment onwards you will have more determination than you've ever had before to hit those targets. You'll have a new-found ability to problem-solve. If any obstacles get in your way you will go around, under or through those obstacles each and every time, calmly and confidently.

> Feel the desire and hunger now deep within to accomplish those targets and live a fulfilled and extraordinary life. The moment you open your eyes, take the actions necessary to achieve the success you deserve in life.

RESILIENCE

the ability to accept unexpected difficult moments,
focus on the best possible outcome and activate
that focus

*'Mental toughness is a lifestyle. It's
something that you live every single day
of your life.' –David Goggins*

9.

BOB THE BUILDER AND THE ART OF RESILIENCE

HOW TO STAY STRONG DURING TOUGH TIMES

NOT SO VERY LONG AGO, my mother, Kitty, lived in a house with no electricity and no running water. Most houses of that time, including hers, had their toilet outside. There was no such thing as an electric shower, while a bath was taken in front of the warm fire using kettles of water once a week. From six years of age, she walked four miles to Ballygunner School every day, even in the depths of winter.

There was no central heating, no mobile phones or washing machines. Nappies were not disposable like they are today and cloth nappies had to be emptied of their contents before washing by hand. High unemployment meant a large percentage of men in the area had to emigrate to England for work, leaving their wives to take care of the children alone. I'm sure your parents or your grandparents will have had similar experiences. In fact, I'm certain that some of them will have gone through much worse and still come out the other side. They showed resilience in the face of real hardship and often it is this older generation who show us, or advise us, how to deal with difficult situations today.

If the coronavirus pandemic showed us anything, it is that psychological resilience has been lost in a lot of the global population and the various lockdowns we have had across the world only proved how soft we have become.

On any given day in any given country the majority of people were actually moaning about having to stay inside in their nice warm houses and watch TV while doctors and nurses were risking their lives every day trying to save others. Have a think about that for a moment.

People were complaining about the fact that they were only allowed travel 5 km, even though it was often raining or snowing outside, everywhere was closed and there was nowhere to go anyway. People were rebelling and starting fights because they had to wear a mask for the five minutes it took them to buy a loaf of bread or a pint of milk in the local shop.

Unlike our parents and grandparents, most of us don't go through real hardship every day. Truth be told, most people of our generation have it handy. If you're sitting on your couch or lying in your bed reading this book, then you most likely have it handy. If you are living in a house or an apartment, however small or sparse it may be, in comparison to somebody homeless living on the street or somebody living in a less developed country, then you are pretty comfortable. Over the last few decades many people have become more and more comfortable. We have become comfortable with our warm homes and oversized TVs, our boring but safe jobs. This is not necessarily a good thing. Being comfortable all of the time will make you less resilient when setbacks in life come your way.

Resilience is the trait we all need to call upon during those difficult moments in life that none of us want to happen. Those unexpected moments like losing a job, a house, or even a loved one that come out of nowhere on an otherwise normal day or night and change everything.

Often when something bad happens, our first reaction is one of shock, disbelief. Suddenly shaken out of our comfortable existence, we often ask ourselves, 'Why is this happening to me?' The truth is that bad stuff happens to everyone on this planet. Whoever we are, we all face adverse moments in life at some time or other. I've had my fair share and I'm sure you have too. Now, some people get luckier than others but ultimately it is our reaction to each of those moments and how we deal with them that is most important. Resilience is what helps you overcome those detrimental moments that life throws at all of us.

Resilience is the ability to look at and focus on the endgame or best possible outcome rather than being trapped in these terrible events that can be sprung on you at any given time. If you get trapped in that moment and engulfed in how bad that moment is at that particular time, then you are going to be dragged down to the depths of despair, anxiety and in some cases depression.

After years of trying to land a TV show with one of the big four US networks, I thought I had hit the big time when the first one, *Keith Barry – Extraordinary*, was a great success. I only ever got to do one of my CBS shows, however, as Janet Jackson's boob-popping performance at the Superbowl half-time show alongside Justin Timberlake that year saw the network slammed with a massive and unprecedented $550,000 fine from the United States Federal Communications Commission. The fine meant that CBS were forced to cut their specials budget and my final three shows were dropped. Just when my career was beginning to accelerate in America, I was reduced to a walk again. I knew if I wanted to break America, I would have to be resilient, dig deep and start over.

A simple yet effective role model for being resilient is the hard-working animated builder, Bob. Now, while it appears that Bob the Builder has had a bit of work done on himself since he first appeared on our screens in 1998, one thing that has never changed is his resilience. Poor old Bob: no matter how much good he does for the people around him, bad things seem to happen to him on a regular basis.

Any time Bob the Builder leaves his building site for whatever reason, he invariably comes back to find that his building project has been accidentally destroyed by some, or even all, of his friends or co-workers. Instead of wasting time blaming people and giving out to them, though, a very resilient Bob immediately accepts what has just happened and soon sets about rebuilding. Instead of fixating on that particular bad moment, he immediately changes his focus to his desired outcome and asks, 'Can we fix it?'

ACCEPTANCE

As an executive coach, I have discovered that the first thought process that resilient people enter is one of acceptance.

Like Bob, when life throws us these bad moments, we need to first do two things. Accept what has happened, and then ask ourselves if we can fix it. Instead of focusing on that terrible event we suddenly find ourselves experiencing, we need to figure out how we can overcome this horrendous situation.

While this may seem a pretty difficult thing to do upon something as serious as the death of a loved one, something I will go into in more detail in another chapter encompassing grief, most of the difficult moments in our lives are not as bad as they appear at the time.

When bad moments hit out of the blue, moments that are out of your control, the first thing you must do is to accept the moment as quickly as you possibly can.

Acceptance is the part of resilience that enables you to escape the reality of those really bad moments – which is actually a good thing. By escaping the reality of these awful moments and instead focusing on *what the best outcome could be* (and that could just be as simple as the fact that you are still going to be alive at the end of whatever you're going through), you can then act upon that visualised outcome and enable yourself to continue moving forward rather than getting trapped in the events surrounding you at that particular bad time. Acceptance is very therapeutic in that moment. It allows you to begin healing. That doesn't mean you are not going to grieve or be in pain emotionally, but if you accept the moment, it makes it a hell of a lot easier. The first time I realised I had to accept a terrible moment and focus on a positive outcome in order to overcome it was in 2007 as I lay screaming in agony on an emergency room trolley in Daisy Hill Hospital in Newry.

Not too long beforehand, I had been driving home from the border town with my then manager after paying our respects at the funeral of iconic Irish promoter Jim Aiken.

It was a bright afternoon and as we made our way home, we chatted and made plans for upcoming gigs, blissfully unaware that we would both end up in hospital within the hour.

Out of the blue (a dangerous place, where most of life's bad moments come from), I was involved in a head-on car collision. I was later told that the combined impact speed of the collision was around two hundred kilometres per hour.

With no time to react, my gold Subaru Legacy was struck so hard that it spun across the road until it hit a stone wall and bounced back onto the tarmac, where it stopped dead. As smoke began to billow out of the engine, I tried to take in what had just happened. With the front of the car wedged in on top of me, I found I couldn't move my legs. I looked down at my left foot to see it had been smashed from its usual place to further up my shin and was now pointing the wrong way.

In an attempt not to pass out, my immediate instinct was to phone my mother.

When the fire brigade and ambulance crews arrived, the front of my car was crumpled like an empty crisp packet, and they had to use the mechanical 'jaws of life' to cut through the car and get me out. Although I could feel no pain in my leg at that point due to shock, the jaws of life had caught my jacket and as it noisily pulled the car apart, it was also pulling my head towards the jagged metal edge of the door. As I came perilously close to decapitation, I was screaming at the top of my lungs to be heard over the loud machinery that was now quickly looking like the jaws of death to me.

Thankfully, the crew heard my screams, cut my jacket away and then cut away the wreckage that had trapped me. Until then my leg had been clamped in place by the car and I thought I had a compound fracture because I could feel a terrible cold sensation all around my lower leg. But now that I was free from the wreckage, they had to straighten my leg and get me onto a stretcher. That was when the pain kicked in.

Unbearable, torturous, searing pain!

I was brought to nearby Daisy Hill Hospital, where I was informed that my kneecap had broken in half, my tibia and fibula were both smashed all the way down, my metatarsals were broken, and my ankle was now located halfway up my shin.

I will never forget the trauma surgeon trying to pull my foot back into place as if I was a human Stretch Armstrong doll. I was screaming my lungs out in agony and tensing my whole body in the process. Each time he nearly got my foot into place, I was in so much agony and my muscles were so tense that it popped straight back out and up my leg.

After a few more unsuccessful attempts, the surgeon stopped trying and calmly leaned over to me.

'Keith, I have about five minutes to get this right. Unless you stop screaming and somehow relax your whole body, then I'm going to have to amputate your foot!'

Hearing those words was another huge moment in my life. I knew I had to accept what the trauma surgeon was telling me. I also knew that if I was to come out of this with two feet, I had to practise what I'd been preaching to so many people for the past few years. I had to use all the techniques I'd learned and used on other people.

I took a few deep breaths, calmed my mind down and began to disassociate from the pain, take my mind out of my body, and basically self-anaesthetise my leg in order to allow the surgeon to pull my ankle back down my shin and into place.

Thankfully, he popped it back on the next attempt.

FOCUS ON THE BEST POSSIBLE OUTCOME

I was then transferred to the bigger Royal Victoria Hospital in Belfast but, as the swelling in my leg was so severe, I had to stay there for three weeks before they could operate on it. Immediately upon hearing this, I put on my invisible yellow Bob the Builder hat and began to look for the best outcome. 'Can I fix this?'

It was the height of the Celtic Tiger boom back then and I knew a few businesspeople who actually owned helicopters. I was thinking, 'Maybe I could get somebody to fly me to a different hospital, maybe a better hospital where I could get fixed quicker or better.' I rang my GP and explained the situation. I told her that I wanted to know where the best place was to get operated on and whether I should consider moving to somewhere else. She told me to stay where I was, that because of the Troubles, when bombings, shootings and knee-cappings were unfortunately common incidents in Northern Ireland, surgeons in Belfast knew how to rebuild legs better than anybody else.

After a successful operation that left me with 13 screws and a 7-inch plate in my leg, the doctors told me they had some good news and some bad news. The good news was that they had fixed my leg as well as it possibly could be fixed, but the bad news was that I'd be left with a permanent limp.

While it's important to accept these detrimental moments that happen, as you have no control over them, you must then take charge of what you can control to overcome the situation you find yourself in. I had accepted everything that had happened to me up until then, but being told I could be left with a limp was a moment I didn't accept. As far as I was concerned, whether I walked with a limp or not was under my control.

I knew there was nothing I could do to make my leg better while it was in a cast, so all I could do was keep my mind really focused on the best outcome. For me, that outcome was to be back on stage walking without a limp. I creatively visualised that outcome every single day and I acted on it as soon as I possibly could.

When I got back home to Sandyford, the first thing I did was ring Aiken Promotions and tell them to book a show in Vicar Street for four months later. They thought I was absolutely crazy when I told them that I was going to walk on that stage without a limp in four months' time, but they booked me in anyway.

When the cast got taken off my leg, I went to former Olympic swimmer Gary O'Toole, who was a consultant orthopaedic surgeon in St Vincent's Hospital in Dublin. He took one look at the staples in my leg and how swollen my ankle still was and his facial expression wasn't good.

'Look, I'm going to be straight with you,' he said. 'Outside of a motorbike accident, this is the worst leg injury I've seen. Did they tell you that you're going to have a permanent limp?'

TAKE ACTION TOWARDS THAT OUTCOME

Still, in my mind, I was going to fix this. I was going to walk around the Vicar Street stage without a limp in four months. As I hobbled out of Vincent's I began to look for solutions to the problem. A large part of my take on resilience is resourcefulness, the ability to quickly discover unique solutions to overcome the moment. I believe every single person reading this, regardless of their social status, has the capacity to dig deep into their resources to find information and make connections to help them get through whatever obstacles they face. I asked myself where the best physios in the world were at that moment in time and concluded that they were either in American football or the Premier League, because the players were worth so much money to their teams that they would surely have the best personnel looking after them.

After many dead ends, I managed to wangle an appointment with Liverpool's head physio, Victor Salinas. On the morning of my appointment, I was pushed through Dublin Airport in a wheelchair by my wife, embarrassed in case anybody saw me. I had two crutches with me but still couldn't put any weight on my injured leg.

That afternoon, I lay on a plinth in Liverpool's Melwood training ground as the renowned Spanish physio did reiki for what felt like an hour and a half on probably the ultimate reiki sceptic in the world. As he hovered his hands back and forth over my leg, I was wondering, 'Jesus, is this it?' Now, looking back, I think that was just his method of getting me relaxed for what was about to come.

When he was finished, Victor stopped and said to me. 'Okay! Now, you can laugh, you can sing, you can shit, you can puke, you can cry, I've seen it all. Take a deep breath and get ready.'

That was when he put his elbow into my leg and began using it as a pointy rolling pin. The pain was excruciating. I actually passed out a couple of times as his elbow ground up and down my banjaxed leg for the next two hours in an effort to get the fluids moving. The next day was exactly the same and, if anything, the pain was even worse. But when it was over, Victor took one of my crutches away and so, having left Dublin Airport in a wheelchair, I arrived back on one crutch. I was walking. Okay, I was walking very slowly sideways and was extremely sore, but I was walking.

For the next three weeks, rather than fixating on how bad I still felt at any particular moment, I focused on the outcome I had in my head, which was walking on the Vicar Street stage without a limp. This visualisation pushed me to drag myself slowly, very slowly, around Sandyford every single day in all sorts of weather. Sometimes I was actually happier if it was raining because then nobody would notice the tears of pain rolling down my face.

Three and a half weeks after my first visit, I went back to Liverpool very happy with my progress. Victor, however, wasn't so happy.

'What the fuck? You bring back the crutch? You should have no crutch now!'

Two days later, after more excruciating treatment, Victor took the second crutch off me, and I hobbled into arrivals in Dublin Airport. I had a bad limp, but I was back on my feet.

With my Vicar Street deadline looming, I wanted to keep my physio up when I got home. I tried to figure out who would have had experience with physios and whose advice I could trust. I managed to get Brian O'Driscoll, the then Irish rugby team captain's number, and asked him where the best physio in Ireland was. He answered, 'Mark McCabe at Sports Med Ireland. Just don't expect it easy.'

Mark put me through a world of pain but, like Victor Salinas, he knew what he was doing. Ultimately, I walked onto that stage in Vicar Street four months after my accident without a limp. I had invited Gary O'Toole to the show and when he saw me afterwards, he was absolutely blown away. 'What I didn't tell you the first time I saw you, Keith,' he said, 'was that I knew you had a form of dystrophy in your leg, and I was certain you were going to have a limp for the rest of your life.'

Now, I don't want you to think that doing that was easy. It came after four months of hard, gritty perseverance and determination to get out the other side of my accident which is, after all, what resilience is.

That whole experience moulded my take on resilience, and I use it in every moment that happens to me now. I use that big life-changing moment to realise that it's okay to be uncomfortable. It's okay to be sick. It's okay to be unemployed. It's okay to be broke. It's okay to have those bad moments, but it's about focusing on the outcome and knowing that it will always get better.

You may be thinking I was 'lucky' to be able to get physio in Melwood training ground, but I don't believe luck had anything to do with it. With a resourceful mindset you can always find a way to dig yourself out of any situation.

Any time you find yourself in a really bad situation, stop and ask yourself these four questions:

> What is the best possible outcome here?
> What are three actions I can take towards that positive outcome?
> Is there an expert I can call on to help me through this?
> Do I know somebody who has been through the same thing?

Coupled with acceptance and action in those moments, you must learn to magnify the positive. There's always a positive, if you look for it. If you look at two cars colliding at that speed, the first positive was that I was actually still alive. The next positive was my leg didn't get amputated. The next positive was that I came away from it without a limp.

On the night of that comeback show in Vicar Street I was still in a lot of pain; I still had to ice my ankle before and afterwards. Even as I write this, 14 years later, I have pain in my ankle every day. In fact, I have arthritis in it now. That's okay. I accept that. I do my best with it and I'm okay being in pain every day, because when I look back on that car crash or see the photos of my mangled car, I know the outcome could have been far worse. That pain I feel every day in my ankle makes me uncomfortable. But I accept it. No whingeing. No complaining. Just pure acceptance that that's life's way of helping me to remember and maintain my resilience at all times.

STEP OUT OF YOUR COMFORT ZONE

So how do you build a foundation of resilience? Well, first you need to step out of your comfort zone. You have to do something that makes you uncomfortable every day. There is a saying that is often used in the worlds of both business and sports that 'everything you want is just outside your comfort zone'. That's where true growth happens.

Think back to when you were younger and you walked to and from school in the rain, swam in the freezing cold Irish Sea, camped out in a back garden or at a music festival, slept on someone's floor or even in someone's car after a party. Most people of a certain age have done stuff like that when we were younger. Yet as we get older and more comfortable in life, we won't stay in a hotel unless it has Wi-Fi, TV and a comfortable bed. We won't wear a pair of jeans unless they have a certain label on them or won't eat food unless it's cooked precisely to our taste. When I was younger jeans were denim, dinner was whatever was put in front of you and calling your best friend involved shouting out of your window or yelling across the street.

Lots of people purposely avoid facing things that make them uncomfortable on a regular basis, things as simple as interacting with a new group of people, doing some exercise, going to the dentist or asking somebody they like out on a date. If you avoid simple things like these, then you are going to crumble at the first sight of real hardship.

As I write this, it is cold, dark and absolutely lashing rain outside. I'm nice and warm inside, though. I have it cushy, so there is no reason for me to get up right now and go for a walk on my own in the dark, cold and rain. But yet, there is every reason to do that. It will make me uncomfortable, and you need to understand that being uncomfortable regularly is actually good for you. Every time I do something uncomfortable, I feel as if I am adding layers of armour around my mind in order to protect it during detrimental moments.

I often hear people say, 'I hate unloading the dishwasher.' Think about that for a moment. Why do you hate unloading the dishwasher? It's a machine that has basically done everything else for you. It has washed the dishes and dried them, so what's the big deal about emptying it? If that's your uncomfortable thing, then unload the dishwasher for a week until it's not uncomfortable anymore.

In my house, unconventionally, my wife puts the bins out almost every week. It's just a pattern that we fell into. Recently, in a discussion about the bins (trash talk, if you like) I caught myself saying to her, 'I hate taking out the bins.' When I took a second to reframe that in my head, I realised I don't actually hate taking the bins out, that it was the most stupid thing ever to say. So now I make myself take the bins out on the wettest, coldest nights of the year.

Another uncomfortable thing that I do every single day is take a cold shower. Now, when I say cold, I don't mean tepid or lukewarm, I mean so cold that I get a full-on brain freeze from standing under the water. It feels like being a prisoner in one of those movies where they spray a cold hose at the inmates and most days, I genuinely ask myself why I am doing this to myself.

Apart from making myself uncomfortable, however, I also know that a cold shower is actually good for me for a number of other reasons.

While hydrotherapy has been used for centuries to take advantage of our body's tendency to become more resistant to stress, in 2007 a molecular biologist named Nikolai Shevchuk carried out a study which showed that cold showers of around two to three minutes, used regularly, can reduce depressive symptoms by activating the sympathetic nervous system to increase production of beta-endorphins, noradrenaline and norepinephrine, all of which can actually make people feel happier.[16]

There are other benefits too. In the same way that ice brings down inflammation in our muscles by carrying warmer, freshly oxygenated blood to the injured area, having cold showers helps blood move through the body more quickly and can help with poor circulation, high blood pressure and even diabetes.

The shock of cold water also stimulates leukocytes in the blood-stream, which help fight infection in the body and can boost your immune system.[17] While stepping into a cold shower may take some getting used to, at first you can start with a comfortable temperature and slowly turn it down over a period of four or five minutes until the water goes cold. If, like me, you have a teenage daughter handy, then simply wait until she's finished showering to have yours. That way there won't be much hot water left anyway!

Now, these are small things to do, but when life throws those bad moments at you – and you don't have to be a mentalist to predict that it will – these small uncomfortable moments will have laid a foundation of resilience and formed layers of armour around your mind for when they do happen.

STOP NOW and choose one of the following things you will do tomorrow to make you feel uncomfortable.

> Go for a walk in the lashing rain.
> Call somebody you haven't spoken to in a long time.
> Make an extravagant dinner for the whole family.
> Apologise to somebody you have fallen out with.
> Try a new healthy food.
> Tell someone you've never told that you love them.
> Make an appointment with the dentist.

Think of five more things that will make you uncomfortable but will help build your resilience. Commit right now to doing these, not just once but on a regular basis.

QUIT YOUR BITCHING

To attain resilience, it's important to consistently let go of negative thoughts and emotions because they will do you no good. Instinctively, when you get bad news, you begin to fear and project the worst outcome. These negative thoughts truly serve no purpose and can stick you to the same spot in life for ages. My mindset is always to accept the moment and take control of what you can control, no matter how many setbacks come at you.

If I find myself having a negative thought or emotion, I break it down and break that pattern by having a little internal talk with myself. My friend Al and I have a saying for whenever one of us begins to moan about something: 'Quit your bitching!' It's simple and effective and has become a sort of motto for the two of us. I now use the same sentence to internally control my own negative thoughts, but you can use whatever words suit you best. You need to look yourself in the mirror and tell yourself to quit your bitching and focus on the best possible outcome.

In my opinion, 99.9 per cent of the time, things are not as bad as they seem, but if you get trapped in the moment rather than focusing properly on the outcome it can result in an endless spiral of inaction, doom and gloom. Let's just stop for a moment and think about that.

Let's take losing a job, for example. A lot of people will get caught up in the moment and go into the depths of despair, worrying about how they are going to pay their mortgage or other bills. A week or maybe months later, they are still worrying about those things rather than focusing on the best possible outcome of this event and actually trying to fix the situation. If you can accept what has happened as quickly as possible and then focus on and put your energy into what you want out of the situation, then you might just seize the opportunity to find a job that you actually like doing or are excited about.

In the past, while coaching an unemployed client, I was very concerned with their lack of understanding of resilience. Our initial conversation went like this.

'So how many hours did you spend yesterday looking for a job?'

'Two.'

'What did you do for the rest of the day?' 'Ah, I was on Facebook. I was on social media. I was on Netflix. I tried to keep myself busy, so I went to the gym. Then I was looking after my kids, and I went for a walk.'

'How do you feel?'

'Not great, to be honest'.

'So, what else did you do?'

'That's it, Keith. That's it.'

Now while going to the gym or going for a walk are obviously good things to be doing, you're not going to find a job in two hours – and unless you're a gym instructor, you're not going to find one in the gym. Nor are you going to find one by watching viral videos on TikTok.

In my opinion, if you're unemployed and are actually serious about getting re-employed then you should be spending 12 hours a day looking for a job. Instead of feeling sorry for yourself because you don't have a job, you need to accept the moment and decide to do something about it. I'm deadly serious about this. If that requires sending out 1,000 CVs and taking 200 unsuccessful job interviews, then so be it. If you haven't been successful after doing that then you need to send out another 1,000 CVs and do another 200 interviews. Doesn't that seem more productive than watching TV or flicking through your social media?

People don't do enough things that they don't like doing in order to build resilience anymore, and that lack of resilience is what stops you in your tracks when those tough moments hit you in the face on a wet Tuesday afternoon. If you are trying to get something done but have little or no foundation of resilience, then you will crumble at the first sign of bad news or rejection.

If J.K. Rowling had crumbled at the first sign of rejection we would never have heard of Harry Potter, a story that has sold over half a billion books worldwide and is now a massive global franchise loved by children and adults alike.

Golfer Tiger Woods overcame racism, alcohol issues, arrest, divorce and no fewer than four career-threatening back surgeries to return to the top of his chosen profession and win the Masters in 2019.

If the Beatles had crumbled at their first rejection by a record label, or even at the second, third or fourth rejections by different labels, the world would never have heard any of their music. Instead, the Beatles went on to sell almost two billion singles in the USA alone and are widely regarded as one of the most influential bands in the world.

Perhaps the fact that all of these people came from relatively poor working-class backgrounds, and each one of them had to overcome various setbacks in their lives before even beginning their careers, enabled them to build a solid foundation of resilience – which in turn enabled them to focus on a positive outcome when bad things happened and continue their actions towards achieving that outcome.

If I had crumbled the first, or even the hundredth, time I was rejected you wouldn't be reading this book right now.

My car crash also made me look at my life up to that point and I remember asking myself, if I had died, should I have done anything different with my life? After sitting down and talking to my wife, I realised the only thing that I would have liked to have done was to have kids.

Towards the end of the following summer, a little under a year and a half after one of the worst things to ever happen to me, one of the best things ever to happen to me arrived in the form of our newborn daughter, Breanna. Now, babies don't come with instructions. Like lots of other new parents, I hadn't a clue how to change a nappy, how to make bottles or, for that matter, how to be a father.

But could I fix that? Yes, I could.

10.

EVERYTHING COMES IN THREES ...

IF YOU WAIT LONG ENOUGH

I N IRELAND, there is an old wives' saying or superstition that 'bad things come in threes'. But if you really think about it, absolutely everything comes in threes ... if you just wait long enough. In fact, if you wait long enough everything comes in fours or fives, or even fifty-fives.

When our daughter Breanna was born the doctor misjudged the size she was going to be, and she got stuck during the birth. In what was a traumatic experience for both me and my wife, the nerves in Breanna's shoulder were damaged – which meant she was left with a paralysed arm.

As my wife and I looked on worriedly, we were handed our baby and literally told, 'I'm not sure if this is permanent or not. Erb's palsy is kind of a toss of a coin. It could be permanent, or it might not be. There's your baby.'

It was horrible news to hear on what should have been one of the best days of our lives, but I couldn't change it. The damage had been done and I had no control over it so, difficult as it was, I immediately accepted that news there and then.

Once I knew my wife was okay and Breanna was otherwise fine and healthy, I immediately began to look into Erb's palsy. I hadn't a clue what it was at the time, but I knew I had to learn as much as I could about it to try to make Breanna better. Within minutes I was on the internet figuring out how to fix it, or at least make the outcome as good as it could possibly be for my daughter.

As well as getting used to becoming parents and the usual shock to the system that a baby brings with it, we were told that our new-born baby would have to have physiotherapy every day in the hope that the mobility in her arm might come back. Upon hearing this and being shown how to do it, I took control of that moment.

Every single day for the next three months, I did physio on my baby daughter's arm with absolutely no improvement. While she was thankfully developing normally otherwise, and I had built up a lovely bond with her over that time, her arm was still paralysed. When we went back to the hospital, there had been absolutely no change and no sign that it would change.

NEVER GIVE UP

I could have given up then, blamed the delivery staff and said there was nothing we could do, and probably nobody would have blamed me for that. In fact, I firmly believe a lot of people would have given up at that point. But I affirmed my intention to continue with the physiotherapy and did so for another few months, without any signs of improvement.

Then one day my wife's parents were visiting our house when her dad suddenly asked who moved Breanna's arm up over her head. We all looked at each other and ran over to see. She was asleep with her arm up and we realised she had started to move it. I kept doing the physio every day until eventually her arm recovered fully. A few months later we were told we didn't need to do it anymore.

Now that I have experienced my daughter's Erb's palsy and my ankle injury, I notice people with paralysed arms, limps and ailments everywhere I go. Maybe it's like buying a new car. Once you have a certain model you suddenly begin to see the same ones everywhere. These types of injury are sometimes hard to get out the other side of and sometimes involve a bit more pain before they get better. We all know people, especially men in my opinion, who won't do their physio after an operation or an injury because they think they don't need to or because it hurts too much. We all know people who will go around complaining about a pain in their back or neck or wherever but when you ask them if they went to the doctor, physiotherapist, sports therapist, or anyone else who might be able to help them the answer is invariably no. 'It's too sore,' 'I don't have time,' or 'It's not going to do any good anyway,' are a few of my favourite excuses. Instead of focusing on the outcome, these people are trapped in the moment and will be stuck there forever unless, like Bob the Builder, they ask themselves how they can fix it and never give up.

Life is going to throw you curveballs that cause you huge distress. Sometimes you are even going to be responsible for those curveballs yourself and are going to cause yourself problems by drinking, gambling, breaking down a relationship or other things. Remember, though, that it's not what happens to you in life that matters, it's how you react to what happens. I firmly believe that.

While Breanna's arm got better, a year or so later we began to notice one of her eyes was starting to turn outwards on occasion. The doctor explained that she had a wandering eye, or intermittent exotropia. Again, we were told that this might or might not be permanent and that she might need surgery when she was a bit older.

Once again, I accepted this bad moment. It was outside my control so I couldn't change it, but, once I knew what the condition actually was, I put on my invisible Bob the Builder hat again and began to figure out what the best possible outcome was and how I could achieve it.

Upon switching my mind into resourceful mode and searching the internet, I found an Australian system where you could train the muscle behind the eye to strengthen it and hopefully draw it back in. While I had taken charge of her arm, my wife took on the task of patching Breanna's eye and making sure it stayed patched for a couple of hours every single day in order to get the best outcome possible.

After six months, we had an appointment with the paediatric ophthalmologist, but upon examination we were told the patch hadn't made much difference. Six months later, we were back again. This time we were told, 'Look it's not really working, so it's up to you guys if you want to throw in the towel or carry on.'

Again, a lot of people would probably have given up at that point because they didn't want to put the child, or themselves, in an uncomfortable position every day. But in those heart-wrenching moments of despair, that's exactly when you need the mindset of never giving up.

With our long-term focus on Breanna's eye returning to normal rather than the frustration and weariness we all felt at patching up her eye every single day, we opted to continue and kept on doing it. We constantly focused on the best possible outcome and visualised her eye getting better every single day.

A number of years later, at home, we noticed that her eye had sort of straightened itself up. When we brought her back to the ophthalmologist for her next appointment she was amazed and told us that she was almost one hundred per cent certain that Breanna wouldn't need surgery, but to continue what we were doing for another few months just to be sure. Ultimately, three and a half years after her condition was diagnosed, Breanna's eye was fixed and now, thankfully, she is a perfectly healthy, if a little cheeky, teenager.

Of course, that didn't mean that life stopped throwing curveballs at me. Small ones, medium-sized ones, and some pretty big ones.

In September 2009 I walked off stage after a show in Limerick and got a phone call to say that my grandfather's home in Waterford, where he had lived alone after the death of my grandmother a few years earlier, had been broken into and he had been beaten up in a botched burglary. All I knew was that one minute he had been sitting down in his house watching television and the next he was in a coma in Waterford hospital.

His door, which had latches and locks all the way down it, had been kicked in and all the locks had been busted with a screwdriver or some other implement. Even at 82 years of age he had obviously tried to defend himself, as afterwards he had a broken arm consistent with holding it up to protect himself. In the mêlée that followed he was either pushed to the ground by his attackers or fell and hit his head on the solid floor and was now comatose.

About five days into that coma, my grandfather, whom I had spent my school lunchtimes and the summers of my youth bonding with and with whom I had maintained a really good relationship since leaving Waterford, died, suddenly and in very traumatic circumstances. To make things even worse, my mother's sister and best friend, my Aunt Betty, also passed away within the week and suddenly, out of the blue, I had lost two people I loved.

I went into what I can only describe as severe grief. I was in a bad way. I was absolutely heartbroken and because of the way my grandfather died, I carried a huge amount of anger around with me for a time. I knew that whoever broke into his house was responsible for his death and in an effort to find out what had happened to him and catch the perpetrators, I used my relative fame to lash out on the radio, in the papers or wherever I could.

This time, it took me a while to realise that those negative emotions weren't serving me well and I needed to process what was going on.

Sometimes I think that people who have a public persona, such as myself, are seen as invincible. Like a gambler, you only ever hear about the times life dealt them a good hand, but you rarely hear about their losses. While I use the techniques I've discussed to deal with those moments when they happen, it doesn't mean they're not difficult. It doesn't mean that at all. I still feel pain, and angst and sadness. But I have a foundation of resilience that enables me to get through those terrible moments. I programme my mind daily to accept things I cannot control and to search for and magnify the positive.

Your brain is the world's first supercomputer. Like a computer, you have the ability to insert files, store information, even get a virus that stops you functioning properly in times of despair. But you also have the ability to dump information that doesn't serve you. For instance, I could no longer tell you one thing about chemistry. Think about how crazy that is. I have a first-class honours degree in chemistry and designed my own men's skincare line and today I cannot tell you one thing about chemistry! Like hitting 'delete' on a computer, I have the ability to hit 'delete' on my brain, and you do too.

Not only can you delete some of the useless information you have stored up over the years, but the really good news is that you have the ability to delete emotions, or at least partition them to another hard drive, or shut them off at certain moments in time. That doesn't mean you won't feel pain or anger or sadness anymore, of course you will, but it will enable you to get out the other side of those feelings much quicker. Most people have that massive outburst of emotion, of grief, of sadness, like I had with my grandfather, but by practising resilience every day I get to the place where enough is enough more quickly than most people. Most people will spend days, weeks, months or even years holding on to their grief or negative emotion, whether that's grief for the loss of a job, the breakup of a relationship or the death of a loved one. They often hold on to that grief for a very long time before things slowly get better.

USE YOUR MIND'S REMOTE CONTROL

They say time is a great healer. So why not think of time as a movie file? If time is a great healer, why not fast forward your movie now, immediately, to the part where you are healed and have finished grieving? Remember, you have the remote control for your own emotions. You control when to change the channel from sadness to joy, from fear to empowerment, from shyness to confidence.

Instead of focusing on your grief, fast forward out of it and then, instead of focusing on the terrible moment that caused that grief, learn to delete it and rewind past it to the good memories, the funny stories, the laughs, and the moments of joy you had before.

After my grandfather passed away, it was hard for me to find anything positive to take from it. I couldn't do anything about his death. It was outside my control and no matter what I did I couldn't bring him back so, after accepting that fact, I first deleted the emotions attached to his death.

I then rewound the video to remember the good times we shared and how privileged I was to have such a good grandparent. I remembered the sunny childhood days I would spend with him and my cousins picking winkles on the beaches of Tramore and Annestown and the afternoons we would spend tasting our wares.

I recalled the visits to see the colour and excitement of the hounds and horses at the hunt after Christmas and the roar of the engine noise and smell of exhaust fumes from days spent watching the Circuit of Ireland motor rally together.

While I couldn't do anything to bring my grandfather back, the positive outcome I focused my attention on afterwards was trying to fix it so that at least this wouldn't happen to anybody else's grandparent or parent. My father and I lobbied the government and had meetings in the Dáil, even had meetings with the Taoiseach of the time, Enda Kenny, and others about mandatory sentencing for aggravated burglary.

While we didn't get that, our campaign highlighted the lack of protection homeowners had when it came to somebody breaking into their house. While my grandfather was never to going to over-power a couple of thugs on his own, even if he had the law on his side, the law was changed a couple of years later. On some small level I'd like to think that because of our lobbying, some people in Ireland have been able to adequately protect themselves in cases we don't get to hear about now, and because of that they are still alive today.

Life is made up of mainly positive experiences that normally outweigh the negative ones. Things go wrong in everybody's lives, no matter how successful they appear to be, and of course the cur-veballs keep on coming.

If you build your resilience by being uncomfortable on a regu-lar basis, accept those moments you cannot control, focus on the best possible outcome, and use the following technique of cognitive reframing on a daily basis during smaller uncomfortable moments, then you will be continuously programming your subconscious to deal more easily with the larger, more difficult situations that arise.

REFRAME THE PICTURE

Think of your mind like the camera on your smartphone. Your pho-tographs are determined by where you point the camera, the aspect ratio you use, whether it's dark or bright, and how you use the zoom and focus functions.

If your camera is set to automatic, then you rarely even think about the photograph you take, because you know that afterwards you can edit the photograph to look sharper, brighter and better.

During difficult situations, your subconscious mind very often takes over and just like a smartphone camera, your mind goes on autopilot. This is why sometimes you are left with a bad picture, often one you never want to see again.

Like a smartphone, though, your mind has editing tools, and if you spend a little time afterwards you can always edit a bad picture to make it look better. You can crop or delete something out of the shot. You can make it bigger, brighter and more colourful and when it's finished you can put it in a beautiful frame and look at it whenever you want. I use reframing daily in any difficult situation, no matter how small or large.

Just a few days ago I was pitching to the director of *Citadel*, a drama series on Amazon Prime. I was showing the director and producers how to manipulate a Zippo lighter through my hands in order to teach one of the lead actors, Richard Madden, how to safely do a few tricks with it.

A couple of minutes into showing them some moves I sliced my thumb wide open on a sharp edge above the flint wheel. With the director looking on and blood pouring all over the lighter and my hand, I could have got stuck in the moment, focused on my badly slit thumb and lost the job.

Instead, though, my daily reframing programming kicked in. I explained that the blood that was now streaming from my thumb and dripping all over my desk was the reason they needed me for the job, that it was my job to get injured and burned to ensure their leading actor wouldn't. I told them how I would work with the props department to ensure the lighters were filed down properly before Richard used them so that he wouldn't injure himself.

Smiling through the searing pain, I continued to show them my fancy lighter moves in between sucking the blood from my thumb or dabbing it on whatever was available at the time to try to stem the flow. Three days later the producers emailed me to say I had the job. So, if you watch the series and notice Richard Madden toying with his Zippo lighter, you now know that it all came from a reframe.

But in order to reframe, you must stop and take a moment in whatever difficult situation you are in and reflect on why you are viewing it the way you are. Like the bad smartphone photo, it's rarely as bad as you think it is and you can always edit it to make it look better.

Cognitive reframing involves programming your mind to perceive a problem or difficult situation from a different, more positive perspective. In doing this, you are not trying to change the situation. You are simply altering your mind to change your perspective on the situation to tackle it from a different angle, and in doing so you will change the emotion connected to it.

We all have different frames of reference in life, depending on our memories and past experiences. When you switch your frame of reference in a given situation, the emotion attached to that particular situation will also switch, which will in turn enable you to deal with that difficulty from a more reasonable perspective.

Let's go back to something small like emptying the dishwasher in the previous chapter. If you constantly say you hate emptying the dishwasher, soon enough, your mind will actually believe that you hate emptying the dishwasher. But you can reframe this by reminding yourself of what it was like, or would be like, if you didn't have one.

In that situation you would have to pile the plates, cups, mugs and cutlery on the counter. Then you would have to fill the sink with hot water and some washing-up liquid. You would have to hand-wash each item individually with a small brush or sponge and then pile them on the other side of the counter. After that, you would have to hand-dry each individual item with a cloth and stack them in their proper place. Depending on the size of your family or the size of your meal, this could take half an hour or longer, every single mealtime. That's a lot of time wasted every day.

So, instead of moaning about emptying your dishwasher, you can remind yourself how long it would take and how tedious it would be if you didn't have the dishwasher. Instead of saying you hate emptying it, you can reframe the experience and reprogramme your brain by saying, 'Thank goodness for the dishwasher. If I didn't have one it would take me half an hour or more to wash and dry the dishes. Right now, it will only take me five minutes to unload it. It's great to have a dishwasher as it allows me to spend extra time doing the things I love.'

Reframing is also a good way to train children's resilience and positivity. A simple task like tidying their bedroom and laying out their school uniform or sports gear for the next day can help develop both if framed properly. Now, most kids will moan and groan when asked to tidy their room or prepare for anything the next morning, but if you can point out to them the advantages of doing this, or even of having a room in the first place, and reframe the whole experience, they will soon come around to your way of thinking.

For example, you can reframe tidying their room and having things ready for school in the morning by explaining that by doing so they will save that time in the morning and can therefore have an extra 10 minutes in bed, or they won't have to leave so early for the match because their gear will already be packed.

Most children naturally have amazing levels of resilience, but they are like sponges and will absorb negativity or positivity from adult behaviours or from personal experiences or little chores they are uncomfortable doing – small things like vacuuming their rooms, hanging out the clothes, or polishing the furniture will help build resilience.

Mollycoddling them and telling them that they are winners all of the time, however, is a pathway to disappointment, leading in some cases to an inability to accept reality when they get older. Children need to be loved, nurtured and encouraged, not lied to.

My friend's son, Jack, has been arm-wrestling with his grand-father every week since he was a very young boy. While Jack's grandfather always made a game out of it, he never let Jack win. At birthday parties during his primary school years, Jack's grandad often took on his grandson's friends and, again, while he made it look close, and had great fun, he never gave in to the temptation of making it easy for them and letting them win. In doing so, the legend of Jack's grandad's arm-wrestling strength was enhanced among the group as they grew into their teenage years.

Jack and his friends are college-going 18- and 19-year-olds now and like most sports-mad teenage boys, they all go to the gym or lift weights at home regularly. One of them is a professional foot-baller. To this day, the lads still arm-wrestle Jack's grandfather at birthday parties or whenever they are gathered together. None of them has beaten him yet. But when they do, if indeed they ever do, they'll know it's not a false victory. It will have come after years of resilience, training and defeat. Jack's grandfather, by the way, is a sprightly 77 years old.

Children must be made aware that nothing lasts forever, including bad experiences. They should know that they have no control over their family circumstances and be raised to understand how lucky they are and to never look down on children or adults who have less.

They need to embrace nature and see that they don't need money to be happy, something we can forget ourselves as adults. Of course, we all admire and wish for material things, but rather than envy anyone with those things, they should appreciate the things they have themselves while working towards those they admire.

In life, the curveballs will inevitably keep coming, some from angles you never thought possible. But if you practise resilience by doing something uncomfortable every day, accept the uncontrollable, reframe the experience to focus on the best possible outcome and take action towards that, it will enable you to bat them away a whole lot quicker.

EVERYDAY BRAIN HACKS FOR RESILIENCE

> It is not failure to accept that things can go wrong, but it is failure to accept defeat when there is a possible solution to the problem.

> Instead of getting stuck in a terrible moment, look ahead to the best possible outcome and, like Bob the Builder, ask yourself, 'Can we fix it?'

> Leave no stone unturned in your search for the best possible outcome.

> Do something uncomfortable every day, whether that is walking in the rain, making friends with new people or apologising for something you did in the past.

> Nip negative inner chatter and emotions in the bud. Look yourself in the mirror and tell yourself to quit your bitching.

> Delete the parts of the movie you don't want to watch. Rewind and fast forward to the best bits.

> Look at things from a different angle. Very often the picture you took can be edited and is not really as bad as you thought.

——— VISUALISATION FOR RESILIENCE ———

An audio recording of me guiding you through this visualisation can be accessed on my website www.keithbarry.com/brainhacks.

Read through the following several times before beginning the visualisation:

> › Sit or lie down in a quiet spot where you can make yourself comfortable. With your eyes closed, visualise a purple light hovering over your body. This is your light of relaxation. Feel the light hovering over your feet and relaxing your feet as it slowly enters them. Focus on your feet and actively allow them to relax. As you do this, repeat silently to yourself over and over, 'My feet are relaxed, my feet are relaxed, my feet are relaxed.'

> › Now allow that purple light to slowly spread up through your legs into your torso, your arms and every other part of your body. As you feel the light entering each part of your body, tell that part to relax. Focus on relaxing each part of your body in sequence.

> › Once your body is relaxed, shift your focus to your breathing. Inhale for 6 seconds and focus on inhaling pure relaxation. Hold for 3 seconds. Exhale for 6 seconds and focus on all the tension leaving your body as you exhale. Repeat this breathing pattern 20 times.

> › Imagine you are looking out of a window in your house, and you notice a storm brewing. See the clouds gathering and the wind blowing violently. Imagine this storm quickly gathering momentum as it becomes a hurricane.

> › This hurricane represents the unexpected and unfortunate events which may happen in times to come.

> › Now think of someone you were once close to who has passed away. I always think of my grandad for this partic-ular visualisation.

> › Feel their love, energy and optimism entering your heart as you see them clearly in your mind's eye. As you do this, gently press the index finger and thumb of your left hand together. Do this for around thirty seconds as you continu-ally and joyfully visualise the person. This will anchor the moment to your subconscious mind.

> › Allow this new-found optimism and resilience to give you the mental fortitude to control this hurricane at all times. You can now begin to shrink the hurricane, slowing the wind down and stopping the rain. You have full control of the hurricane.

Any time you feel yourself being tested past your limits, press your finger and thumb together and allow the power of resilience to flow through you from the memory of your deceased loved one. By prac-tising this regularly you will find you can weather any emotional storm.

POSITIVITY

the practice of living a magical life through a
positive mindset

*'In order to carry a positive action, we must
develop here a positive vision.' – Dalai Lama*

11.

HAPPY HEADSPACE

THE ROAD TO A POSITIVE MINDSET

I WAS ON A RADIO show recently where the presenter introduced me with the words, 'Our next guest is somebody who is so positive it makes me sick.' Perhaps because I have such a positive mindset, I laughed and took the introduction as a compliment.

Having a positive mindset is the one thing that I guarantee will change your life. Like most things in life, though, there is no quick fix to attaining positivity, so I want you to stop here and think for a while. Stop reading for as long as is necessary for you to put serious thought into whether you really want to change your life or not. This will not be easy, so give it careful consideration. Take it seriously. Spend some time thinking about it. Do not begin reading again until you have made up your mind.

Welcome back.

If after some deep and meaningful thought you have decided to commit 100 per cent – and it will take 100 per cent commitment – to changing your life for the better, then read on and I will explain the most successful methods of doing just that. If you have decided that you don't want to change your life and would rather live a life of negativity, then skip this section. It's not for you.

Over the years of doing live shows, seminars and functions all around the world, I've come into contact with so many people asking me for help that I decided to carry out some basic research of my own to see why people felt they needed to change their lives in the first place and what was wrong with the lives they already had.

When I simply discussed these people's everyday lives with them, I soon noticed that the same stories were being churned out again and again, no matter what country I was in or what type of person I spoke to, whether they were young or old, married or single, working or unemployed.

People who seemed to be forever stuck in a rut, never getting anywhere except deeper into the hole they were already in, kept spewing out the same answers when asked why they weren't living as they really wanted to and why they didn't have a positive outlook on life.

'Things are bad out there.' 'The banks have destroyed the econ-omy.' 'I'm too old.' 'The builders have the country ruined.' 'I'm too young.' 'The vaccine rollout is very slow.' 'We're in a recession.' 'It's because of Brexit.' 'It's because of Covid.' 'The weather is too bad.' 'It's the government's fault for letting things get so bad.'

I soon began to realise that every day, in every country, the story was the same. Over the past few years, people have been brainwashed into a negative mindset that the banks, the construction industry, the economy, or even the Chinese government are somehow to blame for them being stuck in a rut in their own lives. People love to play the blame game as it removes the responsibility for their own negative thought patterns.

You only have to read a newspaper, watch TV or listen to the radio in any town in the world and there will be a story about a factory closing down, a home getting repossessed, banks not lending money, Covid case numbers, vaccination rollouts … all pretty depressing stuff. Hell, I've heard it so often they nearly had me brainwashed too!

Regardless of what is happening around you, no matter what the banks are doing, no matter what the government is doing, no matter what the weather is doing, you must stand up and take responsibility for how you think and act. You have the ability to decide whether to think positively or think negatively. That is a choice.

STOP PLAYING THE BLAME GAME

Whether you are reading this book on the train to work in the morning, propped up in bed at night or sitting at the kitchen table with a cup of tea, you have got to stop playing the blame game.

If you don't stop now, then you're not going to solve whatever issues you have right now. Negative thinking will not serve you well and will not help you to problem-solve. You need a positive mindset in order to think your way out of any negative situation you may find yourself in. I'll repeat that. You need a positive mindset in order to think your way out of any negative situation you may find yourself in.

That's right. If you continuously blame other people for the negative situations you find yourself in, instead of thinking positively and trying to change things, you are going to stay in those exact same positions … for the rest of your life! Think about that for a minute. It's a pretty sobering thought. You may be thinking negatively right now about stopping your negativity. 'But I don't know how to stop!' … 'I can't stop!' Don't worry. You can change that. All I ask is that you read on with a positive outlook and think about every single word and sentence in this chapter.

PAY ATTENTION TO YOUR TECHNOLOGY INTAKE

Your brain is like a sponge. It can absorb everything it sees, hears, smells and feels. Everything we do gets locked into our subconscious mind. Of course, we don't knowingly remember every single thing we do or see, but, like files on a computer, it's all in there. If somebody invented a technology to hack into your brain and pull everything out, you would be able to find the exact moment you read this sentence for years to come.

If your brain absorbs everything you put into it, both the positive and negative, then aren't you better off putting in more positive information than negative in the first place? The first thing you need to do is take stock of your tech intake every day. Are you consistently looking at bad news on your TV, smartphone, tablet or computer? You might not think you are doing that but if your phone is always with you, then you are open to a flood of negativity through emails, tweets, messages and social media comments all of the time. If you have a smartphone, have a look at your screen time right now and see how much time you spent looking at your phone this week. If you work on a computer then you can probably at least double that time each day. If you're under twenty-five this is likely to be pretty high. In fact, studies have shown that the younger a child is when they are given a phone the more likely they are to develop technology addiction problems. Thirty-three percent of 13-year-olds never turn their phones off. Ever! Go to any concert, sports event, party or celebration and you will see people recording it on their phones instead of actually enjoying the moment. When it's all over, the only memories they will have will be those video clips they almost never re-watch instead of how it felt to actually be there.

Your phone has been designed to grab your attention as much as possible. Think about how often you jump up to see who just texted you or check what that latest update on your social media feed was. How often do you check to see how many likes your latest post or photograph got? Add in online shopping, gambling and gaming apps and you are like a fish on the end of a digital hook. Heck, they even use the name 'clickbait' for those short headlines that make you want to read more. You know the ones. 'This woman couldn't believe her son's girlfriend did this …' 'You won't believe how a photographer caught these celebrities …'

You might think, 'Well, I only look at positive things like funny dances on TikTok or funny clips on YouTube.' But even light-hearted entertainment can get you addicted, and addiction to anything is always harmful. Dopamine gets produced when you are rewarded with something online. The feel-good chemical can be released by somebody liking your post, a good comment under your photo, or watching a drunk cat trying to climb the stairs. In fact, smartphone manufacturers hire neuroscientists, psychologists and social scientists to make sure this happens.

The problem with this is that people get used to checking their phones regularly to check for those likes and clips and as they do, they gradually get addicted to that dopamine hit. If you don't get that buzz all of the time or get a negative comment or not as many likes as you thought you should, that can lead to anxiety and depression and a consistently negative mindset.

Watch how a child gets cranky and their whole mood changes if you switch off their games console or take their phone off them. Adults are the same. They might not have the same physical outburst as a child, but internally those feelings will begin to build and if the pattern isn't broken this can lead to serious problems. How many times have you seen couples commenting on each other's social media pages when you know they're sitting on the same couch? Wouldn't they be better spending that time together without the distraction of technology?

I was at a hurling match one time with a client who was dealing with anxiety problems. He turned to me in the middle of the game and said, 'Look at this, look at this!' and showed me a video he had received in a WhatsApp group he was in. The video was disgusting so I asked him, 'Why are you showing me that?' I told him that his brain could also never unsee that negative image and advised him to promptly leave the WhatsApp group it came from.

Negativity is the enemy of positivity, but people don't recognise just how much negativity they are subconsciously searching for on a daily basis. Once you see it, it's locked away in your subconscious forever. If you continually watch bad news, or terrible video clips of car crashes, fights, violence, people being ridiculed, bullied or worse, then that is what is filling up your brain and affecting your outlook on life.

STOP NOW and think of the flow of negativity into your brain each day. Ask yourself: where does most of your daily negativity come from? Is it from the television or the radio, from social media or a group chat?

Grab your journal and write down where your negative mental input is coming from. Ask yourself how you can stop or at least reduce this negativity flow as much as possible. If you find negativity coming from the radio show you listen to on the drive home from work, then listen to music or a positive podcast instead. You have to pay attention to what you are paying attention to!

LET GO OF NEGATIVE PEOPLE

The next thing you must stop immediately – not tomorrow, not next week, but immediately – is hanging around with people who add fuel to that fire of negativity. Stop hanging around with people who continuously moan and groan about the same old stuff. Spending time with those people will have a negative effect on your energy levels, it will have a negative effect on your mood from day to day and it will have an effect on your mindset.

In 2009, a study published by professors James Fowler of the University of California and Nicholas Christakis of Harvard Medical School entitled 'Dynamic spread of happiness in a large social network' found that 'whether an individual is happy also depends on whether others in the individual's social network are happy … The happiness of an individual is associated with the happiness of people up to three degrees removed in the social network.'[18]

In other words, if you hang around with happy, positive people, then you are far more likely to be happy and positive yourself. Over the years, I have unfortunately had to make some hard decisions to distance myself from people whom I otherwise quite liked but who continuously moaned and groaned about things they had little or no control over and in doing so had begun to affect my otherwise positive mindset.

If you find that people around you are leeches and are sucking positivity from you, as opposed to building you up and helping you, you can either try to help them better their own mindset or come to the conclusion that you have to cut those negative people out of your life. Even if you are close to them, even if you are fond of them, if they are not good for your mindset, distance yourself as much as possible from them. If they're not predominantly positive people, what is the point of having them in your life? We can't all be positive all of the time, but we do want to surround ourselves with predominantly positive people as much as possible.

In an office environment, for example, often one person will go for a cup of tea and then three others will begin to talk about that person negatively. Perhaps there's a boss who's not a nice person and everybody talks about them behind their back. They have a gripe, a bitch, a moan about them. Perhaps one of your friends or family constantly comes to you with all their problems and always expects you to solve them without ever asking to help with yours. To remain positive, sometimes you need to extract yourself from those situations.

I did a corporate gig recently for a company that I thought was going to be great fun. The whole way through my performance, though, they all sat there with glum faces on them, afraid to crack a smile. That tells me that those people are not happy in their jobs.

They're in such a negative environment that they felt they couldn't react in front of their colleagues. They didn't want to break character and smile. 'Oh, my boss might be looking at me … I'd better not be seen having fun.'

I did the exact same show two hours later for a company that I would regard as being a really serious company and they were roaring laughing, dancing and throwing things in the air. They were two completely different work environments. One company had created a culture of positivity in the workplace while still being serious about their work, while the other company had unknowingly created a toxic, negative workplace. If I hadn't done the exact same show twice within a few hours I might have listened to my inner critic and thought it was me instead of them! Positivity and negativity are contagious. Whichever one you spend more time with is the one you are likely to catch.

I know that you cannot completely eliminate your interactions with negative people in the workplace, but you can definitely reduce your interactions with them considerably, and also check you are not being affected by their negativity and joining in the blame culture they create.

Even positivity, however, can be taken to an extreme and have a negative effect. Online influencers are often prime examples of what I call 'poisonous positivity'. They portray a level of positivity that is unattainable. People are often duped by these influencers apparently living their best lives, going on great holidays, wearing nice clothes or make-up, eating healthy meals or doing whatever it is they do to promote themselves.

While it's all smiles and positivity online, you never see what really goes on in the background. You don't see the fifteen attempts to sound happy in the video. You don't see the twenty photographs that weren't deemed good enough. You don't see the ten items of clothing they tried on but didn't feel good in. You don't see the angry outburst when they get a bad comment.

When you are looking at this type of content, you have to realise that these people are making a living out of this, or trying to make a living out of it. It's literally their job to look positive. What you are looking at is not real.

Regardless of what environment you are in, you must choose how you think, how you interact with negative people and even how you talk to yourself.

NAME YOUR INNER CRITIC

There is a Tommy Tiernan joke about the difference between American and Irish people's attitudes and how they approach the day. If you've spent a few minutes talking to an American on the street or in a store you can be sure to be sent on your way with a smiley 'Have a nice day!' Now, that's a nice positive message to give to somebody. In Ireland, on the other hand, Tommy says the best you can hope for when leaving after a chat with somebody is 'Good luck!' as if the day is fraught with danger and trouble and you'll be doing well to get through it.

Maybe it's an Irish thing, but if I ask somebody how they are, they'll rarely give me a positive answer. 'All right,' 'I'm grand,' 'I'm not too bad.' How often have you heard these answers? How often have you given them yourself? Like the affirmations you learned about in the confidence section, the way we speak and think about ourselves is absorbed into our subconscious mind. If we continuously repeat negative words and thoughts to ourselves, pretty soon we begin to believe them.

In 2013 researchers from the University of Utrecht in the Netherlands conducted a study on patients with anorexia nervosa. Subjects were asked to walk back and forth through a doorway that became increasingly narrower while they were distracted by a memory task at the other end of the room. Those with anorexia turned their bodies to get through the door when the doorway was 40 per cent wider than their shoulders, while those who had no diagnosis only began to turn when the doorway was 25 per cent wider. The negative self-talk the anorexic participants participated in on a daily basis made them believe they were larger than they actually were.[19]

We all have our inner critic, that little voice that tells us, 'I'm not good enough,' 'It's all my fault,' or 'I can't do that.' To maintain a positive mindset, though, you need to catch that internal critic in the act and literally tell it to shut up. I do this all of the time. If I catch myself thinking something negative or getting irritable, I literally stop for a second and tell myself, 'Cranky Keith! Shut your negative pie hole!'

Studies by the University of Michigan and others have shown that thinking of that inner critic in the third person can halt social anxiety and even stop rumination after a stressful event.[20] Give your inner critic a name like Moany Mick, Bitchy Barbara, Negative Noel or Debbie Downer if you like, and the next time you hear that internal voice tell him or her to shut up.

Once the voice is quietened, you then need to argue back with the opposite of whatever it is that voice is telling you. If Negative Noel is telling you, 'I don't know why you're wearing a suit, you still look crap,' change your internal dialogue to 'Shut up, Negative Noel! I look fantastic today. This suit looks really great on me!'

When you hear yourself think, 'Well, I messed that one up and embarrassed myself,' change your internal dialogue to 'Shut up,

Bitchy Barbara! I was very brave to try that. I'm proud of myself for having a go.'

STOP NOW and think about how you speak to yourself on a daily basis.

> What do you say to yourself when you look in the mirror or before going to work or college?
> What do you say to yourself when faced with a challenge like doing exams, making a speech or attending a social event or meeting?
> Are these thoughts predominantly negative or positive? If they are negative, how can you change them to make them positive?

For the next three days, in your journal write down the things Negative Noel or Bitchy Barbara or whoever is saying or thinking and see if there's a pattern. Break that pattern by replacing those thoughts with positive self-talk.

CREATE A MAGICAL MORNING ROUTINE

Most people don't think too much about their morning routine. I suppose that's why it's called a routine. It's a habit, something you've become used to doing. But do you have negative morning habits? If you do, changing them will set you up for positivity for the rest of the day.

In 2014, Navy SEAL commander William McRaven was asked to give a commencement speech at the University of Texas. The man who led the raid that captured Osama bin Laden had simple advice – make your bed:

'If you make your bed every morning you will have accomplished the first task of the day,' he said. 'It will give you a small sense of pride, and it will encourage you to do another task and another and another … if by chance you have a miserable day, you will come home to a bed that is made – that you made – and a made bed gives you encouragement that tomorrow will be better.'

I know lots of people who hit the snooze button a couple of times when their alarm goes off in the morning. When they do eventually sit up in bed, the first thing they do is pick up their phone on the premise of either checking the time or switching off their alarm. Instead, they start checking emails, messages, news feeds or other alerts. They then satiate their craving for coffee before half-eating breakfast and running around trying to get the kids out for school or heading to work. These people have a negative morning routine that is not priming them for a positive day ahead.

Now, I do have off-days like everyone else, but I believe that my morning routine kick-starts my day positively and it helps me have way more positive days than negative ones.

First, I get up an hour earlier than the rest of my household. I label this time my 'magical morning time'. No one and nothing can interfere with this magical time. I have a stone-cold shower, which, as we saw in the section on resilience, helps reduce anxiety levels, increases alertness, improves the immune system and can even help reduce depression. In the shower I repeat my morning affirmations. 'Nobody but me controls this body! Nobody but me controls this mind! I control this body! I control this mind!'

After my shower, I ignore my phone for an hour and focus on getting some fresh air and, if it's sunny out, some sunshine on my face by having breakfast outside. Even if it's raining, opening a window and standing in the sunlight for a couple of minutes will set you up for the day ahead.

I then spend 11 minutes breathing deeply and calmly and listing off all of the things I am grateful for. After that I do one of the creative visualisations that I've outlined in this book, then listen to a motivational podcast or TED talk before I wake my kids up (by dancing and singing loudly in their rooms about how great the day is) and start my day's work. I'm priming myself and my children for a positive day ahead.

STOP NOW and create your magical morning routine. Divide your magical hour into 15-minute segments. For example:

> Spend 15 minutes of quiet time getting some sunlight and fresh air.
> Spend 15 minutes creatively visualising the day ahead and the tasks ahead.
> Spend 15 minutes watching something inspiring.

HIDDEN ACTS OF MAGIC

As previously stated, one of my purposes in life is to is to serve other people. As well as entertaining people, however, I like to do other smaller things on a regular basis to keep me aligned with that purpose and to instil positivity in myself every day.

Hidden acts of magic are very different to random acts of kindness. The concept behind a hidden act of magic is that the other person is left with an air of mystery and wonder that will linger for much longer than the act itself. The only rule is that with each act you must leave an unsigned note of positivity.

While paying for parking on a street in Dublin recently, I noticed that the car beside the meter had an expired ticket on it. After paying for my own parking, I paid for another ticket with two hours of parking on it and stuck it underneath the windscreen wiper of that car. Before I did, though, I wrote the words 'Pass on the positivity' on the back of the ticket so that the person who owned the car would see it and be left with a sense of wonder.

Every town I go to when I'm on tour I make a point of trying to meet at least one homeless person. I sit down beside them and have a chat with them and do a magic trick. Under the misdirection of the trick, I also slip a small envelope into their pocket containing a €50 note and an unsigned letter of positivity to boost their morale.

Another thing I do sometimes is pay for a random couple's meal in a restaurant as I'm leaving. I always tell the waitress or whoever I'm paying not to tell them who paid. That way I'm leaving behind a sense of wonder in those people and a feel-good factor that will last them the rest of the night. It's nice to let people know there is still magic in the world. You can do this in lots of ways.

> Do an online shop for an elderly neighbour and have it delivered to their house with a positive handwritten note, again unsigned.

> Plant daffodils in random places around your neighbourhood with notes of positivity written on biodegradable wooden sticks in the ground next to them.

> Leave sticky notes with positive messages everywhere you go.

> Paint positive messages on rocks and leave them in random places.

> Place a mystery box full of goodies next to a sleeping

homeless person.

> If you can afford it, pay somebody's electricity bill, gas bill or, depending on how much money you have, even pay their mortgage off for them!

STOP NOW and think of three hidden acts of magic you can do this week. Think of at least two that don't involve money. Continue this trend next week and the week after. Notice how amazing you feel afterwards.

KEEP A GRATITUDE JOURNAL

We are in a generation, dare I say it, of self-entitled people. In the instant world of online shopping, online relationships and even online friends we are very often searching for something bigger, better, brighter, without even being conscious of all the good things we already have in our lives.

I'm very privileged to be in the position I'm in. I'm very grateful to have people who enjoy what I do enough to pay to come to my shows. I'm very grateful for my health, my wife and my kids and I put exactly 11 minutes aside each morning to remind myself of those things. I do this because lots of studies have proved that practising daily gratitude and reminding ourselves of the good things in our lives is one of the best ways to retain a positive mindset. A 2008 study by psychologist Alex Wood shows that gratitude can even reduce the frequency and duration of episodes of depression.[21]

Dr Martin Seligman, a psychologist at the University of Pennsylvania, discovered that happiness scores increased hugely in subjects who wrote and personally delivered a letter of gratitude to someone who had never been properly thanked for their kindness, and the benefits lasted for as long as a month.[22] I have personally thanked hundreds of people who have helped or inspired me over the years. Even if you don't know the person you can still send them a positive thank-you message on social media.

The reason my daily gratitude routine takes 11 minutes is because that's how long it takes for me to do my breath work in the morning. I actively practise gratitude every single day as I focus on my breathing.

STOP NOW and grab your journal. List five things you are grateful for today.

Simply write, 'I am grateful for …' and write down what comes to mind. I acknowledge that some people find it difficult to be grateful, especially in harsh circumstances. So start with the simple things. Be grateful for your coffee. Be grateful for rain that helps our plants and vegetables grow. Be grateful for the good memories you have. Be grateful for your heart pumping blood around your body. Be grateful for being able to breathe. Be grateful for life!

List five people you can thank for helping you in life: they could include a parent, a grandparent, a teacher, a friend, a colleague, a sports coach, a spouse or other family member. Express your gratitude with a note or card to one of those people per week for the next five weeks.

FIND YOUR HAPPY HOBBIES

When I was recovering from my car crash injuries and was feeling low, a memory came back to me from my childhood that was one of the happiest moments in my life – snagging a tiny sprat while fishing with my dad off the rocks of Dunmore East in Waterford. We had gone fishing for mackerel that day, but I caught a tiny little sprat instead. To me, though, it was a monster, the first fish I had ever caught, and I can still remember the delight of catching it.

At the age of 32, despite not having fished for almost two decades, I decided I wanted to go bait fishing for the first time, so I went to a local tackle shop and bought two rods, a bunch of hooks and some wriggly live worms for bait. I rang my dad and asked him if he wanted to come with me. He thought it was a great idea and we drove to a beach in Wicklow and started fishing together. Neither of us had a clue what we were doing but we just sat and chatted and laughed for hours on the beach as if we hadn't a care in the world.

I remember sitting in the car on the drive home that evening, feeling refreshed and relaxed, and thinking to myself that the old saying that fishing is cheaper than therapy was right. I began to fish a lot more after that, both on my own and with others, and imme-diately I recognised that this was my 'happy hobby'.

Often, especially in movies, we hear people say, 'Find your happy place.' Lots of people, though, when asked where their happy place is, would find it hard to give an answer. If they do give an answer, it's likely to be a secluded beach in some far-flung place, or somewhere a long distance away, that they can only visit once a year if they are lucky. To me, it's much more beneficial to find your happy hobby, something you can regularly take time to do.

Fishing helps me achieve mindfulness – a way of just emptying my brain and being present in the moment. That's what works for me. I could easily spend six or eight hours fishing, looking at the river or the sea. I forget about my everyday problems, my bills, my job, everything. I turn my phone off for the whole day. I get to focus on nothing and escape the realities of everyday life. I literally don't think of anything apart from where the fish might be.

Allowing your brain to empty is such an important thing to do. There are loads of ways to do it. You can do it through talk therapy, you can do it through hypnotherapy, but you can also do it by simply doing something you love that takes you out of the humdrum of everyday life.

There is a bit of a hunter-gatherer in me. Perhaps I picked it up from my grandfather Gaga in Waterford. Like him, I grow my own vegetables with my kids, and it's great to see the smiles on their faces when we pull up potatoes, carrots, onions, garlic, pick raspberries, whatever it is we plant, and put them on the table for dinner. When I came home from Wicklow that day with a sea bass that I had caught, I gutted it, cleaned it and cooked it. The satisfaction of seeing my family eat that for dinner with a few vegetables from the back garden was a great feeling and, pardon the pun, I was hooked on fishing.

I also enjoy playing board games or card games with my wife and kids. We play together at least three times a week and it's another great way to forget about the rest of the stuff going on in my life, while also spending time with my family. We also garden together, have Nerf gun fights, water fights and lots of other fun activities.

Mindfulness does not necessarily need to be a solitary activity! A friend of mine, a busy businessman with three teenage children, has been playing five-a-side football with the same group of friends for the last fifteen years. Having taken to running during Covid lockdown, he told me he missed his Thursday night five-a-side more than anything. 'When I'm running, I'm on my own and I've nearly too much time to think about stuff,' he said last week. 'But when I'm playing five-a-side, that's all I'm thinking about. I go and meet the lads and we kick a ball around on the Astro and have a bit of craic. For that hour I forget about everything else. It's brilliant.'

Even if you do go to therapy, I would recommend finding activities that make you happy and ensuring you do them on a regular basis. Often, we forget about something we used to do when we were younger. Lots of people played sports when they were younger only to give them up as adult life took over. Maybe you can find a team or group to rekindle that interest. If you are too unfit or too old to play, then why not coach or help out with a local team or group?

Your happy hobby doesn't have to be a physically strenuous activity. Recently I took up the harmonica – I've always wanted to learn to play it. Maybe you loved making jigsaws when you were younger, or painting pictures.

It doesn't matter whether it's colouring, knitting, reading, coaching, volunteering, walking in nature or anything else, as long as you can focus solely on what you are doing and be present in the moment. If you are focusing on that one thing, the analytical part of your brain will relax and so will you. If you do more things that make you happy, guess what? You'll be a happier and more positive person.

STOP NOW, grab your journal and write down two things you used to enjoy doing but which, for some reason, you stopped doing. Decide to return to at least one of those things that bring you joy and happiness.

Pick one new thing that you could try that you think will add positivity to your life.

From this moment onwards I want you to completely flip your attitude around to one of positivity. To do this right now – and I mean right now – I want you to stop wasting time on negative words, thoughts, people, places and actions, start following the tips above on a daily basis and practise the positivity brain hack at the end of this section every day.

All these things are foundations for gaining a happy headspace. If you do one of them, well, that's good. But if you do all of them, then you are going to have a much happier outlook on life within a relatively short period of time and be well on your way towards a more positive mindset.

12.

WHAT ARE YOU AFRAID OF?

HOW TO STAVE OFF FEAR AND ANXIETY

BABIES ARE BORN with only two fears: a fear of falling and a fear of loud noises. If you have more than those two fears now, you learned the rest of them somewhere along the way.

Fear itself, though, is not necessarily a bad thing. When we perceive danger or an immediate threat, our amygdala's red warning light begins to flash and urges us to react as quickly as possible. If somebody comes at us menacingly with a knife our amygdala screams at us to run – which is a good thing. The problem is when people have the same negative emotional reaction to the smallest of threats, or even non-threatening things that they perceive as threats, like meeting other people, getting into an elevator, touching a door handle, giving up a bad habit or even getting out of bed.

The major issue is when fear turns into a phobia and becomes so detrimental to your life that it affects you in negative ways. An unhealthy fear of anything can detract from your positive mindset. I, for example, have a healthy fear of dogs. If I see a strange dog, I'm not going to go over and put my hand near its mouth because the dog might react by biting me. That's a healthy level of fear to ensure I don't do something stupid. Otherwise, though, I like dogs and will play with them and pet them once I know they are friendly and that they don't see me as a threat. On a scale of one to ten, my fear of dogs is probably a one.

Other people have a bigger fear of dogs, a fear that stops them doing the things they want to do. Instead of thinking, 'Okay, well, there's a dog over there minding his own business, so I'll just carry on with mine,' the amygdala tells them, 'Oh no! There's a dog over there! What if he bites me? I might need stitches! Maybe he'll rip my arm off! I'll have to go to hospital! I might never be able to use my arm again! Quick! Run and hide!'

That fear then stops them doing things they love doing and soon they are thinking, 'I can't visit my friend's house because she has a dog … I can't go for a walk in the park because there are always people with dogs there. Okay … I'll just stay inside.' On a scale of one to ten that fear is close to an unhealthy ten and is very detrimental to your mindset. In my time as a hypnotist, I've seen the most extreme circumstances. I've helped people overcome everything from the more common fears of spiders, dogs, snakes, heights and public speaking to people with fears of birds, chocolate, escalators and even balloons.

I had a client once who was afraid of snakes. Well, you might think, there are no snakes in Ireland so there's not much to worry about, but my client was a soldier, and his job was to clear bunkers in foreign countries with his team. Sometimes he would see a snake and be literally unable to move, so his fear of snakes meant that his own life was at risk, as were the lives of his team.

While a fear of balloons might sound funny to some people, the person I cured of that fear hadn't been inside a restaurant for twenty years because they were afraid there might be a party going on and one of the tables would have balloons on it. Fear comes in different forms for different people and no matter how trivial someone else's fear may seem to you, that fear is very real to that person.

I have sold more tickets in the Olympia Theatre than any other artist in history. It's one of my favourite places in the world, but every single time I step out onto that stage, or any stage, I have a healthy fear that I'm going to fail and be booed off the stage. A couple of times I have come very close.

On the opening night of the 'Dark Side' show in Killarney, one of my assistants walked out on stage with the reveal of the first trick facing the audience, which ruined the trick. That night was a disaster. Every single trick messed up. I always have back-up plans, but back-up plans are not nearly as clean and don't look as good. That show felt like the longest show in history.

If we go to see a band and the lead singer hits a bum note, well, that's okay. We know they're singing live. If a guitarist hits a bum note once or twice, well, that's okay. But if a magician messes up a trick everybody goes, 'Ha ha ha! We know how you did it, you gobshite!' A magician spends their whole life running like a rabbit down a rabbit hole with the audience, the fox, chasing them. Audiences can be very unforgiving, and that fear can be very detrimental if you don't know how to handle it.

There is a small spider on your neck right now. It's just after climbing quickly up past your ear and into your hair. You can begin to feel its tiny legs running through your hair now. It's making you itchy. You want to scratch it or rub it and get rid of the spider. Go ahead.

If, like many people, you scratched or rubbed your neck or head, or if you do so in the next few minutes, you will begin to understand how your brain visualises things. If you didn't, change the spider for something you are actually afraid of and read those sentences again.

When you are anxious or afraid and are busy dreaming up the worst-case scenarios for whatever situation you might potentially be faced with, the problem is that you are creatively visualising something and, like the basketball study in the introduction, or the spider example above, it has been proven that your brain doesn't know the difference between you visualising something and it really happening.

Fear can be good. I don't suggest getting rid of all of your fears. What I do suggest is learning to understand your fears and control them. During the Stone Age our amygdala's main mission was to protect us from predators. Back then it was easy to spot a predator – it was usually a big wild animal that came running at you. Nowadays, though, we work at such speed and are used to having so much information thrown at us from all angles, all of the time, that we don't know the difference between perceived fear and real fear.

When it comes down to it, what people are actually frightened of is the thought of fear, rather than the fear itself. When I say I'm fearful of going on stage, I'm not actually fearful of walking onto the stage. I'm fearful of what *might* happen when I get on stage, tricks going wrong, people heckling me, and so on. It's the thought coming into my brain that needs to be controlled and changed. Thankfully, I have learned how to do just that.

My fear of failing on stage comes from the fact that I want to entertain and do my very best for my audience. I know they come to my shows to get away from everyday life, to forget about all of that and be entertained. I want to astound and amaze them so that they leave the show with a sense of wonder and smiles on their faces. I now accept that the fear of failure is always going to be with me, but I have learned to shrink it down so that it doesn't overwhelm me, and at the end of this section I will teach you to do the same.

In 2009 I found myself wondering what the highest number of fearful flyers was that anyone had ever brought on a plane to get them over the fear of flying. The only references I could find were Paul McKenna and Richard Bandler, who each brought one person, so I thought, 'Well then … I'll bring ten!'

In hindsight, letting Dublin radio station 98FM decide who those ten people would be was a bad idea. They ran a campaign where people who were afraid of flying would call in to the radio station and then they picked the ten worst cases out of those callers – people who were so afraid of flying that helping one of them would have been hard enough.

One woman's father had been a pilot and she had actually been in a plane crash. One man had moved to Ireland from New York four days before the terrorist attacks on the Twin Towers. His brother had been killed in the tragedy and he had never flown since. Another man from Dublin had admitted to having been held down while crying on a previous flight. These were the most extreme cases of fearful flyers.

I first met the ten people in Dublin Airport a few days before our flight. I took them to meet pilots, who explained the mechanics, the safety aspect of flying and things like turbulence to them. This, rather than helping them overcome their fears, made them worse. However, I then helped them individually hack their own subconscious minds to push through that fear and ultimately overcome it.

Over the course of two days, I used the creative visualisation for overcoming fears below to finally get those ten people onto a rickety Aer Arann twenty-seater flight to somewhere in Wales. They were all absolutely fine … on the way over.

On the way back, however, one guy, who happened to be sitting right next to me, began to whisper to himself, 'I can't do this! I can't do this!' a few minutes after we had taken off. He then started to unbuckle his belt and tried to get up out of his seat, which caused a few others to turn around and see what was going on.

'Sit down,' I told him forcefully. 'Sit down!'

'I can't do it,' he pleaded, 'I can't, I can't do it!'

'We're on a flight right now,' I said. 'We're in mid-air. There's nowhere to go.'

He was huffing and puffing as if he was about to have a baby, but I knew that if he snapped completely the other nine might get their fear back. There was a possibility they all might kick off and we would have a plane full of screaming, panicked flyers, which would be a very serious situation. As a young hypnotist, I was worried that I had bitten off more than I could chew, but I had to get rid of that fear immediately and concentrate on solving the problem at hand. The hormones released during a stress-induced fight-or-flight moment are the same as the ones released when you are excited, so it's actually possible to flip that moment from panic to excitement.

I've now done it thousands of times to people, but back then I had only done it a few times and this guy was really freaking out.

I got him to quickly close his eyes and visualise everybody on the plane up and dancing, having a rave on the plane. 'Imagine they're all having a dance and a party,' I said. 'Imagine they're all having drinks and they've all got tinsel flying out of their ears! Now I want you to imagine that one of them magically turns into Shrek and Shrek is dancing with Cinderella! Now turn up the volume! Make it bigger, brighter! Turn up the volume again! Now imagine that you're in the middle of the rave and you're the boss of the rave and you're telling them all to dance! Dance, boy!' The man suddenly started smiling and laughing as I continued. 'Imagine now that you're loving flying! Because that's where you are right now! You're on a flight and you're absolutely loving it!'

Suddenly the guy's emotions flipped from panic to excitement, and he was now screaming with a smile from ear to ear, 'I love flying! Whoo-hoo, I fucking love flying!' Everybody else turned around to see what the commotion was, but instead of seeing a panicked flyer, they saw a guy literally screaming with delight and they all began to laugh with him.

I've been on other flights since then where this has happened. One weekend, on the way back from filming *Now You See Me* 2 in London, after a two-hour delay, I boarded the plane exhausted and just wanting to get a bit of sleep on the short flight to Dublin. After a long time sitting on the tarmac in London, this guy got on the plane and within seconds I could tell he was having a panic attack. He had flight attendants and security around him and every few seconds he would flip-flop between taking his seat and getting off the plane. Eventually the pilot came out of the cabin and told him that everyone was waiting for him to take his seat, and the guy looked around and got even more panicked. I called one of the cabin crew over and explained who I was and what I did. It just so happened she had seen me on TV before and knew me. I told her that I had a spare seat next to me, that I just wanted to get home and if she sat him next to me, I'd hypnotise him and there'd be no trouble.

The flight attendant started laughing, but said she wasn't sure if she wanted him on the plane at all. I reassured her that everything would be fine if she just told him that I was a hypnotist and that I'd look after him. A few minutes later they brought the guy down, he sat next to me, and I did the same thing with him as I did with the guy on the 98FM flight. By the end of the flight, he was thanking me and high-fiving me and he was absolutely fine. Now, you might think that was a piece of luck, a fearful flyer sitting beside a hypnotist, but the truth is I didn't really do much apart from explain to him how to think about something differently. All he needed to do was flip the switch.

FLIP THE FEAR

A recording of me guiding you through this technique can be accessed on my website www.keithbarry.com/brainhacks.

STOP NOW and think of a situation that causes you fear.

> In the safety of your current surroundings, allow yourself to visualise that frightening place, person or thing. Feel the feelings, think the thoughts. Feel your palms sweating, your heart beating faster, your breath getting heavier, your temperature rising.

> Now, flip that picture to the happiest moment in your life.
> As you change the picture, continuously tap the back of your left hand with your right index finger. Now really focus on that happy moment and let the feelings of joy spread through your body.
> Allow yourself to physically smile while remembering that moment. Feel the warm glow of happiness flow into every fibre of your body. Turn up the colour and vibrancy of that happy experience and hear the sounds as you continue to tap the back of your hand.
> Now magnify and multiply those positive feelings by a thousand.
> Keep thinking of that moment until you have tapped the back of your hand for about thirty seconds.

Notice how quickly you went from a feeling of physical discomfort, anxiety, and fear to one of happiness simply by changing the image in your head to an image full of joy and happiness. Well, the good news is that if you practise this process regularly, that tapping of the back of your hand becomes an anchor (for more on anchors, see the Influence section), and you can use it any time to shift your mind to induce happiness and allay fear.

Try it again now. Make your mind blank and, after a few seconds, tap the back of your hand again. You will notice that those happy, joyful feelings come back. If you're nervous before walking into Weight Watchers, tap the back of your hand before you walk in. If you're anxious before an interview, tap the back of your hand. Once you take a few minutes to practise this regularly, you will induce happiness and joy any time you tap the back of your hand.

Let's talk about anxiety. It's staggering how many people are suffering with anxiety these days. In fact, I get dozens of emails and calls every week from people who need help with high levels of anxiety, which sometimes results in panic attacks.

What if I told you that, like fear, anxiety can actually be good for you? It's what motivated me to get up out of bed this morning to write this section of the book. I was actually anxious about writing about anxiety! We all experience anxiety from time to time. It's perfectly normal to be anxious about an exam, once the level of anxiety is proportionate to the exam. It's perfectly normal to be anxious about a football final or a job interview, once your anxiety decreases when they are over. In both of those cases, anxiety is really just your body's way of telling you something important is happening.

Anxiety really only becomes a problem if it becomes unmanageable or overwhelming and you begin to avoid certain circumstances on a daily basis due to your level of anxiety. In that case, you may have what is known as generalised anxiety disorder. If you are constantly thinking about future events with a pessimistic frame of mind and predicting negative outcomes, you may have an issue. You are neither a mentalist nor a psychic, so stop trying to predict those negative outcomes!

In 2016, researchers from the University of British Columbia measured the productivity and anxiety levels of 221 participants over a two-week period. For the first week, the group were told to keep all their notifications on and their phones within sight. For the second week they were told to keep their phones out of sight and their notifications off.

When their phones were in sight and notifications were on, the group reported high levels of anxiety, inattention, boredom and hyperactivity, and the researchers anticipated even higher levels when they couldn't see or hear their phones. Instead, the opposite happened. The group was more focused and able to concentrate on tasks better.[23]

STOP NOW and ask yourself if your smartphone, tablet or computer is causing you distress. That can be anything from sore eyes or headaches to a lack of sleep or a bad feeling after interacting with something or somebody online. Do you get anxious when your phone is out of your sight or reach for just a few minutes? How can you ease that feeling?

> Adjust your existing phone settings to turn off notifications?
> Buy a lock box and lock your phone in it for a day?
> Have a 'no phones at mealtimes' rule?
> Set 'do not disturb' between 10 pm and 8 am?
> Delete a messaging group?
> Leave your phone at home for periods or put it on airplane mode in case of emergencies?
> Switch off your alerts?

Pick three of these six ways of reducing your screen time and start right now.

If your level of anxiety is disproportionate to the situation you are in – for example, if you feel you are anxious any time you meet new people or do new things, or if you feel anxious for a prolonged period – this is obviously an issue that needs addressing with a professional.

When I was in my twenties, I did magic absolutely everywhere I went, all day, every day. I did magic for my friends, my family and complete strangers. If I went out for dinner, I did magic for the waitress. If I was on a train, I was doing magic for the passengers around me. I did close-up magic so often that I was very comfortable doing it and enjoyed doing it.

When I did my first big stage show, however, the idea of performing in front of a thousand people increased my anxiety levels tenfold. Thankfully, I had learned additional techniques, which I will share with you below, to help me get over that. The more live shows I did in front of an audience, the more comfortable I became doing them.

When the pandemic hit and I began to do online shows over platforms like Zoom, Microsoft Teams, Webex and others, a new form of anxiety crept in. I was very anxious, not only about the new technology, but about the fact that I was speaking to people in a different way. Again, though, I used the techniques from this chapter, and the more online gigs I did, the more comfortable I was doing them. As I write this, I am in my comfort zone doing online shows.

The problem with comfort zones, though, is that when we get into one, we become reluctant or anxious about trying new things. As I write this, lockdowns and restrictions are due to be lifted soon. Hopefully I will be back to doing live theatre shows again by the end of the year, but I know that when that happens I will be anxious about it because I have become comfortable doing online shows. The wheel has turned full circle again. With experience, I have learned to acknowledge these feelings of anxiety as a message from my subconscious that something important is happening. I use the strategies from this chapter to manage my anxiety levels and you can too.

To overcome anxiety, you need to push your boundaries a little bit further every day. Step out of your comfort zone. If you are anxious about being around a lot of people at a social event, for example, you could prepare for that with stepping-stones. You could start off by maybe having dinner in an outside setting near other people, or inviting a couple of friends over to your house for dinner. The next step could be going out for breakfast, lunch or dinner with those friends in a place you know won't be too busy. Gradually you can build up the number of people around you until you are more comfortable in large groups. It's only when you push yourself to your limits that those limits can expand and grow.

The first step towards reducing your anxiety levels is to map out what makes you anxious, when you get anxious, and how you feel in the moment.

STOP NOW and write down three situations where you regularly feel anxious. Then answer the following questions:

> Why do these situations raise your anxiety levels?
> How long before the situation do you begin to feel anxious?
> How long does your anxiety last?
> What physical changes happen when you feel anxious?
> Do you sweat more than normal, get a headache, feel irritability, experience rapid breathing?

> On a scale of 1–10 with 10 being a full-on anxiety attack, rate your anxiety level in each moment.

The next time you feel that level going above four, use my main go-to strategy below for dealing with anxiety when it becomes an issue.

──────INFINITY CALMING TECHNIQUE──────

An audio recording of me guiding you through this technique can be accessed on my website www.keithbarry.com/brainhacks.

If you feel you are heading towards panic and need to induce calm in a certain moment, you can do this simple breathing exercise to calm yourself down and reduce your anxiety. I use it all the time myself when I feel anxious.

> Begin to trace a calming infinity sign, a figure eight, on the back of your hand with the index finger of your other hand. You can do this openly or secretly under a table, or on your leg if necessary.

> As you slowly trace one loop of the figure eight, breathe in gently but deeply.

> Breathe slowly out for the next loop, still tracing the infinity sign on the back of your hand.

> Continue to trace and breathe like this for the remainder of this exercise. Your mind will be focused on the task of tracing the infinity sign while breathing and this will soon settle your autonomic nervous system.

> In order to magically change your anxiety from the feeling of fear and distress into the feeling of calm relaxation, you have also got to change the picture inside your mind. Think now

of a moment in life where you were most calm, relaxed and carefree. As you do this, continue to breathe slowly as you trace the infinity sign, and feel the calmness and relaxation spread throughout every muscle, nerve and fibre in your body.

> Do this for 60 seconds and then stop tracing the sign.
> Now think of a time when you feel anxious. Allow the feeling of anxiety to begin to take over. Now trace the figure eight on the back of your hand while doing your breathing exercise and visualise the moment when you felt calm again. Bam! Notice what happens. The feelings of anxiety begin to shift into feelings of calm.
> Add in some statements that will help change your internal talk in the moment. 'Right here, right now, I feel calm and relaxed. I am in control right now.' Continue to trace the infinity sign, breathe and think about that calm moment for as long as necessary.

Notice how you went from a feeling of physical discomfort, anxiety, and fear to one of calm and relaxation simply by changing the image in your head. Well, the good news is that if you practise this process regularly, then tracing the figure eight on your hand or leg becomes an anchor (see the section on Influence), and you can use it at any time to shift your mind to induce calmness and allay anxiety.

Try it again now. Make your mind blank and, after a few seconds, trace the infinity sign on your hand. You will notice that those calm and relaxed feelings come back. If you're anxious before attending a social gathering, speaking in public or having an online meeting, use this technique beforehand. Once you take a few minutes to practise this regularly you will induce calmness and relaxation any time you do your breathing while tracing this figure on the back of your hand. If practised regularly, this hack will enable you to feel a psychological shift into calmness any time you feel anxious.

We can all be fearful or anxious about different things. What might make you afraid or anxious might not be a problem for me and vice versa. We are not trying to eliminate fear or anxiety, but you need to learn how to control them so that they don't interfere with your everyday life.

If you can calm your breathing, slow your heart rate, and flip that fear and anxiety into happiness and excitement then you can learn to control those fears and anxious moments. If you can control your fear and anxiety, you will be taking a massive step towards a positive mindset.

As well as fear and anxiety, we often have bad habits that can hinder our progress down the road to positivity. Wouldn't it be great if you could get rid of those bad habits? Well, to do just that, you first need to know how habits work.

13.

DISABLE THE AUTOPILOT

HOW TO MAKE BAD HABITS DISAPPEAR

Have you ever taken a shortcut through a field or a park to get to your friend's house, to school, to the shops, or somewhere else you go regularly? Maybe at first, the grass was pretty high, and you had to stomp down nettles or weeds to make an easier route to your destination. After regular use of any new shortcut, though, the trail improves bit by bit until eventually there is a clear pathway to your destination worn into the ground. The more you use this pathway the firmer and clearer it becomes, and you don't think of it as a shortcut anymore. It's simply the way you go. Well, your brain works in exactly the same way.

If you find yourself regularly eating popcorn while watching a movie at home, having a cup of tea and something sweet after your dinner, having a cigarette when you drink, browsing on your phone when you are bored, or even regularly putting yourself down when you talk to yourself, it's because you have done it so often it has become habitual. You don't need to think about it anymore. You are on autopilot.

Any time we do something new, neurons in our brain fire a signal and create a new neural circuit. At the start, when we are trying to learn something new, like how to play a musical instrument or pick up a sporting skill, the signal is weak and slow – like the initial days of dial-up internet access, for anyone of a certain age who can remember such things.

When we do the same thing regularly, though, those circuits get coated with myelin, a sort of fatty insulation. Repetition increases the thickness of that insulation and the thicker the insulation, the stronger the signal becomes. The more we repeat things and practise them, the more insulation we provide for those circuits, the signals go from slow dial-up to ultra-fast fibre-optic broadband, and we can play a song or hit a sliotar with a hurley without thinking about how we did it. There is an old scientific saying for this. 'Neurons that fire together wire together.' In other words, those habits become hardwired in our brains.

When neuroscientists began learning about how habits form, they discovered that as new things become more and more automatic, your brain starts working less and less. Habits actually make the thinking part of your brain, the prefrontal cortex, go into sleep mode. It literally thinks, 'I've done this a thousand times. I can do it in my sleep.' This means you don't notice most of your habits because you don't need to put any conscious thought into them. That's why you don't remember how many cigarettes you smoked, how many video games you played, or how many biscuits you ate. These neural pathways established by our habits actually never get deleted. Like the shortcut to school, the pathway is still there for us in case we need to go back and use the same route again, which is great for simple things like getting dressed, eating food, brushing our teeth, tying our laces, kicking a football, and so on, but not so great for the bad habits we pick up along the way. Now, that doesn't mean you can't lose your bad habits. It just means you have to work harder and smarter to override those neural circuits you have created in your brain.

Like fear and anxiety, sometimes a habit can be a good thing. Putting your seatbelt on when you get into a car is one example. Washing your hands after using the toilet or brushing your teeth before you go to bed are two more.

Other habits, however, such as overeating, biting your nails, picking your nose, excessive alcohol consumption, smoking, playing video games endlessly, watching too much TV or even being sedentary can be very detrimental to our health and in some cases bring with them serious repercussions – even death.

All habits have three parts: the prompt, the habit itself and the perceived reward. The key to breaking a habit is taking the time to recognise these three parts and acting upon them.

> **The prompt**: something always prompts you that it's time for your habit. That prompt could be a time of day, a place, a person, an activity or a feeling.
> **The habit**: the act you are prompted to do, like putting on your seatbelt, eating that bar of chocolate, smoking that cigarette or backing that horse.
> **The reward**: what you feel you get out of your habit, for

example, a feeling of safety, a sugar rush, a feeling of calm or an adrenaline hit.

For example, the prompt of getting into a car precedes the habit of putting on your seatbelt, for which the reward is a feeling of safety.

DISCOVER YOUR PROMPTS

Before writing this chapter, I began to think about my own bad habits and realised that this week, every single time I have a cup of coffee it prompts me to want to have something sweet, like a biscuit or a piece of chocolate, with it. My problem is that I have three to four coffees a day, which means I am being prompted to have chocolate or something sweet far too often. The good thing is that because I am aware of my prompt and my habit, I have already started to take control of it.

STOP NOW and figure out what the prompts are in relation to your bad habits.

> Do you always have a cup of coffee when you feel tired?
> Do you always have a cigarette after a meal?
> Do you always have a sweet snack when you need a break from work?
> Do you bite your nails after a stressful conversation?
> Do you do something immediately after a certain activity?
> Do you do it because you feel a certain way?

In your journal, write down as many prompts as you can think of for your bad habits. In order to take control of your prompts you must first become consciously aware of them.

DECIDE

The next thing you have to do to lose a bad habit is decide whole-heartedly whether or not you actually want to lose it. Some habits can be quite easy to lose. The habit of not switching off a light when leaving a room can be easily remedied by putting a note on the back of the door or somewhere else it will be seen. Not putting dirty clothes into a washing basket would have the same solution. Other habits, bigger 'keystone' established habits, however, may take more time and more effort to lose, which is probably why a lot of people never try.

People often say they want to give up smoking, for example, but they don't really want to give up smoking. It's their mother, father, sisters, brothers, kids and friends who want them to give up smoking.

Despite all of the studies that tell us smoking promotes tumour growth and causes lung cancer (among other serious diseases), people continue to smoke and vape. As with a lot of bad habits, people don't actually think about why they're smoking or vaping. The thinking parts of their brains go to sleep. Habits become ingrained into our subconscious over time, so you must first make a conscious decision to lose your bad habit, followed by reprogramming your subconscious mind to eliminate it.

When questioned about their habit, I have even heard people say, 'I love smoking. It relaxes me.' But that feeling of 'relaxation' after a cigarette comes from the fact that your body has been so busy trying to combat the poison you're putting into it that when you finally stop sucking it in, and your system finally stops trying to save your life, it then calms down. If a cold bucket of water could calm you down, you wouldn't set yourself on fire every five minutes just so that you could throw one on yourself.

STOP RIGHT now and decide on a bad habit you want to lose. If you don't want to lose a bad habit, then skip the rest of this chapter.

What I hear a lot from people who want to quit a habit is 'All right, Keith, let's set a date for me to give up smoking,' or 'Let's set a date for me to start losing weight.'

This whole thing of setting a date or starting on a Monday, which is also a very popular phrase among people who don't really want to do anything about their current situation, is just an excuse for avoiding the issue and prolonging the pain. You are the master of your own mind. When somebody tells me they want to set a date for doing something, my reaction to this is usually something along the lines of 'What are you talking about? We don't need a date. We're doing this now! This is the exact second we're doing this!'

STOP NOW and have a look at your watch or a clock. Do it immediately, don't waste any more seconds. Note the time and date. In your journal, write down in the present tense whatever it is you need to overcome, for example:

> 'This very moment I have decided I am a permanent non-smoker.'
> 'This very moment I have decided I no longer bite my nails.'
> 'This very moment I have decided food is my pharmacy and I am a healthy eater.'

By doing this your subconscious mind will begin to recalibrate itself towards taking actions that are conducive to losing your bad habit. It becomes far more 'real'.

DECLARE

From now on, with discipline, when you look in the mirror you will begin to see a non-smoker, an active person, a responsible spender, a good eater, whatever it is you now are. Go to a confidant and declare to them you are doing this. Get support from a partner, a friend, a work colleague or your children. There is no better motivator than a child who wants their parent to get healthier so they will be around longer.

You also need to declare your intentions as a written statement in your journal. Start a WhatsApp group with your family or close friends and explain what you are doing and that you will need support from them beforehand. Join a social media page dedicated to supporting people giving up the same habit.

If you feel your own social media page is a safe and secure environment, then why not declare it on that? Once it's out there you will feel a level of responsibility to do it. Declare regularly. Put up regular posts on your progress and reward yourself for positive results.

Most importantly, handwrite a commitment contract with a friend or family member. Researchers at the Norwegian Centre for Learning Environment and Behavioural Research in Education found that handwriting something keeps it in our brains far longer than if we type it out.[24] You can even write out a contract with a dead loved one. I've seen people do amazing things when they declare to their dead loved one that they are going to do something they had trouble doing before.

Declare that you will do whatever it is you are going to do by a certain date and that you will pay a financial penalty if you don't. If you declare to a dead loved one that you will stop eating fast food within three weeks but don't do it, then donate the amount in your contract to a local charity.

If you tell your children that you will treble their pocket money or give them each a big reward if you don't lose a certain amount of weight, don't walk a certain number of kilometres, or don't halve your screen time within a certain timeframe, those children and that penalty will be a constant reminder to lose that weight, walk those kilometres or halve that screen time. (If you have sneaky kids like mine, though, be aware they may not remind you ever again until the deadline arrives, and then they will come to you with their hands out!)

DISASSOCIATE

I did a stop smoking seminar in Carton House a few years ago. At the beginning I welcomed everybody with the words 'Okay, folks, thank you for coming. I know you're all here to give up smoking. I want you to be absolutely honest with me. If you've got cigarettes with you, just take them out of your pockets and hold them up.'

Most of these people had stacks of cigarettes on them – at a stop smoking seminar. Think about that for a moment. They said they planned to give up smoking but had still brought cigarettes to the seminar. Imagine if you went to a weight loss meeting with two bags of McDonald's and a bag of sweets in your hand. They'd probably throw you out.

For a while before my first child was born, I had an unhealthy relationship with a games console. It probably began as a means of passing time when I was recovering from my car crash and then became a bad habit. While my wife was in work, I could sometimes be sitting playing video games for five hours a day. After our daughter was born, if my wife left me in charge of the baby when she went out, she'd often return to see me sitting on the couch with my baby daughter on my knee and a remote control in my hands playing *Call of Duty*.

Pretty soon I realised this habit was taking away from my family life and my own life. When I realised this, I declared to my wife that I was giving up playing video games and then I immediately disassociated myself from the habit.

The first thing I did was remove the physical temptation. For you, this could be crushing and binning your cigarettes, putting your phone in a timed lock box, unplugging your Wi-Fi, cutting up your credit card or deleting your social media. For me, it meant snapping every single video game I owned in half. One after another, I snapped them and binned them. Even though each one of those games had cost me a lot of money, it felt so liberating to do that.

The second part of my disassociation with my habit was to eliminate the account I had with the game store. That way I couldn't buy any more games.

A few years ago, I was at a neighbour's fortieth birthday party in our local pub and enjoying a bit of down time with my wife. After a while, one of the partygoers, who was a bit worse for wear, came up to me and said, 'I need to give up smoking!'

While he wasn't overly rude or boisterous, he was pretty drunk and, perhaps forgetting that he had already told me, he continued to repeat the scenario quite a few times over the course of the night. I told him a few times that because he'd had some drink on him

I wasn't going to hypnotise him. But he insisted and kept coming up to me and repeating the phrase over and over. 'I need to give up smoking. I need to give up smoking.'

While I had been enjoying the party and the chance to have a few quiet drinks with my wife and friends, by the last time he came up to me I was so fed up with it that I stood up and said, 'Okay! You want to give up smoking? Here we go!'

Within seconds I had done an instant handshake hypnosis induction on him and laid him out on his back in the middle of the packed pub. As he lay there, I guided him to see his own funeral. I had him see his adult children revert to young babies and watch them as they crawled around on their tummies puking cigarettes up on top of him – real shock hypnosis stuff. The whole thing only lasted about sixty seconds before I stood him up in front of me at the bar and asked him if he was a smoker.

'Fuck no! I'm a non-smoker,' came the reply.

I asked him why he had a pack of cigarettes in his pocket. He didn't believe he had.

'Take them out and break them in half right here, right now.'

The man rummaged around and was amazed to find his own packet of cigarettes in his pocket. He took them out and broke them up there and then.

'Now, that's the last box of cigarettes you'll ever touch,' I said.

Delighted to have halted the inconvenience and return to a few quiet drinks, I completely forgot about the incident until about six months later, when I opened my front door to a bottle of Gentleman Jack whiskey on my doorstep with a lovely thank-you note attached. As far as I know the man is still off the cigarettes, which shows the shift somebody can make in the blink of an eye.

STOP NOW and ask yourself what you can do to cut out temptation and disassociate yourself from your habits.

CREATE A NEW YOU

Try not to imagine a really tall purple giraffe with white wings. Now try not to imagine that giraffe cycling past your front door waving at you with a cheesy grin on his face. When somebody tells you not to think of something you can't help but immediately think of it. A lot of people find it hard to stick with something that doesn't have an instant effect, but your brain doesn't know the difference between thinking something and seeing it.

That's why it's important to think of yourself from this very moment as a non-smoker, as a person with healthy habits, as an outgoing person, as a calm, rational person, as a frugal person, or whoever it is you want to be.

When you say, 'I don't want to smoke,' all your subconscious mind hears is that you're still a smoker. If you say this, your subconscious mind actually eliminates the negative and only hears, 'I … want to smoke.' The best way to stop smoking is to immediately begin to think of yourself as a non-smoker. Tell yourself, like the man in the pub, 'I am now a permanent non-smoker!'

If you've decided today is the day to give up cigarettes, you are already a non-smoker. You stopped seven minutes ago. By now you should already have broken every cigarette in the house. Do it and feel brilliant about it. As you are doing it, tell yourself, 'I'm a permanent non-smoker. These mean nothing to me!' Break them in half. Put them in the bin.

If you've decided that you are going to lose the habit of eating a sweet treat every time you have a cup of tea or coffee, then do as I did and bin all of your sweet treats. Don't mull over it. Don't do it one at a time. Do the lot. Do it now!

From now on you are a new person. You are the person you want to be. For your brain to really believe you've become a healthier person, you should create a screensaver on your phone. Find a photo of yourself when you were fit and healthy and in your prime and set it as your lock screen and screensaver. That way, every time you pick up your phone you will be reminded of what you are doing and why you are doing it. You can also stick this photo on your computer screen, on the door of the treat cupboard or inside your wallet or purse, depending on what habit you are trying to lose. Understand that you don't ever need to compete with anyone except yourself.

REPLACE BAD HABITS WITH GOOD HABITS

Replacing bad habits with good ones is so simple it seems like cheating. At first, though, swapping an old habit with better new ones may take a while.

When I decided to stop playing video games after my daughter was born, I replaced the habit by bringing her out for a walk in her pram or spending some quality time playing with her any time I felt the prompt to play a video game. I also began to invest in myself by studying books that helped me move forward in my career and as a parent.

It may take a while to find a replacement habit that gives you the same reward as the old but, like bad habits, good habits are only formed after repetition.

You need to identify the reward of the old habit. Is that reward something to reduce a mid-afternoon hunger pang? Is it something to give you a break from work? Is it something to keep you in touch with other people?

A lot of people who work in an office, for example, will get up from their desk at around 3 pm and go to the canteen or the kitchen and make themselves a cup of tea or coffee – and while they are there, they'll grab a couple of biscuits or some sweets and have a chat with whoever else is there.

If you are one of these people, you need to ask yourself why you get up from your desk at 3 pm in the first place. Do you want something to satisfy your hunger? Do you want something to give you an energy boost? Do you want something to relieve the boredom of work?

If your answer is that you are hungry, all you need to do is replace the unhealthy snack with a healthier version. Have a bottle of water and a piece of fruit instead.

If you find that you have a cup of coffee at 3 pm because that's when you are feeling tired, replace that habit by getting away from your desk and doing some exercise for five minutes instead to revitalise yourself.

If you're stuck in an office, you may find that walking or running up the stairs or stretching for a few minutes in the bathroom will get the blood flowing and your heart rate up enough to get you through the rest of the working day.

If you find that you leave your desk at 3 pm because you need a break from work, then instead of going to the canteen, where the biscuits and other temptations are, go and have a chat at somebody else's desk, take a walk outside or ring a friend instead.

A 2002 study by Duke University habit researcher Wendy Wood and her colleagues found that approximately 43 per cent of our daily behaviours are habits,[25] so be kind to yourself as you undergo this process.

None of us are born drinkers, gamblers, or smokers. We aren't born procrastinators, over-spenders, nail-biters, cake-eaters or fidgeters. Habits take time and repetition to form. To create good new habits, at first we need to repeat them and pay attention to them until our neural circuits get hardwired so that they become habitual.

The problem is that people consistently look elsewhere to solve their problems. A lot of people tell me, 'I tried hypnosis, I tried acupuncture, I tried yoga, I tried everything.' I always ask them if they ever tried themselves. Did you try yourself? Did you really put 100 per cent of you into this? You're searching for an answer that's within you.

Positivity is attainable for everyone. While fears, anxieties and habits can stem from different aspects of your life and can affect your positive outlook on life, none of that matters. What matters is that you can change them all. If you really want to.

You can build a positive mindset. Whether you are positive or negative is a choice you make regardless of your circumstance or situation. You will always have a brighter, more fun-filled life if you attack each day with a positive frame of mind. Any time you feel that negativity creep in, use the relevant techniques in this section and combine them with the visualisation at the end of this section to achieve a more positive mindset.

EVERYDAY BRAIN HACKS FOR POSITIVITY

> Stop complaining about what other people are doing. Take control of, and take responsibility for, your own life.

> Stop the negative feed to your brain. Delete negative social media accounts or messaging groups.

> Stop giving time to people who are negative and drag you down. You are not here to continuously solve their problems. Stop listening to gossip.

> Give that little negative voice in your head a nickname. When you hear them saying something negative, tell Bitchy Barbara or Negative Noel to shut their pie hole. Turn their chatter into positive self-talk.

> Get up early. Make your bed. Give yourself a magical hour before you check your phone.

> Give your time, expertise or money to somebody who needs it, without seeking anything in return. Be sure to add mystery to the moment by leaving an unsigned note.

> Spend time each day counting your blessings. Write a note of thanks to somebody who helped you in life.

> Find a few things you love doing that take you out of the moment. Do as many of them as possible, as often as possible.

> Use the Flip the Fear visualisation to switch from fear to excitement.

> Trace the figure eight on your hand or leg to calm yourself down in anxious situations.

> Figure out what prompts your habit and what is the real reason for doing it.

> Make the decision to lose your habit now. Record the moment.

> Tell anyone who will listen that you are losing that habit. Join a support group.

> Get rid of the temptation. Ditch the video games, cigarettes, sweets or whatever it is you're losing.

> As soon as you decide to kick your old habit, tell yourself you are a new person. Pick a photo that suits your habit change and make it your screensaver.

> Take time to figure out the reward and replace your habit with a good one that fulfils the same emotional rewards.

− VISUALISATION FOR A POSITIVE MINDSET −

An audio recording of me guiding you through this visualisation can be accessed on my website www.keithbarry.com/brainhacks.

Read through the following several times before beginning the visualisation:

> Sit or lie down in a quiet spot where you can make yourself comfortable. With your eyes closed, visualise a purple light hovering over your body. This is your light of relaxation. Feel the light hovering over your feet and relaxing your feet as it slowly enters them. Focus on your feet and actively allow them to relax. As you do this, repeat silently to yourself over and over, 'My feet are relaxed, my feet are relaxed, my feet are relaxed.'

> Now allow that purple light to slowly spread up through your legs into your torso, your arms and every other part of your body. As you feel the light entering each part of your body, tell that part to relax. Focus on relaxing each part of your body in sequence.

> Once your body is relaxed, shift your focus to your breathing. Inhale for 6 seconds and focus on inhaling pure relaxation. Hold for 3 seconds. Exhale for 6 seconds and focus on all the tension leaving your body as you exhale. Repeat this breathing pattern 20 times.

> Allow your imagination to take over and fill your mind with thoughts of peace, happiness, joy and hope for your future, regardless of what obstacles may face you. See the best possible outcome in every circumstance.

> Now visualise a new future version of yourself. A person who has a profound ability to maintain a positive mindset on a daily basis. What does this person look, act and sound like? How are they different to the current you?

> Begin to feel the positivity of that new version of yourself being absorbed into your mind and body in this present moment. Feel the positivity as a tingling sensation in your stomach at first. Now allow that tingling sensation, that shimmering, vibrating force of pure positive energy, to spread into every part of your body. As this happens, gently squeeze your right earlobe with your right hand to anchor this feeling.

> Accept in this exact moment that being a more positive person, with a positive outlook on life, will benefit not just you but also your loved ones.

> Say to yourself three times, 'I am and always will be a person with a positive mindset.'

> Take a moment to think about a current issue where you need to feel more positive. Allow your inner positivity guide, your own inner voice, to share thoughts, ideas and words on how you can address this situation from a more positive perspective.

> Finally, imagine a force field of positivity surrounding your whole body and mind. See it as a silver mist surrounding you. This is your positivity shield. This is the mental force

field that will prevent the bullets of negativity from entering and wounding your mind. You, and only you, can control what enters through the force field. Continue to squeeze your right earlobe gently.

Any time you need to activate your force field or need to flood your mind, body and soul with positivity, simply squeeze your right earlobe. You will feel positivity spread through your body and your force field will activate.

INFLUENCE

having the skill to subconsciously influence people
and steer their decisions in the direction you need

*'The secret of my influence has always been
that it remained secret.'* – Salvador Dali

14.

INVISIBLE INFLUENCE

THE SECRETS OF NON-VERBAL COMMUNICATION

We all try to influence other people every single day of our lives. Think about that for a moment.

Every decision you make is influenced by somebody or something. It could be as simple as your partner influencing you to make them a cup of tea or coffee in the morning. It could be a sales rep influencing you to book a holiday or buy a certain brand of car. It could be that girl in the bikini on TV influencing you to buy another packet of that green tea you hate the taste of, just because she says it's good for you.

As a baby, you quickly learned how to draw your parents' attention by crying when you were hungry or wanted to be picked up, influencing them to feed you, cuddle you and play with you. As a child you knew how to get around your grandparents to give you sweets just before your dinner when your parents weren't looking. Now, your granny or grandad knew you wouldn't eat your dinner after a big bar of chocolate or a pile of sweets. They also knew they would more than likely face a tongue-lashing from your parents when they found out about your sugar-filled 'appetiser'. So why did they do it? The answer is simple. Five-year-old you influenced them to do it.

On the other end of the scale, why do some people still smoke or vape, in a time when smoking and vaping have been proven so dangerous that all advertisement is either extremely limited or banned altogether? Again, somebody or something influenced them to start smoking or vaping despite the widespread knowledge of their harmful effects.

Maybe a friend, or circle of friends, putting peer pressure on them at the beginning was enough, or maybe there was a more subtle influence, such as an older sibling or parent always smoking or vaping around them. Even if a parent warns a child of the dangers of inhaling toxic substances, leaving cigarette packets and fashionable vapes lying around the house tells the child that they really think otherwise and often influences them to do the same.

As a series of experiments carried out by Robert Cialdini and Noah Goldstein in 1999 on the best way to persuade hotel guests to reuse their towels discovered others can influence you even if they are not around.

When guests read a message in their bathroom that 'most other guests' reused their towels, they were 26 per cent more likely to reuse their towels than those who saw the standard message, which cited saving water and the environment as the reason for doing so. When the message told them that 'most other guests who stayed in this particular room' reused their towels, then that percentage jumped to 33 per cent more than those who saw the standard message.[26]

The advent of social media has brought with it a whole new world of influence and even a career path where online influencers are rewarded for making you watch their video clips, tag people in their posts, like their photos and buy their sponsored products.

These new forms of influence are now being used to change the face of global politics. Voters have been tracked online and influenced to vote certain ways without them even knowing it's happening.

The US political scandal involving up to 87 million Facebook users saw the online platform fined $5 billion by the US Federal Trade Commission after their users' data was harvested and used by Cambridge Analytica to display customised messages and tailored advertisements to help elect Donald Trump to the White House.

In fact, it doesn't matter whether the effect of influence is positive or negative, you are still susceptible to it – especially if that influence is invisible to you.

Now, you might be thinking that you're smarter than that. Maybe you're the type of person who is just not susceptible to invisible influence. But what if you could be made to think of something by just using three little words?

Ask yourself this – what image do the words 'Just do it' conjure up for you right now? If you're thinking of a brand of running shoe or clothing, then you've just been invisibly influenced. Invisible influence is used every day by people wanting you to buy something, wear something, eat something, do something. Why? Well … maybe it's *because you're worth it.* If you thought of a hair product just now, then you've been invisibly influenced again.

The good news is that you too have the ability to influence people even more than you ever realised. In fact, you yourself are invisibly influencing people every moment of every day and a lot of the time you don't even realise you are doing it.

At first, I didn't really believe these influence techniques could be used in everyday life. But after discovering that hypnotism actually worked when 14-year-old me convinced my classmate David Burke to strut around our Irish class thinking he was a chicken, I began to delve deeper into the subject of the subconscious mind.

I devoured any books I could find on philosophy, psychology, neuro-linguistic programming, behavioural analysis, non-verbal communication, lie detection and even business books about marketing and strategy. I then practised and honed my new-found skills and began experimenting with my own strategies until I perfected my own invisible influencing technique.

The first time I used a basic version of this new technique was as a chirpy, fresh-faced 22-year-old at the check-in desk of Continental Airlines on the way from Dublin Airport to Newark.

Back then I was still dreaming of getting my very first TV show. To do so, though, I often had to fly to Los Angeles to pitch my ideas to US network executives.

Like most people on those flights, I was crammed into the not-quite-roomy-enough economy seating and often wondered what it would be like to fly business class.

As I walked up to the girl at the Continental Airlines check-in desk that fateful morning, I distinctly remember thinking to myself, 'I wonder if I could invisibly influence her into giving me an upgrade?'

BUILDING RAPPORT

The very first thing you must do when trying to influence somebody is build rapport with them in order for them to like you. Rapport is that sense of connection you get when you meet someone you like and trust, or discover that you share interests, opinions or values in life with them.

Doing everything you can to ensure that other person likes and trusts you will strongly increase your chances of getting the decision you need, and there are a few ways of doing this.

In terms of body language, the first thing you need to do is smile. Now, this seems so obvious, but it's something many people seem to have difficulty doing for some reason. I've held numerous seminars for people who should be the best in the world at connecting with others and building rapport with them, but they can't even manage a smile at the beginning of the talk. Charm is such an underrated attribute. You've got to smile, be happy, give a little grin even, to encourage people to like you.

If social guidelines allow, a firm handshake is also another important tool. You wouldn't believe the number of high-powered businesspeople I've met who have a wet-fish handshake. It drives me bonkers and, if it drives me bonkers, you can bet it drives other people bonkers too. People might think that, because of the pandemic, the handshake is a thing of the past, but I believe that once people are vaccinated, and we get back to normal life, the handshake will return.

The handshake is said to have originated in early Greece as a way to demonstrate that you weren't carrying a weapon. Although we no longer need to show we have no weapons on us, a firm handshake, or a hug if it's socially acceptable, also triggers oxytocin.

Nicknamed the 'trust molecule' and 'the essence of empathy' by Paul Zak, professor of neuroeconomics at Claremont Graduate University in California, oxytocin is released from the brain into the blood. Its levels rise when we hug, touch, sit close to someone else or even simply hold open a door for them, resulting in that person being more likely to trust you.

Good eye contact is very important when trying to build rapport and make a connection. If there is more than one person in a social or interview situation, try to keep eye contact with the person who is speaking at the time. By maintaining eye contact when they are talking, you are showing that you are engaged and interested in what they are saying. If you break eye contact with someone when attempting to invisibly influence them, their mind may wander to other things, and they may begin to lose interest. If you are feeling put off by this, remember the tip from the Confidence section of this book and look at a point between their eyebrows instead. Another top tip is to practise blinking at a slightly slower rate than you normally would. To keep the person as interested as possible in what you are saying, slow your blink rate to around twelve blinks per minute, or once every five seconds. This way you will be gazing at the person for slightly longer periods of time than you ordinarily would. You will keep their attention and focus and add to your rapport-building with that individual.

As a hypnotist I've asked people to 'look into my eyes' hundreds of thousands of times. When they do and I am about to influence them to fall under my spell, I never blink at that moment. Even in social situations where I might be speaking to new people for a while, I have often overheard them say afterwards, 'Jesus, the way he looks at you … it feels like he's looking into your soul.'

As well as good eye contact, you also need good listening skills. Ensure you don't cut the person off. You need to listen to every single word that comes out of their mouth. Now, that may sound obvious, but effective listening is an acquired skill. Become an active listener rather than a passive listener and let the other person know this by casually repeating two or three words they've said, every now and then.

MIRRORING

The next step in our set of rapport-building tools is mirroring. When you mirror somebody, you become like them and will begin to create a bond with that person. On a very basic level, when you become like somebody then that person begins to subconsciously like you, because most people inherently like themselves.

Whether we notice it or not, we move away from things we dislike and we move closer to things we like. In order to invisibly influence somebody, you need to mirror them. You can begin by leaning slightly towards them, without invading their space. If you are seated and lean back in the chair, you are distancing yourself from that person, showing them subconsciously that you're not really enjoying the experience. Instead, sit or stand upright and angled slightly towards the person you're talking to. In preparation for mirroring, make yourself comfortable, but don't close your hands; leave them in an open position, either on top of a table or desk, or on the arms of your chair.

Mirror neurons were first found in the brains of monkeys in the 1980s, and since then various neuroscientists have argued that mirror neurons in the human brain help us understand the actions and intentions of other people. In a UCLA study published in March 2005 Marco Iacoboni and his colleagues reported that mirror neurons could tell whether somebody picking up a cup of tea intended to drink it or clear it from the table.[27] Iacoboni has also argued that mirror neurons are the neural basis of the human capacity for emotions.

This is why we yawn when someone else yawns, or we shake our own leg when we see a spider crawling up someone's leg. Mirroring displays empathy with the person and if you do it right, you will begin to create a subconscious bond with them.

While mirroring somebody's body language, you must be subtle. If you cross your arms every time someone else crosses their arms or scratch your ear whenever they scratch their ear, then it will become noticeable, if not a little bit weird for the other person. Instead of crossing your arms, you could simply place one hand across your opposite forearm or, if they wave a pen around, you might pick up a pen. Basically, you want to alter your own expressions and gestures to echo their expressions and gestures.

During a conversation, set yourself a target of subtly mirroring three of the other person's physical gestures or actions approximately three times over the course of your chat. For example:

> If they take a sip of a drink take a sip of yours a few moments later.
> If they fold their arms, cross yours.
> If they scratch their chin, scratch your cheek.

STOP NOW and think of five other actions or gestures that you think you could easily mirror.

You will know that you have developed mutual rapport if the other person begins to mirror you in return. After a while you can have fun with it in your head. If you are standing talking to a friend you could lean against a wall, cross your ankles, or put your hand on a countertop and see if they copy you. Fold your arms and see if they do the same. If they do, that's a subconscious signal of trust and rapport on their behalf. After all, imitation is the sincerest form of flattery. If they don't, then maybe you haven't quite made that connection yet.

The next time you see me on stage or TV, watch for how I always mirror a person I'm meeting for the first time in order to gain an instant rapport with them. Mirroring is not just copying body language, though. In essence, you are trying to become subliminally symbiotic with that other person by not only mimicking their body language but by breathing at the same rate and even trying to replicate their speech patterns.

While trying to match the other person's rate of breathing may seem advanced, it is easier than you think. If a person is nervous and breathing heavily, I will first begin to match their heavy breathing to subliminally connect with them. I will then mirror their physical actions and slow my breathing down to lead their breathing into a slower pace in order to make them feel more comfortable.

The top tip for mirroring somebody's speech is to repeat back one to three words from a sentence they say to you. I once had a client who told me he had no confidence when meeting people, so I brought him to a corporate barbecue event full of strangers. I told him, 'All I want you to do is repeat back one to three words of a sentence people say to you, and you will find you will gain rapport that way.'

By the end of the evening, after mirroring everybody at the barbecue and using this simple language mirroring technique, my client was surprised to notice how popular he was among the other guests there.

THE ART OF GIVING

Giving something away is also very important when it comes to big decisions, job interviews, major purchases, business deals and daily interactions. Robert Cialdini, the Regents' Professor Emeritus of Psychology and Marketing at Arizona State University, found that reciprocity is one of the few social rules that is followed worldwide. Reciprocity means that when you give somebody something for free, they feel obliged to give you something back.

This is why you invite somebody to your party after being invited to theirs. It's also why you often get free samples and treats from sales reps as you walk through an airport or even your local supermarket. After smelling that nice perfume or tasting those fresh sausages, you are more likely to engage with the person selling the items (thereby giving them back your time) and indeed purchase those items at some time in the future.

In fact, the art of giving doesn't have to involve a physical product. I have found that even giving away ideas or information for free is also likely to influence the other person into giving you something in return.

Decide on one person right now who you need or want to influence and what you are going to give them in order to influence them towards a desired outcome. This doesn't have to cost any money and can be your time, help, expertise or information.

Expect nothing in return, but in the back of your mind know the law of reciprocity will look out for you. This can be used in both your personal and professional life.

YES-SETTING

The next part of my invisible influencing system involves combining an age-old technique called 'yes-setting' with subliminal anchors and triggers. On a basic level, yes-setting is a language pattern technique which is used in order to get people into a 'yes' frame of mind so that you can ultimately tip them towards agreeing, either subconsciously or consciously, to whatever it is you finally suggest to them.

To get people into a 'yes' state of mind you need to get that person either thinking or saying 'yes' truthfully at least three times. This can be done during the general chit-chat you almost always have at the beginning of any conversation.

Simple yes-setting questions work best and are usually used in the course of normal everyday talk. Like on *The X-Factor*, three yeses would be the minimum requirement, but you need to extract as many truthful yeses as possible before asking your final question. You always want the other person to answer truthfully so, if it's a lovely day out, you may say something like 'It's a lovely day out, isn't it?' while using your subtle anchoring motion (which I will describe below) immediately after the question. Nodding your head slightly as you ask the question will fire up their mirror neurons and help get a yes answer.

'Yes.'

If the person looks tired you may say something like 'I'd say you'll be glad to get home and relax?' using the same anchoring motion.

'Yes.'

Neurologically, what's happening is that the person's subconscious mind is now making a pathway or connection between that small anchoring motion or gesture and them saying yes. By yes-setting them and anchoring those yeses you are priming the person to enter an emotional yes state when you trigger that final response. Habituate them into a yes-set.

'The weather is lovely today, isn't it?'

'The traffic was crazy today, wasn't it?'

'Your eldest is in university now, correct?'

STOP NOW and think of five extra questions you could easily extract a yes with. Provided you don't make it too obvious and do everything with charm and a smile, the person should already be leaning towards a positive response to your final decision-making question, even before you have finished asking it.

ANCHORING

My invisible influence system enables you to change people's emotions not only by yes-setting them but by combining this with body language and hypnotic techniques and then subliminally anchoring and later triggering those truthful yeses. In hypnotism, anchoring involves associating an internal emotional response to an external stimulus which can then later be used to subconsciously trigger a desired psychological state. These anchors can be visual, auditory or kinaesthetic.

In my system, simple visual anchor movements can be used each time the person says or thinks 'yes' during general chit-chat. These movements would be very minimal, something the other person might only see peripherally, and therefore subconsciously, like tapping your finger on a desk or clicking a pen each time they say yes. If you scratch your chin or pull your ear every time the person says yes, then it's going to look really weird. These anchor movements should be small enough that in the worst-case scenario your subject might go away thinking you have a slight tic. The most important thing is that this anchor must be consistent. Decide now on an action that feels natural to you that can act as a visual anchor. So you need to get that minimum of three truthful yeses, anchoring each yes with a subtle, barely perceptible stimulus at the exact time the other person says yes.

Using invisible influence, the person is now getting into a state of mind where their subconscious mind, not their conscious mind, is recognising that this little motion of touching the back of your hand or drumming your finger, or whatever it is you are doing, is related to them thinking or saying yes.

TRIGGERING

When you arrive at the final decision-making question, that small anchoring gesture changes into a trigger at the optimum moment of the conversation. When you want somebody to make a particular decision, this trigger sets off the same neurochemical reaction they got when you anchored those earlier yeses. The trigger is now priming the person to say (or think) yes to your final question where perhaps ordinarily they might say no.

This final trigger, though, is where a lot of people can fall down. Although the subliminal signal used will be exactly the same as during the anchoring process, using my system, instead of waiting until they answer yes, the signal is used on the very last word of the final decision-making question. What happens then is that the person's brain associates this anchor with thinking 'yes', and they are subconsciously ready to say yes before even hearing the end of your question.

Back in Dublin Airport, I began to try my new invisible influence technique on the unsuspecting check-in girl. As she was taking my passport and going through the motions of checking me in, I leaned in to express interest in her, therefore making her subconsciously interested in what I was saying.

I mirrored her body language, and I began to yes-set her by asking her questions. During our smiley chit-chat about how busy the airport was, how early she must have to get up for work, how nice the weather was and how she could probably do with a holiday herself, I lightly drummed my fingers on the check-in desk each time she said yes.

Having already yes-set her and then anchored those yeses during the general chit-chat, I then used the same finger-drumming motion to subconsciously trigger that 'yes' again when I wanted her to answer the question that I knew perhaps she was going to be resistant to.

Now, most people have tried to get an upgrade at some point in their lifetime, but the approach has probably been somewhere along the lines of just bluntly asking, 'Any chance of an upgrade?' – a question which the check-in staff probably hear a hundred times a day and have a standard negative reply to. What I said, while all the time smiling and trying to be as charming as possible, was 'I'm flying to LA on my own today. I'm so excited! I wonder if there is any possibility at all of getting an upgrade? I'd be really, really apprecia-tive.' On the last word of the sentence, I triggered her final response by drumming my fingers lightly on the desk again.

Now, the girl didn't say yes straight away. Instead, she said, 'I'll take a look.' But I knew that, subconsciously, she wanted me to have that upgrade and, sure enough, within a few moments she handed me a business class ticket to Los Angeles. I was so delighted that I actually roared laughing all the way through Dublin Airport and onto the plane.

Up until that morning, I wasn't sure if my new invisible influence technique was a real thing or not. As I sat in the luxury of business class for the first time in my life, though, I realised that it was. This stuff works. It is real and I have been using it positively ever since. But like a new saw for a carpenter, this technique is just another tool to add to your influencing toolbox. Most of the time, though, a saw won't get the carpenter's job done on its own and neither will this.

PREPARE, PREPARE, PREPARE

Preparation is absolutely vital for any situation where you want to influence someone. As a mentalist, I have no limits to where I will go to in order to pull off a mind trick or some grandiose illusion in front of a live crowd on stage. People don't realise that I can sometimes be preparing for one big trick for twelve months, or even longer. I have the same work ethic when it comes to preparing for other occasions. Before I got buried in a tonne of ice for my TV show *Brainhacker* I immersed myself in ice baths every single day for a year.

If I'm attending an important business meeting or social event, you can bet your bottom dollar that I take enough time to do massive amounts of research on the person, or people, I'm going to meet.

You would be surprised by the number of people who still have their privacy set to 'public' on their various social media accounts. Because of this, you can find out what they look like, where they live, whether they like cats or dogs, what their hobbies are, even where they went to school or college.

Some people might think this is invasive but it's not. If people have their life up on social media and their settings are public, then the way I see it is, they want me to know all about them. The more I know about the person I'm meeting, the better chance I have of invisibly influencing them. If you find out that somebody loves dogs, horses or a certain football team, you can use that to start a conversation and build a bond.

You can prepare in other ways too. For example, if you need to persuade your kids to tidy their room, prepare what you are going to say to them in advance and rehearse it in your mind. Create the illusion of choice by altering the language you use. Children want to be in a position of power, so use the skills of a mentalist to create that illusion. Ask questions like the ones below to create the illusion of choice:

> Which book would you rather read for the next twenty minutes?
> Would you prefer broccoli or carrots with your dinner?
> How long would you like to exercise for today? For fifteen minutes or thirty minutes?

BE AN AUTHORITY

Commanding authority is an essential part of influencing. If you are trying to sell a product or explain a concept to somebody, you'd better know that product or concept inside out. If the person you are meeting knows more about it than you, there is a good chance you will lose their respect straight away and they are very unlikely to cut a deal with you.

I successfully combined all the elements of my invisible influence technique in order to get a job as mentalism and magic consultant on the first *Now You See Me* movie a few years ago. When Brian Tucker, an Irishman working on the movie, heard the production company was looking for a mentalist and recommended me, I doubt very much that the guys in Summit Entertainment had ever heard of Keith Barry. Yet I flew to Los Angeles, walked into a room with the movie's top executives and landed the job. Here's how.

I prepared as much as possible for the meeting, knowing that other potential magic and mentalism consultants wouldn't go to the same lengths that I would in order to pull off that job. Not enough people prepare for difficult conversations or other obstacles they might face in daily negotiations, so I tried to pre-empt anything that might come my way. As discussed in the section on my TARGETS formula, spending time in your preparation period to guess or predict what those obstacles or difficult questions might be, and having solutions to those obstacles on hand, is absolutely key.

Before I flew to LA (business class again, of course), I guessed that most of the top magicians and mentalists in the world had already auditioned for the consultancy position. I figured that everybody else had probably gone into that room and performed their very best tricks for those executives and had absolutely blown their minds. I decided to do something a little bit different.

I walked into the room and, with some of the top executives in the movie business looking on confused, I placed the movie script down on the table and announced, 'There are three spelling mistakes in that script.'

Doing this instantly made them sit up and pay more attention to me. It also demonstrated my authority as a consultant. I had read the script and found flaws in it. As well as throwing them off their usual interview pattern, I now had authority in the conversation.

After a shocked pause, a reply came that it was only a 'rough draft'.

'Well, that's as may be, but there are still three spelling mistakes in it,' I insisted.

In doing this, I also wanted to make sure that those executives knew that I was serious about that job and that my standards were not only the same as theirs, but actually above theirs at that moment in time. Next I began to build rapport with those executives. I leaned in, showing interest in what they were saying, and expressed interest in everybody in the room. I then mirrored the body language of the key decision-maker in the room and matched his breathing and language pattern in order for him to immediately make a connection with me. As I was doing all of this, I began to yes-set them slowly over the hour-long meeting, while continuously mirroring to get them to like me subconsciously.

I then threw out ideas for the movie. I gave those movie moguls a whole bunch of great ideas, absolutely free, which made them feel great. I also anchored their yeses by tapping the fingers of one hand on the back of the other. By the end of the meeting, I hadn't done any tricks in the room. No magic. No mentalism. Nothing.

After an hour of using my invisible influence technique, the meeting came to a close and I wanted to trigger those yeses one final time. I flashed a cheeky smile and asked, 'Alright, so ... have I got the gig?' making sure to tap my fingers on the back of my hand on the final word of the question.

Remember, doing this automatically shifts a person's mindset from being hesitant in that moment to being in a 'yes' frame of mind. I did it so quickly that nobody even noticed, but it was announced immediately: 'Keith's got the job. Cut the deal!' I also got the job for *Now You See Me 2* a few years later.

Now, I don't believe I'm special. I don't believe I was born with a gift, or that I'm any smarter than you or anybody else. In fact, a while back I took an IQ test that revealed that I'm not exceptionally smart, contrary to my own belief!

Sometimes, of course, I don't get exactly what I want. After almost getting a TV project across the line, often the final negotiations are conducted by an agent and my influencing tactics are taken away from me. Yet I've had dozens of TV shows on networks all over the world, consulted on a couple of movies and actually grown my business during a worldwide pandemic.

Ever since that first successful trial at the Continental Airlines desk in Dublin Airport all those years ago, I have tested, improved and perfected my invisible influencing technique. I have now used this technique positively in all types of negotiations from buying and selling to networking, hiring people and cutting business deals all over the world. Now you can too.

15.

INFLUENCING ONLINE

HOW TO INFLUENCE IN THE DIGITAL AGE

MORE THAN thirty years ago, golden tortoise beetles became the first known insect species with the ability to rapidly change colour. What really sets the colour-changing tortoise beetles apart, however, is that the colour change is controlled by them, in response to specific events in their environment, such as being poked by a curious human or stumbling upon a willing mate.

During the Covid pandemic, we have all had to become like a golden tortoise beetle and adapt to changes and shifts in our daily lives and working patterns. Thankfully, after decades of perfecting my skills, I have found that my invisible influencing technique doesn't even need to be done in person and can even be done online.

Even yes-setting can be done during online meetings. If the other person cannot see you, it can be done using an auditory anchor. Over the phone, for example, a simple tap on the phone or click of a pen at the correct time provides the same anchor as scratching your chin or tapping your hand while speaking to somebody in person.

The beauty of it is that the other person doesn't notice – and even if they do, they simply think there's a crackle on the line.

DRESS TO IMPRESS

My grandmother Nancy always told me that I should always be the best-dressed person in the room. That was a real lesson to me. I went to Heroes clothing in Waterford and rented a suit complete with dickie bow and shiny shoes for my teenage magic shows – and I still try to look dapper whenever I appear on stage or online.

Since my corporate gigs went virtual, I'm amazed at how many people turn up to online meetings or shows wearing pyjama bottoms. The old rule still applies. Be the best-dressed person in the room. By dressing well, you will be perceived as a leader and will gain respect more easily. People will listen more intently to your words as you will have their attention. You only get one chance to make a first impression.

CONNECT WITH PEOPLE THROUGH THE CAMERA

To effectively influence people, they have to feel that you're talking to them – not at them. I've recently noticed a lot of people pretending their Wi-Fi isn't great and not turning on their camera at all. Don't expect to have as much influence if you don't turn your camera on.

When I'm doing my online gigs, I'm very cognisant of the fact that my eye line is in line with the camera on my device. A lot of people look at the middle of their screen instead of looking into the camera or light at the top. This makes the person on the other end of the conversation feel like you are not listening to them and are focused on something else.

Position your device so that you are framed properly in the middle of the screen. If you need to raise it, you can put a couple of big books or a shoe box underneath your device. Do not have your keyboard to the side and be looking at that instead. You should look into the camera lens most of the time (see below).

LIGHT UP THE ROOM

There is nothing worse than talking to somebody you can barely see or who is pixelated because their lighting is so bad. If the room lighting isn't great, then position a lamp nearby or buy an inexpensive ring light. Make sure you don't sit with your back to a window as this will underexpose your image, leading to one of those horrendous dark silhouettes we've all seen too frequently.

Do a dry run with a friend or host a fake meeting with no guests to check it out. You'll know within seconds if your lighting is bad.

CREATE A CHEAT SHEET

If you've got to remember lots of information for an online interview or presentation, make clear and concise notes and stick them on a piece of cardboard taped to the back of your device behind your camera. That way, you can still glance at them throughout your presentation.

If you are doing this, though, it's important that you don't continuously stare down the camera during the interview. Yes, it is important to make eye contact, but if you do it all through the call and then, suddenly, you glance at your notes to remember something it will look suspicious. Instead, as you are chatting, you should glance around the room every so often so that it looks normal when you do check out your cheat sheet.

SAY THE OTHER PERSON'S NAME

On most online meeting platforms, if not all, the person's name is written directly below their face. As the forefather of influence, Dale Carnegie, once said, 'A person's name is to him or her is the sweetest and most important sound in any language.'

Simply saying somebody's name three or four times during a call can make them feel important and valued. Saying somebody's name engages them, especially virtually, and also helps build rapport. People love to feel seen and heard. There is no easier way to create a connection with someone than saying their name aloud several times.

GET A CREDIBILITY BOOKSHELF

Have you ever noticed that whenever an 'expert' in something comes on TV they almost always have a bookshelf full of books behind them in full view of the camera? American channel CNN is a great place to check this out. Having books behind you gives off an air of intelligence and lends credibility.

I suggest you fill your bookshelves with books on whatever topic you are supposed to be an expert in. If you are a car salesperson, have car books or manuals on the shelf. An architect would have books about buildings, architecture, planning behind them. I often have fun trying to read the titles of some of these books.

A credibility bookshelf will add an air of authority and

professionalism to your presentation and help make you look like an expert in your field. Prince Charles, Joe Biden and actor Sean Penn have all made use of credibility bookshelves during recent online presentations and interviews.

DISPLAY YOUR AWARDS

I did a gig recently for a top business network and while some of the participants did have bookshelves behind them, very few, if any, had awards on their wall. Awards and qualifications behind you are always good.

Framed certificates, diplomas or degrees lend you credibility and they also make you feel more confident. All these small things add up to build your confidence and demonstrate you are an authority in your field of expertise.

ABSORB THAT SPACE

As in real life, you should sit up with your back straight, elbows on the arms of your seat, and your arms uncrossed and open. While crossing your arms might make you feel comfortable, the person you are talking to will subconsciously see this as a sign of resistance, that you are closed off or that something is wrong.

Like a TV correspondent, though, don't just sit there static. Lean in to show you are interested in the other person. Move your body a little and express yourself when necessary. Absorb the space you are in and use hand gestures when applicable.

In a study into charisma by expert Vanessa Van Edwards, she discovered the most popular TED Talkers in 2010 used an average of 465 hand gestures during a 15–20-minute talk, almost twice as many as the least popular speakers.[28]

But be careful what gestures you use. In another study of eight lecturers giving the same talk to different audiences, results showed that when they used mostly open palms-up gestures throughout the talk, the reviews afterwards were 84 per cent positive. When they used mostly palm-down gestures, however, the positive reviews dropped to 52 per cent. When they delivered the exact same presentation to another audience using finger pointing, though, it dropped again to 28 per cent – with some students even walking out during the lecture![29]

Whether you want a better deal for your next contract, a better price for your next car or simply to get your kids to bed on time, the techniques above will help you do just that. In fact, they will help you in all aspects of your life. After decades of perfecting my invisible influencing techniques, I firmly believe that when you master these methods you too can use invisible influence to have all the success you desire.

EVERYDAY BRAIN HACKS FOR INFLUENCE

> Try to build a bond with the other person. Smile, shake hands, listen and find common ground.

> Lean towards the person. Try to mirror one or two physical gestures and repeat a few words from two or three sentences without obviously mimicking them.

> Give something away for nothing, whether it's your time, a gift or a piece of information.

> Elicit three truthful yeses from the person in general chit-chat.

> Anchor these yeses with a simple visual or auditory stimulus.

> Change your anchor to a trigger just before they answer the final decision-making question.

> Use all resources necessary, including contacts or social media, to find out as much as you can about the person you wish to influence.

> Know your product or concept inside out. Be prepared for questions.

> Be the best-dressed person in the room, even if that's a virtual room.

> In online meetings look at the camera to make eye contact.

> Make sure your lighting is correct so that the other person can see you clearly.

> Make clear notes and stick them to your computer behind your camera.

> Say the other person's name three or four times in conversation.

> Have a bookshelf behind you filled with books relevant to your expertise.

> Hang degrees or awards in view on the wall behind you.

> Sit up straight, with your arms open. Express yourself with palms-up gestures.

—— VISUALISATION FOR INFLUENCE ——

An audio recording of me guiding you through this visualisation can be accessed on my website www.keithbarry.com/brainhacks.

Read through the following several times before beginning the visualisation:

> Sit or lie down in a quiet spot where you can make yourself comfortable. With your eyes closed, visualise a purple light hovering over your body. This is your light of relaxation. Feel the light hovering over your feet and relaxing your feet as it slowly enters them. Focus on your feet and actively allow

them to relax. As you do this, repeat silently to yourself over and over, 'My feet are relaxed, my feet are relaxed, my feet are relaxed.'

> Now allow that purple light to slowly spread up through your legs into your torso, your arms and every other part of your body. As you feel the light entering each part of your body, tell that part to relax. Focus on relaxing each part of your body in sequence.

> Once your body is relaxed, shift your focus to your breathing. Inhale for 6 seconds and focus on inhaling pure relaxation. Hold for 3 seconds. Exhale for 6 seconds and focus on all the tension leaving your body as you exhale. Repeat this breathing pattern 20 times.

> Imagine for a moment you are on stage in front of 80,000 people, giving a motivational seminar. See yourself as the most charismatic and influential version of yourself possible. Notice how confident, mesmerising and fascinating you are. Those 80,000 people are hanging on your every word, awaiting your advice and open to your influential words. As you do this, pinch your left earlobe gently with your fingers. This will anchor this influential version of you internally.

> Now jump into that picture and allow the feeling of charisma and influence to flood into your mind, body and soul. Imagine you are really there in that moment, oozing charisma and influence.

> Hear your influential words and how you speak them. See your confident body posture as you guide and influence the audience with your words and body language. Allow this vision of you to be absorbed into your very being.

> Now think of a situation where you need to influence someone. Visualise yourself in that moment speaking with authority, subtly mirroring them and using your new-found charisma from this exercise to invisibly influence them, always ethically.

> See yourself briefly pinching your left ear during that moment to trigger the feelings of charisma and influence from this exercise. Notice that when you do this you see a shift in your mindset. An almost imperceptible shift, but when it happens you become the most influential version of yourself imaginable. Understand now that you are unique. You are special. You are influential.

Repeat the above exercise as necessary to embed the feeling of being an influential leader deep into your subconscious. Any time you wish to be more charismatic or influential, simply pinch your left earlobe gently for a second and allow those feelings to flood into your very being.

DECEPTION

Conning, tricking and cheating

'Here's something to think about: How come you never see a headline like "Psychic Wins Lottery"?' – Jay Leno

16.

THE MIND READER WHO CAN'T READ MINDS

HOW THE PSYCHICS SEE YOU COMING AND HOW TO USE THEIR TECHNIQUES TO YOUR ADVANTAGE

ONE OF THE MOST POPULAR parts of my stage show 'The Dark Side' was when I brought four members of the audience up on stage and performed a comedy psychic routine inspired by famous psychics from the 1940s.

For that routine, I would randomly fire four foam darts from a Nerf gun into the audience. If a foam dart landed on you, you were invited up on stage. Of the four people on stage, one was assigned the role of a sceptic whose function was to oversee a 'test' of my psychic abilities. The other three people on stage each wrote down the first name of a deceased person they would like to contact on a single piece of paper, folding it into quarters and sealing it in an envelope. I never asked any of the three people their full name or the name of the deceased person they wanted to contact. I never touched any of the three envelopes, all of which were then handed to the sceptic, who sat on them for the rest of the routine.

After declaring to everyone that I am not actually psychic, I proceeded to give each of the three people in turn a psychic reading live on stage, while using comedy to try to lighten things up. The routine was designed to be a parody of psychics. By the time I was finished I had told each of the participants how they were related to the person they were trying to contact, what the deceased person's job or hobbies had been, how the person had died, the age of the person, their star sign and some other random information that only the audience member would have known. The only piece of information left to reveal was the deceased person's name.

When I had revealed all three names, each of the three participants would leave the stage stunned and bewildered as to how I had contacted the other side and found out so much information about the person they were thinking about. It really was the most talked-about part of the show.

In another tour, in a different psychic routine, I had a girl on stage and simply told her, 'The name Johnny comes to mind.' Not only did she completely freak out when I said the name, but her boyfriend got up from his seat in the audience and walked out of the theatre. Everybody noticed him walking out. She left the stage and ran after him.

About a week later, I got an email from that girl saying that she'd split up with her boyfriend, who had walked out because he had suspected her of having an affair with her boss, whose name was Johnny. So when I spat out the name Johnny on stage it created this whole chain reaction. The crazy thing is that, about a year later, she emailed me again thanking me. She wrote that the breakup was the best thing that ever happened to her. While she hadn't been having an affair with Johnny, that night made her realise how possessive and untrusting her boyfriend was and she was now much happier.

But here's the thing. I am not a psychic. I can't contact dead people and I don't believe anyone else can either. I do believe that people who call themselves psychic or even actually believe they are psychic can unethically influence your choices in life, and that some of them are making a lot of money out of this. Psychic practices include, among other things: tarot card reading, palm reading, numerology, faith healing, astrology, clairvoyance, evangelists and even psychic surgery.

A lot of psychics and mediums say they can contact dead people. You might say, 'Well, some people get comfort from that …' But I would say that this only prolongs the natural grieving process that people must undergo to get through the death of a loved one.

Most importantly, fake psychics are taking a lot of money from people under false pretences, to the extent that I've heard of people selling their houses in return for advice on health, love or money.

The global 'psychic services' industry is worth $2.2 billion and is unregulated, which means that anyone can say they are psychic and set up a business. A report by the American National Academy of Sciences into psychic abilities stated there is 'no scientific justification from research conducted over a period of 130 years for the existence of parapsychological phenomena'.[30] Yet one in five

Americans have consulted fortune tellers or psychics, according to a 2017 study.[31]

A lot of people think that psychics do no harm. I respectfully disagree. You only have to look into the history of psychics to see that they can actually do great harm. Psychics and evangelists have advised political leaders, kings and queens for hundreds of years. My comedy psychic routine for 'The Dark Side' was based on two of those people, Wolf Messing and Erik Jan Hanussen.

Messing was a circus performer who built a reputation in the '40s and '50s for being able to read minds, predict the future and use hypnotism and the power of suggestion to get what he wanted. His reputation grew so much that Marilyn Monroe, Mahatma Gandhi, Sigmund Freud and Albert Einstein were among those to visit his touring shows.

When Einstein and Freud met Messing to conduct some experiments, he is said to have asked Freud to make a wish and that he would make it come true. Messing then went to Einstein and pulled three hairs out of his moustache, which was, Freud admitted, what he had wished for.

When Hitler came to power, Messing predicted that 'If Hitler goes to war against the East, his death awaits him.' The prophecy saw Hitler place a 200,000-Reichsmark reward for Messing's capture – but when he was arrested in Warsaw, he convinced his captors to come into his cell with him, then walked out and locked them inside.

When Joseph Stalin heard about Messing, he sent him a private jet and flew him to the Soviet Union, where he tasked him with getting into his country house, which was under armed guard. Messing convinced the guards that he was the Commissioner General of State Security and made it into Stalin's house, where Stalin gave him a tougher task of withdrawing 100,000 roubles out of the state bank without any documentation.

Again, Messing passed the test, put the money in a briefcase and returned to the Kremlin, where he correctly predicted the impending outbreak of war and had 'visions' of Soviet tanks entering Berlin, all of which had an impact on Stalin, who was said to be afraid of him. Erik Jan Hanussen was also a mind reader and hypnotist when his performance at the Scala in Berlin propelled him to the attention of Adolf Hitler. Hanussen is known for teaching Hitler his crowd control techniques, how to stage meetings for dramatic effect and the techniques of mass psychology. Predicting the Reichstag fire, the event that gave Hitler absolute power over Germany in 1933, was his most famous feat of clairvoyance, quite possibly because he was allegedly the person who hypnotised the fire-starter. The prediction, however, led to his assassination by Hitler's men shortly after.

Whether psychics' claims are real or not is down to your own belief system. The big problem is that most people haven't studied and don't understand fake psychic techniques, so it is very easy to be deceived. Of all the 'psychics' that I have seen and visited from all over the world, I've yet to find one who I believe is truly psychic. I actually offered €10,000 to any psychic who could prove to me, under strict conditions, that they were actually psychic.

Even with ten grand on offer, nobody seemed to want to take up the offer until 'Psychic Wayne' decided to accept the challenge. But when we organised for it to happen in a radio station studio, he suddenly got cold feet and disappeared. Nobody has ever taken up the challenge since.

I am not alone in trying to find a true psychic. In 1964, magician and sceptic James Randi offered a $1,000 prize to anyone who could prove their psychic powers under strict test conditions. By 1996 the prize had grown to a whopping one million dollars, but despite thousands of people applying for it over the years, nobody passed the test, and it was eventually withdrawn in 2015.

Since 2000, the Centre for Inquiry Investigations Group (CFIIG) in America, under the leadership of Jim Underdown, has offered a large reward to anyone who can prove they have supernatural, paranormal or psychic abilities under scientific test conditions.

Again, lots of people have tried, and the group has raised the reward to a cool quarter of a million dollars, but so far nobody has even passed round one of the tests. The CFIIG also did an exposé of psychic TV shows a few years ago featuring well-known 'psychics' James Van Praagh and John Edward. 'We recorded everything in studio and compared it to what aired,' said investigator Jim Underdown. 'They were substantially different in the accuracy. They're getting rid of the wrong guesses. Once you pull back the curtain and see how it's done, it's not impressive at all.'

For my 'psychic' routine in 'The Dark Side', I utilised some of the tricks and techniques of the psychics in order to get inside others' heads – ethically and with their permission. Now, while I'm not going to give away all of my secret techniques here, I will share a few with you.

The first thing any 'believable' psychic will do is analyse you. In business or in life, when you want to get inside other people's minds, the first thing you must do to is go from being a passive listener to being an active listener. Most people are passive listeners. All you are really doing is waiting for the other person to stop talking so that you can have your turn, and most information goes in one ear and out the other. A psychic, however, is continually listening for clues, hints and tips about you that they can actually use over the course of an hour to make it look like they have given you an accurate reading.

Lots of people have told me they've had a good psychic reading. They say to me, 'Oh my God, Keith, it was so amazing. They told me about my dead dad Paul and that I had a ring from my Granny Anne. They said the names and everything! They even knew I had a clock in the shape of an apple beside my bed! There's no way they could have known that.'

Whenever this happens, I always answer them with 'So you've described thirty seconds of your sixty minutes with the psychic. Can you tell me what happened for the other fifty-nine and a half minutes?'

They will think about it for a while, but the answer is always no, because here's what happens. The psychic extracts information from the customer without their knowledge and then feeds it back to them later as if it is coming from them.

Psychics also purposely put in timeline misdirection at the end and wrap up the thoughts you unknowingly gave them into a thirty-second package that makes you believe that's what you heard them say and do. That thirty-second package at the end is the package you end up walking around with in your head.

COLD READING

One of the techniques psychics use is cold reading. Cold reading is used where the psychic has never met you before and must figure things out about you 'cold'.

Psychics are great observers. Hair, nails and hands are all give-aways, as are shoes. There are lots of farmers and mechanics in Ireland and no matter how hard you scrub, if you're a mechanic, there will be oil on your hands somewhere. If you smoke, there will be nicotine stains on your fingers. If you're married there will be a ring or, if you have taken it off for any reason, the outline of a ring on your finger. If a person's hands are soft, depending on what they look like I'd guess they are an office worker, beautician or computer worker. Jewellery and tattoos can also be giveaways.

If a very well-dressed prim and proper lady is the customer, you can almost bet that the lady's granny was similarly prim and proper. Statements like 'Even when she was close to the end, she'd never leave the house without her hair or her make-up done' will make it seem as if you are in contact with her.

On the other hand, if a woman arrives not wearing too much make-up and seems more relaxed with her attire, then the psychic could say, 'I sense that this person really cared for other people and, to the end, maybe cared for other people more than themselves. They didn't mind if they were seen with no make-up or if their hair wasn't done.'

Psychics will almost always ask why you are visiting them. People will tell them they want to talk to their dead granny or whoever, straight away. Then they forget in the excitement of later 'revelations' that they ever told them anything at all. If they don't ask who you are there to contact, they usually begin with a fishing technique, like 'Okay, I get a sense that somebody's coming through with a name beginning with M, does that make any sense to you?'

FORKING

Psychics have wildly vivid imaginations and are prepared to 'fork' a conversation at any moment. 'Forking' is the ability to change the conversation in many different ways, based on their counterpart's reaction. This is a fantastic attribute that you can use in any negotiation. For example, if a psychic says, 'I have a person coming through from the other side whose name begins with an ...' but there is no physical or verbal reaction from the client, the psychic will now 'fork the conversation' and say something like 'Maybe not an M but like an M, an N perhaps ...?'

If the client begins to smile or show a small glimpse of acknowledgement, the psychic now will spread out the prongs of the fork further by saying something like 'I think it's a man ... Nicolas ... Nick or Noel, does that make sense to you?'

Forking can be used in any situation where you want to lead the conversation. To become really good at forking or, if you like, to become forking brilliant at it, you must practise the ability to improvise in every situation. You can practise forking by doing improvisation routines with friends or family, or any other games where you must come up with a convincing story quickly off the top of your head. If you are being interviewed for a new job or promotion, have a few different answers ready with endings that will fork in your direction for the next question. Try to do it smoothly and without hesitation. The next time you are about to have a team meeting think of three different ways you can improvise and fork the conversation. Consistent practice is essential if you want to become great at it.

If a psychic's guess is wrong, then it's brushed over very quickly and moved on. It's all about moving on, swiftly forking and reframing 'misses' into hits.

'I have someone here with a name beginning with P who's passed on. Is there somebody with a name beginning with P who has passed to the other side?' If you are from Ireland, you are very likely to know somebody named Pat, Patrick, Paddy, Patsy, Patricia. Later you will not remember that the 'psychic' only got one letter correct. You will misremember and be convinced they told you about your deceased grandad Paddy.

Psychics always use the openers 'I believe …', 'I get a sense …' or 'I get a feeling …' Each of these statements is open to interpretation and they are great for creating empathy. When talking about a dead relative, a psychic will almost always put their hand on the centre of their chest and rub around the area, saying that 'I get a sense or a feeling of pain here …'

In Ireland, respiratory disease, heart attacks and cancer are the top three killers. By rubbing their hand in a circular motion that takes in the heart, the lungs, the liver, and everything else internally, the psychic can't really miss. Most of the time, though, if a loved one has died of an illness relevant to that area, the person will freak out and think they're getting a great reading.

Depending on your age, a psychic will know whether you are more likely to have a grandparent or parent who has passed away. If I know that you're thinking about your dead granny I will always say something like 'There's a smell coming through … It's like baking in the kitchen … Yeah … I'm smelling apples … like apple tart …' and the person will lose their mind. But most people's mothers or grandmothers will have baked apple tart at some stage in their lives.

THE FEEDBACK LOOP

A psychic is running a two-way operation, feeding information and covertly gaining information that they then feed back in a manner which will connect with the subject. Over the course of an hour, they will spread their bets and eventually hit on a name. At the end of the whole hour, they will tidy it all up into a gift-wrapped thirty-second mental present complete with fancy ribbon.

To feed back information to somebody, the psychic needs to figure out their primary mode of language and mode of thinking. You can learn to do the same to communicate more effectively with other people. We all think and speak predominantly in one of three different modalities, as they are known in neuro-linguistic pro-gramming. Some people are auditory, some are kinaesthetic and some are visual.

If somebody says, 'It sounds like …' or 'I hear what you're saying,' then they are an auditory thinker, and the psychic will use auditory language to gain rapport with them. If somebody uses phrases like 'It feels like …' or use touch-based language consistently, then the psychic knows they are kinaesthetic. If somebody uses language like 'I can see that,' 'I can picture that,' they are thinking in a visual manner, and the psychic will try to construct pictures inside their head in order to reach their subconscious. Psychics use this all the time to gain rapport and feed back information to the subject. Now you can too.

HOT READING

Hot reading is where the psychic would have done research on the person they are about to meet and would have 'hot' information on that person.

This can be done in a variety of ways, whether that's through social media or physically, by excusing themselves to go to the toilet and while doing so rummaging through the pockets of a coat left hanging in the hallway or out of sight. A box of cigarettes, a tissue, a receipt or a piece of paper in a coat pocket can give a psychic enough information to give you a pretty 'accurate' reading.

Hot reading can also be done by using an accomplice posing as a customer, who asks you questions while seemingly waiting their turn before feeding the answers back to the psychic.

Hot readers will know you have a dog because they saw it on Facebook, they will have read that tweet where you said you were 'done with men', they will have seen that Instagram post of your kids playing in the park or eating ice cream, or the profile picture of your dead loved one. Nowadays, there are even online services that facilitate people who want information, all the way from your name and address or marital status right through to your medical history.

EMPATHY

Well-versed psychics are fantastic at creating empathy. They connect with people based on shared feelings, or pretend feelings on their part. Empathy is now recognised as an essential skill for good leadership. To create a sense of empathy with someone, that person needs to feel as if you're connecting to them with compassion and that you understand where they are coming from emotionally.

Highly empathetic psychics have the ability to step inside the shoes and minds of their customers. They immediately try to comprehend why the other person is talking to them, why they need the advice of the psychic and what advice they want to hear most. We can all use empathy to connect better with people we meet every day.

A friend of mine once worked as a doorman in a large pub. Part of his job was to go around telling everyone when it was time to go home so that the pub could be closed. Every Saturday night for about ten years a customer we'll call Derek sat at the bar and was always last one out of the pub. In all those ten years Derek was jovial and chatty, even when it came to being told to leave. One night, however, as my friend was ushering people out of the pub, Derek became argumentative and said he was staying where he was. My friend passed it off and went about his business, but long after everyone else had gone Derek was still at the bar despite being asked to leave on numerous occasions by other staff. He became aggressive, even throwing a bar stool at one of the other doormen before my friend calmly talked him down and walked him to the door.

The following Saturday, Derek returned to his usual spot at the bar, but before he did, he apologised to my friend for his erratic behaviour the previous week. It turned out that his brother had died that morning and he had taken his frustration and anger out on the bar staff that night. The moral of my friend's story is that you never know what is going on in another person's life and should always try to treat everyone with respect and empathy.

Instead of judging people all day long (which is what a lot of people unfortunately do), make a habit of spending the first sixty seconds in someone's company trying to figure out how that person is feeling in that exact moment. This can have a profound effect on your interactions with people, and they will open up more easily to you, just like people do with psychics, who are naturally brilliant at this.

The next time somebody is late for a meeting or interview, think about how anxious or frustrated they might feel rather than getting frustrated at them. If somebody gives you an excuse you believe to be a deception, ask yourself, without judging, what they must be feeling in that moment and why they might be doing it. If someone aggressively knocks your opinion, take a moment to wonder why they are behaving that way. If somebody is yawning or seems bored, ask yourself if it could be because of a young baby at home, an early start to get to work or lack of sleep.

In the world of the psychic, there are some people who are known as shuteyes. A shuteye is someone who actually fully believes they are psychic but are not psychic. They are delusional, and are deluding other people too. Thankfully, shuteyes are rare, but while they're quite innocent in their belief systems they can have very damaging effects on people.

About three years ago I was in the White Horse pub in Ballincollig for a charity fundraiser. Afterwards, I was having a few drinks with my friends when a woman approached me. She eyed me up for a minute before stating, 'I just want you to know, Keith, that you don't look well and you're going to have a medical emergency in the next three days. Look after yourself.' Not sure if she was joking or not, I laughed. 'I'm a psychic, Keith,' she said very seriously. 'I know these things!' She then turned on her heel and walked off. Now, that's a horrible thing to say to somebody. For a minute I began to wonder, 'Jesus, do I not look well?' I then started to get panicky feelings in my chest for a minute before I copped on and told myself, 'Jesus, Keith, you know all the rubbish they go on about. Wipe it out and get rid of it!'

Just as quickly as it entered my head, it was gone, but the next day, I thought about how detrimental those few words could have been to someone who wasn't in such a strong frame of mind as I was at the time. I thought it was a disgusting thing to do to somebody.

This, for some reason, has happened to me a couple of times – self-proclaimed psychics have approached me after shows and said more or less the same thing: 'You don't look well, and I sense there's a tragic accident coming your way in the next few weeks.' While nothing has ever happened to me at all afterwards, imagine if something randomly did happen in the next few days! Then I might have thought this woman was a real psychic and got sucked into a world of spending money to 'find out' what was going to happen next.

Words can have a profound effect on another human being. Think wisely about the words you use, online or in the real world. An online version of this happening to you is a message on social media or even a text or WhatsApp message telling you that 'if you don't pass this message on to five others you will have bad luck for the next week' or even worse. Other messages include comments like 'Only real friends will repost this message' or 'If you stand for such and such you will repost this message.' Teens and young people can be especially susceptible to these messages.

Maybe the next message you're asked to pass on is something controversial, or something that could incite violence or hatred, and you may have already fallen into the pattern of passing these things on out of superstition or fear. Ignore these messages.

Phones are the new psychics. Your social media feed is the new psychic. Have you ever talked to somebody about a certain product or looked up a certain product only to find it suddenly appears on your social media feed and everywhere else you go online? Much like a psychic, your phone relays information back to you that you've given to it. All of the follow-me ads you are being targeted with online are the end result of information you have given your phone or computer, through your search history, through speaking, through your geographical location. To counteract this, you can change your privacy settings, but most people don't do this.

People simply don't know that your smartphone's tracking can tell not only where you've been but lots of other information too. If you go to the settings on your iPhone, for example, then go to the Privacy section, then click on Location Services, scroll to the bottom, and click on System Services and then go to Significant Locations, you will find where you've been, how long you spent there and even how you got there!

You can do the same by launching Google Maps on Android. Tap the 'more' button (three horizontal lines) on the top left corner. Tap your timeline. Tap the calendar icon to view a particular day. Swipe left or right to switch months. Tap a date to view your location history including the routes travelled and the duration of overall journeys.

Nowadays, even our cars are psychic. Have you ever sat into your car only for the sat nav to tell you it's twenty-two minutes to home or work? How does your car know where home or work is? Like a visit to the psychics, you've already told it without knowing you did, and it's just feeding back the information.

Another way to make you think you've got a really good reading is through Barnum statements.

For *The Keith Barry Experience* on RTÉ, I did a piece called the 'red envelope experiment' where I would walk up to a complete stranger and offer them a red envelope containing a letter.

'This red envelope is for you,' I would tell them before handing them the envelope. 'It couldn't possibly be for anyone else. It's for you and only you. But there are a couple of rules. If I give you this red envelope you have to read it silently to yourself and you can never tell anyone what it contains.'

When they agreed to accept the envelope in front of the cameras I would say, 'If this letter is for you, I just want you to let us know right now.'

Every single time, the person would slowly read the letter and have a really emotional reaction, to the extent that we decided not to air the full experiment. We showed one or two snippets but, out of respect for the people involved, we didn't show a full recording because the experiment had too powerful an effect on them. They were having huge emotional reactions to what was inside the envelope, even though I had told them I wasn't psychic.

What was in the envelope was what's commonly known as a Barnum statement, named after the famous circus owner P.T. Barnum, who is alleged to have said, 'There's a sucker born every minute.'

Also known as the Forer effect, this technique was first used in 1948 by psychologist Bertram Forer on his psychology students. Forer gave each student notes based on their individual personalities and asked them to rate their accuracy out of five. It was only after the students had revealed their ratings, which garnered an average of 4.3 out of five for accuracy, that Forer revealed he had given them all the same notes:

> You have a tendency to be critical of yourself. You have a great deal of unused capacity which you have not turned to your advantage. While you have some personality weaknesses, you are generally able to compensate for them. Your sexual adjustment has presented problems for you. Disciplined and self-controlled outside, you tend to be worrisome and insecure inside. At times you have serious doubts as to whether you have made the right decision or done the right thing. You prefer a certain amount of change and variety and become dissatisfied when hemmed in by restrictions and limitations.

You pride yourself as an independent thinker and do not accept others' statements without satisfactory proof. You have found it unwise to be too frank in revealing yourself to others. At times you are extroverted, affable, sociable, while at other times you are introverted, wary, reserved. Some of your aspirations tend to be pretty unrealistic. Security is one of your major goals in life.

If you read that note and thought, 'Actually, these statements relate to me too!', there is a good reason for this. The Forer effect works because, like most psychic readings, the statements are vague, and you can read your own meaning into them. People look for meaning everywhere. The lines apply to almost anyone, so the statement becomes personal to you. It works best when you're hearing things about yourself that are positive or at least understandable and sympathetic. An updated variation of those lines might be 'While you are sometimes seen as the life and soul of the party, very often you feel shy and reserved. You know that you spend far too much time on technology and need to spend more time outdoors. As a result of the recent pandemic, you feel uneasy sometimes in small spaces with strange people. I sense that you recently received an email or social media message that played on your mind for a few days ...'

Forer's study was updated in 2011 so that the statements applied to organisations rather than individuals and it had the same results. Forer put the results of his original study down to his students being gullible and even named the study 'The fallacy of personal validation. A classroom demonstration of gullibility.'[32] The word 'gullible', by the way, is the only word in the English language that rhymes with 'orange'. Say it slowly and see what happens!

I can't believe you just did that! Anyway, moving swiftly on … Michael Birnbaum, professor of psychology at California State University, summed up the world of psychics in 2017 when he wrote, 'The moral of the Barnum Demonstration is that self-validation is no validation. Do not be fooled by a psychic, quack psychotherapist, or a phony faith healer who uses this trick on you! Be sceptical and ask for proof. Keep your money in your wallet, your wallet in your pocket, and your hand on your wallet.'

17.

IT'S ALL IN THE LIES

HOW TO LOOK FOR SIGNS OF DECEPTION

IN FEBRUARY 2020, Hollywood superstar Tom Cruise joined the social media app TikTok. In his first post, he knelt down and spoke to the camera. 'You guys cool if I play some sports?' he asked before hitting a golf ball and mysteriously adding, 'If you like what you're seeing, just wait till you see what's coming next!'

Within hours, his TikTok video had gone viral and had been seen all over the world, but there was one slight problem. Tom Cruise hadn't joined TikTok, hadn't said those words, hadn't hit that golf ball or even known anything about it. The video was made by special effects wizard Chris Ume and Tom Cruise impersonator Miles Fisher and instantly became the best of what are now known as 'deepfake' videos.

Deepfake videos use footage of a real person combined with a digitally replaced face and sometimes a digitally altered voice. In the Tom Cruise deepfakes, Fisher had Cruise's face digitally transplanted onto his and mimicked the actor's voice well enough to convince most people that it was in fact Tom Cruise.

Despite the makers openly announcing the fact that the clips were digitally made and false, the results were so realistic that people still believed it was Tom Cruise trying to fool people. Therein lies the problem. No matter what evidence there is to the contrary, often, people simply believe what they want to believe.

In 1987, American televangelist Peter Popoff was earning almost $4 million a year – until he declared bankruptcy in September of that year, after magician and sceptic James Randi aired video footage on the *Tonight Show* of Popoff's wife feeding him information about his audience through an earpiece.

Despite several more warnings of fraud and later investigations by several media outlets and broadcasting regulators, people still believed Popoff. By 2005 his 'ministry' was taking in over $23 million. Since then, Popoff has changed his business to a tax-exempt religious organisation, so his financial details are no longer available, but today you can buy such everyday necessities as 'miracle spring water' and 'faith healing handkerchiefs' on his website, or you can simply donate. If you do so, beware of giving a small amount. According to the site, 'Whoever sows sparingly will also reap sparingly.'

Even when I declare in front of a live audience that I am in no way psychic, as soon as I do some mind-boggling mind-reading, some people will convince themselves I am a real psychic. The more I announce that I am not, the more they believe I actually am!

A study conducted by University of Massachusetts psychologist Robert S. Feldman in June 2002 found that, on average, 60 per cent of people told two to three lies during a ten-minute conversation.[33] In fact, according to lie-spotter Pamela Meyer, you will be lied to between ten and two hundred times every day.

The advancement of technology means that the way people watch their news is going to become one of the biggest problems in the world over the next few years. While you may have sat down to get the six o'clock or nine o'clock news on TV from the national broadcaster, younger people don't do that anymore. Why sit through a half–hour programme when you can get a snapshot of it in ten seconds by just reading a headline or a post on social media?

Social media outlets have already been blamed for the election of Donald Trump, the advent of Brexit and other global happenings. With deepfake videos now getting harder and harder for even the experts to identify, what chance do the rest of us have?

People who never watch the national news networks will soon see 'politicians' or 'celebrities' giving speeches on the internet and will have no way of knowing whether it is actually that person giving that speech. Indeed, a lot of people won't care whether they are real or artificial intelligence-based deepfakes.

While he may not have been the first person to use the phrase, Donald Trump will be forever associated with the words 'fake news'. While Trump called everything that didn't serve his side of the story fake news, there is a lot of fake news out there. We are being lied to by people in power all the time, from salespeople to politicians.

It may be increasingly tough to spot digital fakery, but there are still some ways to know you are being lied to. There's no guarantee but these are important tools and techniques that can give you some advantage when trying to tell if somebody is being sincere.

To accurately determine if someone is lying or concealing information, we need to determine their baseline. This is where most human lie detectors go wrong – this is a must!

We then look for deviation from the baseline through studying facial expression, body language and vocal patterns.

One deviation is not enough. We must see three or more to determine if someone is being dishonest. Only once we notice a cluster of leakages can we begin to assume that someone may be lying to us. If you are in any doubt, ALWAYS assume a person is telling the truth.

OBSERVE THE BASELINE

Like a psychic, the first thing you need to do is observe somebody for a while. Look at how quickly or slowly they talk, how slowly or quickly they breathe. How do they behave? Do they gesture big or small? Do they sit with their legs or arms crossed or uncrossed? Do they stay still or shift in their chair or stance? Do they gesture a lot? Are their shoulders moving? What descriptive language do they use? What is the pitch and tone of their voice like? Is there any redness in their skin? Do they look hot or cold? What size are their pupils? What is their blink rate? Are they looking directly at you or constantly shifting their gaze?

Observe as much as you can to gain a baseline of how that person behaves when they are acting in a truthful manner. While gaining the baseline ask three questions you know they will answer truthfully. You can verify the answers by using simple questions such as 'The traffic was crazy today, wasn't it?' or 'The weather is amazing, isn't it?' Both of you know whether the weather is good or bad, if the traffic is heavy or light, so you begin to get a feel for how the person reacts when telling the truth.

This baselining generally happens during the first five minutes of a conversation, during general chit-chat when your counterpart has no reason to deceive you.

When you have established that baseline, then you can look for deviations from it. A deviation is basically where the person does something that makes you question what they are saying. Now, over the course of a longer conversation you are going to be looking for deviations from the baseline that set off a bell in your head. I think of it like a carnival bell: 'Ding-ding-ding! Something's up here, something is weird about this picture.'

Think of yourself as an old Polaroid camera. When you hear the bell going off in your head, take a mental snapshot of that moment. What did that picture tell you? For example, if somebody hasn't touched their face at all during the conversation and they suddenly touch their face when asked a tricky question, then 'Ding-ding-ding, jackpot, snapshot!'

MICROEXPRESSIONS

Microexpressions are another thing to look out for. From my experience the top ones to look for when attempting to detect deception, the ones I find most accurate, are asymmetric lip movement or an involuntary one-sided shoulder shrug. When this happens it's like a subconscious tic, hence it doesn't feel unnatural. Asymmetrical lip movement can be one side of the lips going up or one side going down. An asymmetrical lip movement or a one-sided shoulder shrug is easy to spot in a photograph, but the problem in real life is that these happen in a millisecond so they can be very hard to spot. That's where the Polaroid camera idea comes in handy!

When Donald Trump was asked during the 2020 presidential debate if he was willing to condemn white supremacists he answered, 'Sure I'm willing to do that …' but his left shoulder shrug at that moment hinted otherwise. He didn't actually condemn them until two days later.

These indicators may not signal the moment a person is telling lies, but they do reveal that their body is under pressure. The fight-or-flight system has kicked in, adrenaline has kicked in, which means that something they have said has, for some reason, made them uncomfortable – which suggests to me that they may be about to tell a lie or are thinking of a lie. Practise looking out for these indicators by watching TV interviews that you can slow down or rewind. An asymmetrical lip movement is a subconscious movement. Even if you are aware that you don't want to do it, you are powerless to stop yourself doing it.

It's actually really hard to do voluntarily in the course of a normal conversation. A one-sided shoulder shrug is the same. Try saying something truthful and doing a one-sided shoulder shrug as you are speaking. It feels unnatural.

INCONGRUENT HEAD MOVEMENT

In 1971, psychology professor Albert Mehrabian found that people give away the emotional intent behind their words from mostly non-verbal sources. When the two are in conflict, we should always believe the non-verbal.

The non-verbal truth spotter I find easiest to see is an incongruent head movement. An incongruent head movement is moving your head in disagreement with what your mouth is saying, nodding when you are saying no or shaking your head when you are saying yes.

Again, it feels weird to do consciously. Try it now. Say, 'I am [your name here]' out loud but shake your head in disagreement when you're doing it. Or, vice versa, say something out loud that you know is a lie and nod your head. It feels unnatural, right? But to somebody doing it in real life, it's a subconscious movement; their body knows the truth and is moving their head that way without them even noticing. There are plenty of examples of videos online where the movements are so blatant it's almost comical. Once you start to notice these movements, you will see them on people from politicians to sports stars to celebrities.

For example, if a politician tells you, 'Yes, things are going to get better,' or 'Yes, if I am elected I will reduce the price of electricity,' but they are shaking their head as they are saying these things, then you can take it that things are not going to get better and the price of electricity is not going to be reduced.

In an interview with CNN's Larry King, prior to being stripped of his seven Tour de France wins for doping, cyclist Lance Armstrong states, 'I've said it for longer than seven years. I have never doped,' which seems like a pretty clear-cut statement. The problem is that on the words 'I have never doped' Armstrong clearly nods his head twice. You can see the video on YouTube for yourself. When he says he never doped, his head nod is not agreeing with what he is saying.

When former US President Richard Nixon made his infamous 'I am not a crook' speech during investigations into the Watergate scandal, he also clearly nodded his head in disagreement when he said he wasn't a crook. That statement was later found to be false, and Nixon became the first ever US president to resign.

Watch the politicians of today on TV. See if you can spot these incongruent head movements. When you see these, you need to take a mental snapshot there and then and store it to add to other possible indications of deceit.

BODY LANGUAGE

Researchers at the University of Granada used thermographic cameras to discover that when a person lies or has an anxiety attack, they experience an increase in the temperature around the nose and inner corner of the eye.[34] When being deceptive, chemicals called catecholamines are released in your body. These chemicals cause the tissues inside the nose to swell.

During Bill Clinton's 1998 testimony on his affair with Monica Lewinsky, for example, he did not touch his nose at all when he answered truthfully. When he lied, he consistently touched his nose. In fact, he did it twenty-six times while lying! Now, some people naturally touch their face more than others, while colds and sniffles can cause more nose rubbing than normal. If someone normally touches their face a lot, then I would ignore them touching their face when they are being asked a question. However, if they didn't touch their face during baselining and they suddenly touch their face, their lips, their ear, I would be wary. I also look for when someone attempts to cool themself down by adjusting their collar or taking a sip of water.

A pacifying gesture is another way of telling when somebody is under stress of some sort when they are being asked a question. In moments of stress, your brain sends a message to your body to soothe itself and, in an effort to stimulate your nerve endings and release calming endorphins, you will often use pacifying gestures like playing with your hair, twirling an earring, touching your face, touching the back of your neck, holding or rubbing your upper arms in a self-hug or playing with an object.

Smaller pacifying gestures may go unnoticed, things like rubbing your thumbs together or rubbing your thighs under the table. The hardest pacifying gesture to spot is probably somebody rolling their tongue around inside their mouth, when their mouth dries up.

If somebody's blink rate suddenly increases, or even stops for long periods, at a particular question or moment during your conversation, this may also be an indication they are stressing out or lying.

Our normal resting blink rate is 12–15 blinks per minute. Again, I have found this varies from person to person, so you need to observe your counterpart's blink rate during your baselining.

Another thing I look for is reddening of the skin. When women are being deceptive, I see this reddening mainly on the chest, while with men I observe it on the neck.

In moments of stress, our brain tells us to go into fight-or-flight mode. If you are in flight mode and want to run away, your brain will send extra energy to your limbs to help you run away. If the person can't run away, look out for nervous fidgeting, shaking legs, arm movements or sudden gestures.

An increased heart rate or rush of adrenaline may see the person moving their hands, legs or feet.

For my TV show *Deception with Keith Barry*, I performed lots of lie detection experiments on various members of the Garden Grove Police Department. While there, one of the things I noticed was that their interrogation room wasn't set up correctly. Instead of making the person they were questioning feel hemmed in so that they could see these signs of fight-or-flight, they had the person being questioned sitting beside the door.

When I got them to change the furniture around so that the person being interviewed had a desk and a police officer between them and the door, they found that these gestures were much more prolific, and their interviews got better results.

LISTEN TO THEIR VOICE

When a question which requires a simple yes or no answer results in the subject rambling on without expressly answering yes or no, this is known as smoke screening. This is most often used by politicians, who rarely answer a question with a simple yes or no.

Some people attempt to use their voices to try to conceal lies. When a person gets stressed or aroused, positively or negatively, the limbic system fires up, resulting in the vagus nerve being stimulated, and in turn their vocal cords get stressed.

To spot these deviations from the norm, you will have to look out for changes in rhythm, speed, volume and pitch. Sighs, swallows, or any noticeable mumbling or stumbling over words may be signs of distress.

Any noticeable changes in tempo of a person's vocal pattern should also set off your internal carnival bell, and you should take a mental snapshot of this moment and what was being discussed. Watch for deviation from the baseline by someone either slowing down or speeding up during a conversation.

Sounds such as 'tut', 'um', 'mmm', 'eh', 'ahh', 'errrr' are worth noting. If they stammer or stumble during a particular sentence it is usually something they are stressing over.

If a person begins speaking in a higher-pitched voice than during their baseline analysis, this is a signal that they are trying to show their innocence with the 'poor me' voice. We've all heard the high-pitched voice of a child saying, 'It wasn't me. I didn't do it.'

A proficient liar will often get excited by the lie they are trying to tell and raise their voice. In doing this, they are also trying to 'sell the lie' by increasing their volume to display their confidence in their version of the truth.

When someone is lying, they often distance themself from the lie by using fewer personal pronouns when they speak. For example, instead of saying, 'I wasn't there when that happened,' someone might say, 'There is no way it could have happened like that.' Instead of saying, 'I didn't take the sweets,' a child caught sneaking sweets might say, 'The sweets are still there.'

Of course, even with all these tips and hints, spotting lies is not an easy task. Some people are very good at hiding their inner emotions and, indeed, the truth, as I found out to my cost in one of my stage shows.

As part of my 'Brain Hacker' show, I brought an audience member up on stage each night and asked them to conceal a €50 note in one of their hands behind their back. When they had done so, I then asked them to hold their closed hands outstretched in front of them so that I could guess which hand the note was in. I was so confident in my lie detection skills that I offered them the €50 if I guessed the wrong hand.

I have performed this routine hundreds of times around the country, and even did it for a whopping €10,000 with five members of the audience on the *Late Late Show* one night in 2018, and had never lost – until one night I had a guy on stage who was a very, very good liar.

I used the exact same techniques I had used on everybody else over the years. After he beat me and won my €50, I offered him a double or nothing chance to beat me again, which he duly did. This continued until, at the end of the routine, I found myself down €400. The point here is that even a skilled human lie-detector can be wrong at times!

While this chapter may not make you an expert lie-detector, if you remember to look out for all of the things I have listed and practise on your friends, or by watching videos of proven liars, you will begin to have an instinct for when somebody is telling you the truth and when they are not.

Among other things, I am a deception artist. I use tricks, illusions and misdirection all of the time, but I only deceive people with their permission, either when they're on stage, or when I'm in front of an audience that have come to be entertained. You will soon notice, however, when you start really looking, that there are a lot of people who don't ask your permission to lie to you.

Try lie-spotting for the next few days. Watch some speeches on TV and see if you can figure out who is lying. Can you spot the deviations in news interviews or even chat shows? Have fun with it and write down your results. Practise the hidden note trick on your friends. Just don't gamble anything on it.

EVERYDAY BRAIN HACKS FOR READING MINDS

> Be observant. Notice hands, hair, nails, wedding rings, anything that may give you an advantage in your conversation.
> Lead the conversation in your direction. Quickly pass over mistakes and be prepared to fork if necessary.
> Use social media, Google or other ways to research the person you are meeting.

> Have patience. You never know what is going on in the other person's life. See the moment through their eyes.

> Use everyday small talk to ask questions you know the answer to in order to get a baseline of how the person ordinarily behaves.

> Watch for asymmetrical lip movements, one-sided shoulder shrugs and other microexpressions at awkward moments.

> If somebody is saying yes, watch to see if their head is really shaking no, and vice versa.

> Watch out for leg movements, collar tugs, nose touching, self-hugs and other pacifying gestures.

> Listen for changes in tempo or pitch and even long pauses when asked an awkward question.

——————— DECEPTION TEST ———————

Give a coin or a small object to your subject and ask them to hide it in one of their hands while your back is turned. When they have done that, ask them to close both fists and hold both hands out in front of them.

Begin with some easy baseline questions and watch their body language when they answer. Next, tell them that they must answer 'yes' to whatever questions you ask them and that you will try to guess which hand the object is in. After a few of these questions, you can ask, 'Is it in your left hand?' or 'Is it in your right hand?' Remember, they must say yes to both questions. Keep asking questions and try to read their body language to predict the correct hand.

This will take a lot of practice but over time, you will get better at it. If you don't, there is an easier solution later in this book!

A MAGICAL

MIND

How to improve your memory and spread magic
everywhere

*'Those who don't believe in magic will never
find it.' – Roald Dahl*

18.

DON'T FORGET TO REMEMBER

TIPS AND TRICKS TO IMPROVE YOUR RECALL

WHERE WERE YOU and what did you do at 8 pm on Monday five weeks ago? Have a think about it for a minute or two.

Unless you do the same thing at 8 pm on Monday every week, or Monday five weeks ago was a special occasion, it's very unlikely you will be able to answer that question. Now ask yourself one or more of the following questions, relevant to your age and whether you were around at the time.

> Where were you on September 29 1979, when Pope John Paul II came to Ireland?

> Where were you on June 25 1990, when David O'Leary scored

a penalty against Romania to put the Republic of Ireland into the quarter finals of the World Cup in Italy?

> Where were you on September 11 2001, when the Twin Towers came crashing down after a terrorist attack?

> Where were you on January 20 2021, when Joe Biden was named President of the United States of America?

> Where were you on the night you got your Leaving Certificate results? (Don't worry, I'm not going to tell your parents!)

If you are old enough, you will probably be able to remember all of these. If not, you will be able to remember the ones that relate to you. I can remember walking down a street in Dublin on September 11 2001, when one of my friends phoned me to tell me about the Twin Towers. I walked into Sinnott's Bar and stood there with my mouth agape, watching it unfold live on television. I was so shocked by what was unfolding on the screen that I bought myself a pint of Guinness even though it was barely lunchtime. I also remember what I was doing on the night of my Leaving Certificate results but, as my own parents might be reading this, I'm not telling you.

Memory was a valued tool not so long ago, but the emergence and technological progress of computers and smartphones has changed the way we remember. If we want to remember a recipe, an email address, or the measurements or price of something, we simply take a photo on our device and it's there when we need it again. Instant recall. But technology has its drawbacks. Where we once would have known somebody's phone number off by heart, we now just look at our contacts list and press the call button. Do you know your kids' or parents' phone numbers off by heart? The chances are you don't, because there is no need to anymore unless, of course, your phone battery dies, and you have to use somebody else's.

In 2015, psychological scientists Pam Mueller and Daniel Oppenheimer had two groups of college students listen to the same five TED talks. One group were allowed use laptops to take notes, the other group only pen and paper.

Afterwards, both groups were tested on facts from the talks and on their understanding of the talks. The students using laptops were able to take more notes, but as they tended to type everything word for word, this 'mindless transcription' seemed to cancel out the benefits of being able to take more notes and diminished their learning.

While each group memorised about the same number of facts from the lectures, the laptop users did much worse when tested on ideas based on information contained in the lectures.

Those who took fewer notes, but took them in longhand and processed the information so that they could more easily understand it, did significantly better than the quickest 'mindless' typists.[35]

PAY ATTENTION

How often have you done something only to realise later you can't actually remember doing it? Maybe you were lying in bed when you wondered if you'd locked the front door or put on the house alarm? Maybe you turned off the iron but couldn't remember doing it? How come you can remember something as far back as 2001, or even further, but you can't remember where you left your keys half an hour ago? Seriously, where did you leave those keys?

The reason we can remember big events in our lives is that we were actually paying attention at the time. Attention is the main ingredient necessary to create a memory. If you want to remember somebody's name, a shopping list, where you left your keys or even why you just walked into your bedroom again for no apparent reason, you must pay attention in the first place.

Something shocking like the Twin Towers attack, or something extremely happy like a wedding or birth, concentrates your attention on that moment and therefore it's much easier to remember it long after it has happened.

The main reason you can't remember something you did is that, instead of concentrating on the task at hand, you found yourself engrossed in something else instead. Maybe you were paying attention to something that was going on in *Emmerdale* when you put down those keys? Maybe somebody asked you a question or sent you a text message while you were locking the front door and therefore you didn't create the memory of locking that door in the first place? If so, you will be glad to know that this is all perfectly normal, and I have a few hacks to help improve your memory.

MNEMONICS

Mnemonics have been around since the days of Plato and Aristotle and are used to help remember things by turning them into a song, a rhyme, an image, an acronym, a sentence, a word or a phrase.

If somebody asked you how many days there are in July, for instance, you may recall the mnemonic you learned in school: 'Thirty days has September, April, June and November; All the rest have thirty-one, except February alone, with twenty-eight days clear and twenty-nine in each leap year.'

Your English teacher may have taught you 'I before E, except after C,' to remember how to spell tricky words like 'receipt' or 'believe'. If you are a sportsperson, you may know how to treat a sprain by using the mnemonic RICE; Rest, Ice, Compression, Elevation.

Here's how to remember the value of pi in mathematics, which is 3.1415927. You can remember this with one simple sentence: 'Ted, I have a large container of rashers!' If you count the number of letters in each word of that sentence, you will see they make up the value of pi. If you picture Father Dougal walking down the road on Craggy Island holding a large container of rashers, when Father Ted pulls up in a car beside him and asks him what he's got, you will help that mnemonic stick even better.

A friend of mine told me they learned the phrase 'Steven Gerrard Robbed My Lollipop' to remember the counties in Connacht – Sligo, Galway, Roscommon, Mayo, Leitrim. They also learned the words Fat Dad for the counties in Northern Ireland – Fermanagh, Antrim, Tyrone, Derry, Armagh, Down.

The next time you need to remember something, see if you can turn it into an easy-to-remember sentence, song, acronym or word.

REPEAT NAMES

The main reason I got such good results all the way through college wasn't because I was the smartest student in class. It was because I trained my brain to memorise vast amounts of information. When I first moved to Galway, however, I was more interested in meeting new people and making new friends than my college work. That's where I began to develop my technique that will help you to remember names and faces.

When meeting somebody new, the first thing you need to do is hear the person's name properly. Now, you might think, 'Well, obviously I hear the name.' But do you? The main reason you forget another person's name is that you weren't actively listening to it in the first place. Technically you haven't actually forgotten the name, you just haven't heard it in the first place.

When you meet somebody for the first time, you have to be genuinely interested in them and use that first meeting to remember their name. When I meet somebody new, I like to have a sort of script in my head that goes, 'Hi, I'm Keith, what's your name?'

If they answer that their name is Jack, I will respond with 'Jack! Nice to meet you, Jack. I met somebody named Jack a couple of weeks ago, but they spelled it ... weirdly enough, J.A.C. How do you spell your name?'

'J.A.C.K.'

By using this technique, within a couple of seconds of normal conversation, I have not only said the person's name three times but have asked them to spell it too, so I am much less likely to forget it.

Once you have the name of the person, you can help yourself remember it better by turning that name into a picture. So, if the name was Jack, I would picture the person with a jackhammer or a car jack on top of their head. You can do this for any name. If somebody told me their name was Keith, I would use the first part of Keith, the Kei sound, to remind me of a giant key, one that opens a lock on their mouth by going through their teeth, the eith sound of the name. I see a key going through teeth ... Keith. Sinéad could be somebody with a plaster covering a deep cut on their shin – shin aid, if you will.

For Eithne you could see a volcano, Mount Etna.

Rory could be a lion. A lion who roars – a 'Rory' lion.

For Pat, I would visualise myself patting the person on the head.

This technique of repeating a person's name, spelling it out and then picturing an object to go with it is a great way to remember names. It might take a few minutes at first, but soon you will get the hang of it and every name will become easy. If you like to go one step further, have a deck of cards and a marker at hand for a great memory recall trick.

A MAGICAL SHORTCUT TO REMEMBERING A NAME

A recording of me guiding you through this technique can be accessed on my website www.keithbarry.com/brainhacks.

Have a spectator examine and shuffle the deck of cards. Have them select any card that they think suits their personality. Have fun here explaining how different cards represent different personalities – people who choose diamonds are more motivated by money, those who pick spades are very career driven, those who pick hearts are actually quite devious, and people who pick clubs are more outdoors people than indoors.

Once they select a card have them print their name on it. Remember to ask them the exact spelling of their name and also repeat their name multiple times during this process. 'Print your name, "Jill Byrne", across the card, please … Is it Jill with a J, as I met a Gill recently whose name began with a G?' The idea is to embed their name naturally in your mind during this trick.

Once the card is signed, explain, 'In a moment I will place the deck behind my back and attempt to find your card.' As you explain, you demonstrate what you will do and place the deck behind your back. When you do this, secretly turn the whole deck over, so all the cards are now facing up. Now flip the top card over to face down.

As you bring your hands out front again, everything will look the same, but in essence you have easily and secretly turned the whole deck over bar the top card. Now, without fanning the deck out, have the spectator place their card anywhere they like, face down, back into the deck as you hold the deck tight. Now place the deck behind your back again and state that you will find their card.

Again, this is a wonderful time to repeat their name. 'Would you be amazed if I found your card, with your signature, "Jill Byrne", behind my back? Let's use some magical words to try and find it. What could be more magical than your name? Jill Byrne, Jill Byrne, Jill Byrne.' As you say this, with the deck behind your back, flip the top card face up and turn the whole deck face down again. Their card will now be the only card reversed in the deck!

Bring the deck forward and spread it to show their card is indeed the only card face up! Take the card out, hand it to them as a souvenir and ask them to pose for a quick photo with the card.

By the end of the card trick you should have definitely remembered their name, but how cool would it be a year later to bump into the same person and not only know their name but also tell them what card they had picked? Well, it's easier than you think.

At home with the photo you need to create an imagined scene with the card and the person's face. For example, if their name was Jill Byrne and they picked the two of hearts I would imagine Jill tumbling down a giant hill (from the Jack and Jill rhyme) and Jill's face on fire (Byrne – burning). They are also getting shot through the heart with two arrows shot from my imaginary bow, with blood squirting everywhere. The crazier, more outlandish, more nutty the images are, the easier they will be to recall months or years later.

Developing crazy, outlandish images to remember things was how I came up with my body warehouse system below. In my early years, I used the 'Mind Palace' memory system (as seen in the TV series *Sherlock*) and other methods, but I still struggled with my memory.

THE BODY WAREHOUSE

I discovered that the reason we forget things is largely based on how those very things were stored to begin with. Luckily for us, unlike a computer, our brain has an unlimited storage facility. To remember information, both short-term and long-term, we must learn how to encode memories properly and how to retrieve that same information hours, days, weeks or even years later.

To do this, I developed my own memory system, which has served me well ever since. I now no longer need to write lists or make notes, as I can remember huge amounts of information relatively quickly with this system. You can use this to remember shopping lists, speeches, passwords, PINs and other information.

As we are all familiar with our own bodies and our bodies are with us 24/7, I thought that an amazing way to memorise objects and lists would be to use my body as a warehouse of sorts, to store information. I found that creating crazy, funny images of these body parts is the best way to remember.

Here is how my body warehouse works. First, you convert a part of your body into an easy-to-remember, zany, colourful image. For example, your hair is made of spaghetti. This spaghetti can move all over your head and grow and stretch to grab things.

You then give outlandish images to the other parts of your body, working your way down to your eyes, nose, mouth, ears, shoulders, elbows, hands, knees and feet. Below is an example of how the body warehouse works. In this example, you start at the top of your body and work your way down. Take a few moments to visualise the following body parts and what each one represents. Be sure to really visualise each element as clearly as possible.

> Hair – Your hair is made of spaghetti. This spaghetti can move all over your head and grow and stretch to grab things.

> Eyes – Your eyes have powerful red laser beams that can burn, cut and melt through anything. The lasers are no ordinary lasers but are super wide. When they shoot out from your eyes, they are almost one inch in diameter.

> Nose – Your nose is green like an ugly dragon and giant green flames shoot from your nose whenever you blow it.

> Mouth – Your mouth is now a bright yellow duck beak, and you talk like Donald Duck.

> Ears – Your ears are guns, and they shoot shark bullets with super sharp teeth which eat everything they hit.

> Shoulders – You have 100 sharp metal spikes, 20 inches long, on each shoulder to protect them from attack.

> Elbows – Your elbows are arrows made from Lego and always turn an object invisible when they hit it.

> Hands – Your hands are made of purple diamonds worth $100 million.

> Knees – Your kneecaps can twist open to reveal amazing surprises wrapped in shiny tinfoil inside your knees.

> Feet – Your two feet have cartoonish eyes, nose and a mouth and can talk to you!

Read through the above list a couple of times. Give yourself a few minutes and see if you can recall your newly formed body. Test yourself and read through the list again until you have all of the parts memorised.

Once you have this list of parts memorised you can then begin to associate or store a random list of ten objects on your body. This sample list contains: newspaper, orange juice, toilet roll, beans, nappies, butter, crisps, dishwasher tablets, milk, broccoli – typical things you might have on a shopping list. Here's how to memorise that list.

Imagine the following:

> Your spaghetti hair grows and grabs a newspaper, getting it covered in tomato ketchup. You tear your imaginary spaghetti hair out in order to save your newspaper. You see the spaghetti has left a stain across the front page.

> Using your powerful, red laser beams from your eyes, imagine you burn the top off the orange juice and, using the beams, you boil the orange juice so much that the orange turns purple.

> You then imagine the green flames from your nostrils setting fire to 10,000 toilet rolls on a bonfire, with 100 people surrounding the bonfire sitting on toilets!

> You now imagine yourself as Donald Duck and, using your yellow beak, you are trying and failing to open a can of beans. Eventually you hit the tin so hard with your beak the beans spill all over your bed.

> Imagine your ears shooting shark bullets at nappies all over your car. The shark bullets begin to eat not only the nappies but also your car. Now you notice the shark bullets puking and regurgitating the nappies all over your car!

> You now imagine the Hulk throwing giant green blocks of butter at you and the only defence you have is the

spikes on your shoulders. As the green blocks of butter hit the spikes you shake them off and they fly directly into the fridge.

> Your green, white and gold Lego arrows now shoot at a bag of crisps. Amazingly, the bag disappears for a second only to reappear on the other side of the room. You shoot again and again, and time and time again, the crisps disappear and reappear as if by magic.

> Imagine the dishwasher tablets you need are in the supermarket window, but you are a minute late to the shop and it is closed. You use your purple diamond hands to cut through the glass and grab the tablets. But you notice the tablets actually have the ability to dissolve diamonds, so you have to juggle the tablets all the way home.

> Next you imagine you unscrew your kneecaps and unwrap the tinfoil inside your hollow knees. To your delight, you find the foil is full of milk, so you grab a long straw and take a sip of the warm milk from inside your knees!

> Finally, your feet begin to talk to you and tell you to get some broccoli, but you notice your right foot is choking. To help your foot, you reach inside its mouth and pull out a saliva-covered piece of broccoli!

Although initially this might feel strange, once you get the hang of it you will be able to memorise long lists within a few seconds.

You can also create your own system right now that's unique to you. To add more and more body parts, you can split your body down the middle, using the left ear for one object, the right ear for another. The same with your shoulders, eyes, biceps, triceps, wrists, hips, hands, thighs, feet and so on.

You can even split body parts. Instead of storing one thing on your hands, feet or mouth, you can turn each of your ten fingers into an image, each of your ten toes, even your teeth. And don't forget your back, buttocks, hamstrings, neck, temples and more.

If you run out of space, you can even go internal! Use your lungs, brain, spleen, heart, liver, kidneys and other organs.

19.

FUN BRAIN HACKS

TRICKS TO AMAZE YOUR
FRIENDS AND FAMILY

IMAGINE FOR A MOMENT you have a new superpower, the ability to enter people's minds and extract their innermost thoughts. Well, after this chapter you will have to imagine no more. The following brain hacking demonstrations have been in my working repertoire for over twenty years. I struggled with whether to reveal them in this book but, after careful thought, I decided that the world needs wonder now, more than ever before.

These trick and hacks are designed to make it look like you can really hack into someone's mind. When you learn the secrets to these tricks, please follow the Brain Hacker's rules:

Rule 1: Never reveal the secret.

Rule 2: Commit to performing as if you are a real brain hacker.

Rule 3: Act the part. See Rule 1.

Rule 4: Scripting is everything! Be sure to have a loose script to 'sell' each effect.

Rule 5: Did I mention rule number 1? If they really want to find out how to do it, tell them to buy this book!

EXTRACT A NAME FROM SOMEBODY'S BRAIN!

A recording of me guiding you through this technique can be accessed on my website www.keithbarry.com/brainhacks.

I shouldn't be giving this away. Seriously! I use this all the time in impromptu situations to make it look like I am inside someone's mind.

Effect: You ask someone to think of a person they haven't thought about in a while. You hand them a slip of paper and ask them to clearly write the person's name in the centre of the piece of paper while you look away. They are instructed to fold the paper in quarters, so the name is hidden from view. You tear up the piece of paper and drop the pieces into your pocket. You then hack into their brain and reveal the name!

Props: You'll need a piece of easy-to-tear paper approximately three inches square. I often have these prepared in my wallet but, when needed, I have torn out a square from boarding passes, ticket stubs, newspapers and magazines.

Sample introduction script: 'Did you know the brain is the world's first supercomputer? And just like a computer the brain can not only have information input and extracted but it can also be hacked! I've just started learning to hack into people's minds – is it okay if I try to hack your brain right now?'

Method: You are going to use a technique as old as the hills called the centre tear. Draw a circle in the centre of the paper and fold it in half and then in half again, making sure the circle is on the inside. Show this folded piece of paper to your spectator and tell them to think of someone they haven't thought of in a while, then to open the piece of paper and print the name inside the circle. Tell them that by printing the name inside the circle they will lock that thought into their subconscious, which is what you will try to hack. Ask them to fold it back into quarters and give it back to you.

Now you will apparently tear up the piece of paper into small pieces in front of their eyes and tell them the name they have written down.

Here's how you do it: take the folded paper back from the spectator and position it in your right hand with the folded centre positioned to your top right. This centre should be held between your thumb and first two fingers.

Now tear the paper in half vertically from top to bottom. This will leave the centre circle undamaged, still positioned in the top right corner. Place the pieces from your left hand in front of the right-hand pieces and rotate everything a quarter turn to the right. The circle will now be towards you on the right-hand side, still being held by your thumb and fingers. Now tear the paper in half again vertically from top to bottom.

Place the torn pieces in your left hand in front of the right-hand pieces once again. The torn circle will now be behind all the torn pieces facing you. Now drop all the torn pieces into your right-hand pocket but as you do so slide the circle back towards the middle joints of your fingers. Hold on to the circle.

The situation is as follows: The spectator will now think you have torn up the name into shreds and dropped them into your pocket. The reality, however, is that you now have the circle, still folded into quarters, hidden in your right hand. You now need to secretly open the circle and look at the name. There are many ways to do this:

If you are at a table, drop your hands naturally to your lap and open the paper. Leave it on your lap for a few moments and then take a peek at it.

If you are standing, place your hands behind your back and open the circle secretly behind your back. Keeping it hidden in your hand, you can now bring your hands forward and take the pen from the spectator.

If you now hold the pen in your right hand your hand will look natural, and you can ask them to stare at the tip of the pen as you look down and look at the circle with the name on it. As they stare at the pen, you ask them to imagine the first letter of the name hovering like a neon sign over the tip of the pen. Then begin to reveal the name, letter by letter. To clean up, simply ditch the circle in the same pocket as the torn pieces.

Don't underestimate this piece of (apparent) mind-reading. I've used it to get free dessert in restaurants after freaking out waitresses and free drinks in bars after freaking out the bartenders!

THE PSYCHIC ENERGY TOUCH

A recording of me guiding you through this technique can be accessed on my website www.keithbarry.com/brainhacks.

Here is a trick that Woody Harrelson performed on set and behind the scenes on the *Now You See Me* movies. Little did anyone know that I was secretly assisting Woody every time!

Effect: You leave the room and ask a spectator to touch any object in the room. When you are called back in, you wander around the room attempting to pick up on the psychic energy emanating from that object. You eventually find the object, leaving everyone completely stumped.

Props: A room full of objects and a secret accomplice.

Sample introduction script: 'Did you know that by touching an object, your energy transfers into that object and can be still vibrating within that object for up to three hours? I've discovered I have a weird ability to pick up on that energy. Let me prove it.'

Method: This method is super simple, which allows you to focus on your acting ability to pull off the trick with style and flair!

You instruct a spectator to touch any object in the room, while you are outside and the door is closed. Upon your return you wander around the room, touching objects at random in order to get a feel for the 'psychic energy' left behind. As you touch the objects, you continuously look towards the spectator who has touched the object. However, what you are really doing is looking at your secret accomplice within your peripheral vision. If their feet are apart that means you are not touching the object. When you touch the object, your accomplice will touch their feet together.

Once you know the object you are looking for, keep moving around touching other objects. This will put your audience off the scent. Acting is key here! Pretend you are a real psychic trying to pick up on the energy from the objects, before you eventually go back and amazingly pick up the item the spectator has touched and declare that it's the one!

What if your accomplice is seated and you can't see their feet? No problem!

They simply behave as normal as you wander the room. Again, you are looking at the spectator throughout, but also looking at your accomplice in your peripheral vision. When you touch the selected item, your accomplice will purposely not blink for a few seconds. This is almost impossible for people to spot as your accomplice knows not to stare at you! They will simply not blink for five seconds, even if they are talking to another person or apparently looking in another direction not paying attention.

If it's good enough for Woody Harrelson it's good enough for you!

PSYCHIC CONNECTION CARD TRICK

A recording of me guiding you through this technique can be accessed on my website www.keithbarry.com/brainhacks.

I've been using this for years in impromptu situations as my favourite go-to card trick. It can be done any time, anywhere, even with a borrowed deck of cards.

Effect: A spectator selects a card which is then lost inside the deck. You flip through cards and ask a spectator to merely think of the word 'stop' when they see their card. Miraculously you find their card.

Props: Deck of cards.

Sample introduction script: 'Do you believe in mind-to-mind communication? Let's test my mind-reading abilities with a deck of cards.'

Method: After a spectator shuffles the deck of cards, have them return the deck to you. Spread the cards face down and ask them to freely select any card. As they show the card to their friends, you need to glimpse the bottom card of the deck discreetly. Have them place the card back on top of the deck, split the deck into two segments and move the bottom portion to the top. If they like, they can do this a couple of times. No matter how many times they do this, their card will always be positioned beneath the card which you have glimpsed, which in magic terminology is known as the key card.

Now, presentation is everything. You hold the deck face down and state,

'In a moment I will deal the cards face up onto the table. When you see your card, please don't say anything, don't flinch, just merely think of the word stop. I will psychically connect with you and stop at your card. Remember, please, not to say anything at all for the next sixty seconds.'

Deal through the cards, flipping them face up one at a time. You are keeping an eye out for your key card, the card that you peeked at on the bottom of the deck earlier. When you see the key card, you know the next card is theirs. However, you deal past their card and continue.

They will now assume you have missed it, which is exactly what we want them to assume! Continue for about five more cards and then stop with a single card face down in your hand. State EXACTLY as follows:

'Would you be amazed if the next card I turned over was your chosen card?'

They will be convinced you are going to turn over the card in your hand so they will agree they would be amazed. That's when you reach down into the spread you have already dealt out and turn their card over. Watch their absolute shock when you do this. It really is a class trick which I've done weekly for the past thirty years! I love this trick and really want you to enjoy spreading magic and mystery in the world, so give it a go.

FIND THE HIDDEN OBJECT

A recording of me guiding you through this technique can be accessed on my website www.keithbarry.com/brainhacks.

Remember the hidden note trick from the lie detection chapter? Well, there's an easier way to find out which hand a person is holding a hidden object in. As long as the lighting is right wherever you are doing this trick, this method works every time.

Effect: You give a coin or small object to your subject and ask them to hide it in one of their hands when your back is turned. You turn your back and tell them that once they have decided which hand to hide the coin in, they must hold that hand up to their forehead for about ten seconds and keep thinking, 'The coin is in this hand, the coin is in this hand,' in order for them to send that thought to you and help you read their mind and body language. When they are done, they hold both hands closed into fists out in front of them. You turn around and correctly reveal which hand the coin is in.

Props: A coin or something small that can be hidden in a person's hand without being seen.

Sample introduction script: 'Do you believe I can read your mind and your body language in order to tell which hand you hide a coin in?'

Method: After ten seconds of holding their hand to their forehead with your back turned to them, ask the person to hold both arms out in front of them so both hands look identical. You turn back around and gaze into their eyes as if trying to hack their brain. You now look at their hands. When they place both hands out in front of you, the one that has been held up to their head will be slightly paler due to the lack of blood flowing to it when it was held up against their forehead.

Rather than select the hand straight away, however, you can play around with 'reading' their body language before revealing the correct hand. Now, they may say that you had a 50-50 chance of predicting the correct hand, but they will be amazed when you can do it several times in a row, even using different people. If the results are not clear to you then maybe they didn't hold their hand to their head when you turned your back.

Once you have done this correctly a few times, you can announce that you have now built such a good connection with the person that you don't need a coin or object anymore. You say, 'I might even be able to tell which hand you think the object is in ...' Repeat the trick without an actual object and the results will be the same as long as they hold their hand to their forehead for long enough.

This will require some practice on your part, but once you get proficient at it, you really will feel like a real mind reader!

PRECOGNITION

A recording of me guiding you through this technique can be accessed on my website www.keithbarry.com/brainhacks.

Effect: You hand a spectator a folded piece of paper which you declare is a prediction of things to come. A spectator selects a word at random from a book as you flip through it. When they open up the prediction it says, 'On my arm.' It appears as if you have messed up the trick. You then take some coffee granules and spread them on your arm. The word the spectator is thinking of appears on your arm as if by magic!

Props: A thick paperback book, a coin, some clear ChapStick and some coffee granules.

Sample introduction script: 'Did you ever hear about Nostradamus? He was a famous psychic who apparently could see into the future. I've read his book *Les Prophéties* and have learned to see exactly three minutes into the future. Let me show you something.'

Method: Before you begin, secretly place the coin into a book – closest to the spine, towards the front half of the book. For example, if you are using a 300-page book, then you would place the coin around page 50. Remember the first word at the top of the left-hand page. Let's imagine the word happens to be 'brain'. Using the ChapStick, secretly write the word 'brain' big and bold on your arm. It will be completely invisible. You are now all set to perform a miracle. Shut the book and place it on a table, being careful of course that the coin does not fall out.

Introduce the premise to your spectator and hand them your folded prediction, which says 'On my arm'. Next, grasp the book with the front cover facing you and the back of the book facing the spectator. Grasp the book tightly with the spine of the book held in your left hand and you should be able to feel the coin through the pages. Now flip through the pages from back to front with your right hand and ask the spectator to call 'Stop'. As they call 'Stop', you will allow all the pages to flip by until you naturally stop at the page where there is a break from the coin. Try it now with this book! Grab a coin and place it at page 50 where the word 'approached' is at the top left of the page and flip through the pages as described. You will notice how easy it is to stop at the page with the coin. With practice you will be able to time this so that you naturally stop at this page the moment the spectator says 'Stop'.

Open the book, still holding the coin through the spine, and ask them to think of the word at the top of the page in your right hand, which in our example is 'approached'. It is obvious to your spectator that you cannot see the page or word they are looking at, but to make it even more impossible feel free to close your eyes and turn your head the other way as you open the book.

Tell them to remember the word as you allow the book to close. Ask them to open the prediction. This is your moment of misdirection to allow the coin to fall gently into one of your hands and pocket it. Don't worry – all eyes will be on the prediction. When they open the prediction, and it says, 'On my arm', you ask if it was correct. Of course, they will say you are wrong. You ask what their word was and that's when they tell you, 'approached'.

You then state, 'My prediction is actually correct – it's on my arm!' Grab a handful of coffee granules and rub them on your arm over the ChapStick. The word 'approached' will reveal itself – watch them freak the freak-out of all freak-outs! The best part is that everything can now be thoroughly examined!

Go now and amaze your friends and family. When they ask you how you did it, tell them Keith Barry taught you and they must buy this book to find out how!

ACKNOWLEDGEMENTS

I would like to thank Sarah, Aoibheann, Teresa, Claire, and all in Gill Books for all their support, guidance and help in creating the book that's now in your hands.

Thanks to Ger for the endless late nights spent putting my thoughts onto paper.

Thanks to Michele and Alanna for picking thousands of cards over the years; to Al for your endless curiosity and support; to Rhona, Ian and Marie for endless laughs; to Sean for your level head in tough times and to Bart for listening to all of my crazy ideas over the years.

Thanks to Jose for being my invisible ninja for all these years; to Joe for locking yourself in a cabin with me for eighteen months; to Colly for being 'positronic' through thick and thin; and to Gerard for your ideas and inspiration.

Thanks to Burkie for allowing me to hypnotise you in Irish class – and for the fishing trips; to Cian for encouraging free thinking; to Fergus for guiding my business decisions and to Bro for all the late-night brainstorming chats.

To Noel, Denis, Caroline and the MCD team – thanks for having faith in me for all these years.

To Tony Sadar for your amazing wisdom; Doc Shiels for your mysterious ways; and Ann and Declan for putting up with my madness!

Above all, thanks to my amazing parents, Ken and Kitty, for a life filled with magic.

ENDNOTES

1   Richardson, A. (1967). 'Mental Practice: A Review and Discussion Part II.' *American Association for Health, Physical Education and Recreation, 38*(2), 263–273.

2   Adams, A. J. (2009, December 3). 'Seeing Is Believing: The Power of Visualization.' *Psychology Today.* https://www.psychologytoday.com/ie/blog/flourish/200912/seeing-is-believing-the-power-visualization.

3   Clance, P. R.; Imes, S. A. (1978). 'The imposter phenomenon in high achieving women: Dynamics and therapeutic intervention.' *Psychotherapy: Theory, Research & Practice, 15*(3), 241–247.

4   Rutherford, G. (2020, February 19). 'Up to 70 per cent of us feel like a fraud, says U of A psychologist.' University of Alberta. https://www.ualberta.ca/folio/2020/02/up-to-70-per-cent-of-us-feel-like-a-fraud-says-u-of-a-psychologist.html

5   Roese, N. J.; Summerville, A. (2005). 'What we regret most... and why.' *Personality and Social Psychology Bulletin 31*(9): 1273–1285.

6   Lucas, C. G. et al. (2014). 'When children are better (or at least more open-minded) learners than adults: developmental differences in learning the forms of causal relationships.' *Cognition, 131*(2): 284–299.

7   Clouse, A. M. (2016). 'Human Psychological Response to and Benefits of Interior Water Features.' (Honours thesis, University of Southern Mississippi). https://aquila.usm.edu/honors_theses/418/.

8   Chellappa, S. L. et al. (2014, April). 'Photic memory for executive brain responses.' *Proceedings of the National Academy of Sciences, 111*(16): 6087–6091.

9   Sander, E. J.; Caza, Arran; Jordan, Peter J. (2019) 'Psychological perceptions matter: Developing the reactions to the physical work environment scale.' *Building and Environment, 148*, 338–347.

10 Slepian, M. L.; Ambady, N. (2012). 'Fluid movement and creativity.' *Journal of Experimental Psychology: General, 141*(4), 625–629.

11 David, J. B.; Naftali, A.; Katz, A. (2010). 'Tinntrain: A multifactorial treatment for tinnitus using binaural beats.' *Hearing Journal, 63*(11), 25–26, 28.

12 Barrett, D. (1993). 'The "committee of sleep": A study of dream incubation for problem solving.' *Dreaming, 3*(2), 115–122.

13 Wagner, U.; Gais, S.; Haider, H.; Verleger, R.; Born, J. (2004) 'Sleep inspires insight.' *Nature, 427*(6972), 352–355.

14 Gao, C.; Fillmore, P.; Scullin, M. K. (2020) 'Classical music, educational learning, and slow wave sleep: A targeted memory reactivation experiment'. *Neurobiology of Learning and Memory, 171*, 107206.

15 Adams, D. R. (2020, August 31). 'Survey: Smartphones distract employees for hours on end during the workday.' *TechRepublic.* https://www.techrepublic.com/article/survey-smartphones-distract-employees-for-hours-on-end-during-the-workday/.

16 Shevchuk N. A. (2008). 'Adapted cold shower as a potential treatment for depression.' *Medical Hypotheses, 70*(5), 995–1001.

17 Beard, A. (2018, March). 'Cold Showers Lead to Fewer Sick Days.' *Harvard Business Review.* https://hbr.org/2018/03/cold-showers-lead-to-fewer-sick-days.

18 Fowler, J. H., et al. (2009). 'Dynamic Spread of Happiness in a Large Social Network: Longitudinal Analysis of the Framingham Heart Study Social Network'. *British Medical Journal, 338*(7685), 23–27.

19 Keizer, A.; Smeets, M. A. M.; Dijkerman, H. C.; Uzunbajakau, S. A.; van Elburg, A.; Postma, A. (2013). 'Too fat to fit through the door: First evidence for disturbed body-scaled action in anorexia nervosa during locomotion.' *PLoS ONE, 8*(5), 64602.

20 Kross, E.; Ayduk, O. (2017). 'Self-Distancing.' *Advances in Experimental Social Psychology*, 81–136.

21 Wood, A. et al. (2008) 'The role of gratitude in the development of social support, stress, and depression: two longitudinal studies.' *Journal of Research in Personality 42*, 854–871.

22 'Gratitude Letter.' (n.d.) *Positive Psychology Toolkit.* (PDF). https://positivepsychology.com/wp-content/uploads/Gratitude-Letter1.pdf.

23 Kushlev, K.; Proulx, J.; Dunn, E. W. (2016). '"Silence Your Phones": Smartphone Notifications Increase Inattention and Hyperactivity Symptoms.' *Proceedings of the 2016 CHI Conference on Human Factors in Computing Systems*, 1011–1020.

24 Ose Askvik, E; van der Weel, F. R.; van der Meer, A. L. H. (2020) 'The

Importance of Cursive Handwriting Over Typewriting for Learning in the Classroom: A High-Density EEG Study of 12-Year-Old Children and Young Adults.' *Frontiers in Psychology,11*, 1810.

25 Wood, W.; Quinn, J. M.; Kashy, D. A. (2002). 'Habits in everyday life: Thought, emotion, and action.' *Journal of Personality and Social Psychology*, *83*(6), 1281–1297.

26 Goldstein, N. J. et al. (2008) 'A Room with a Viewpoint: Using Social Norms to Motivate Environmental Conservation in Hotels.' *Journal of Consumer Research*, *35*(3), 472–482.

27 Iacoboni, M. et al. (2005) 'Grasping the intentions of others with one's own mirror neuron system.' *PLoS Biology*, *3*(3), e79.

28 Van Edwards, V. (2021, April). '60 Hand Gestures You Should Be Using and Their Meaning.' Science of People. https://www.scienceofpeople.com/hand-gestures/.

29 Phillips, B. (2013, October). 'Can You Become 56 Percent Better At Presenting – Instantly?' Throughline. https://www.throughlinegroup.com/2013/10/16/can-you-become-56-percent-better-at-presenting-instantly/.

30 National Research Council. (1988). *Enhancing Human Performance: Issues, Theories, and Techniques*. National Academies Press.

31 Bame, Y. (2017, October). 'How common are psychic moments? 1 in 3 Americans feel they have experienced one.' *YouGovAmerica*. https://today.yougov.com/.

32 *Journal of Abnormal and Social Psychology*, *44*(1), 118–123.

33 Feldman, R.; Forrest, J.; Happ, B. (2002). 'Self-Presentation and Verbal Deception: Do Self-Presenters Lie More?' *Basic and Applied Social Psychology*, *24*,163–170.

34 Moliné, A.; Dominguez, E.; Salazar-López, E. et al. 'The mental nose and the Pinocchio effect: Thermography, planning, anxiety, and lies.' *Journal of Investigative Psychology Offender Profiling*, *15*, 234– 248.

35 Mueller, P. A.; Oppenheimer, D. M. (2014). 'The pen is mightier than the keyboard: Advantages of longhand over laptop note taking.' *Psychological Science*, *25*(6), pp. 1159–1168.